SPIRITS AND SCIENTISTS

SPIRITS AND SCIENTISTS

Ideology, Spiritism, and Brazilian Culture

David J. Hess

THE PENNSYLVANIA STATE UNIVERSITY PRESS

University Park, Pennsylvania

Library of Congress Cataloging-in-Publication Data

Hess, David J.
  Spirits and scientists : ideology, spiritism, and Brazilian
culture / David J. Hess.
      p.   cm.
  Includes bibliographical references and index.
  ISBN 0-271-03367-3 (alk. paper)
  1. Spiritualism—Brazil.   2. Science and spiritualism—Brazil.
3. Religion and culture—Brazil.   4. Brazil—Religion.   I. Title.
  BF1242.B6H47   1991
  133.9'0981—dc20   90-39780
                                                          CIP

It is the policy of The Pennsylvania State University Press to use
acid-free paper for the first printing of all clothbound books.
Publications on uncoated stock satisfy the minimum requirements of
American National Standard for Information Sciences—Permanence of
Paper for Printed Library Materials, ANSI Z39.48–1984.

To my parents

CONTENTS

ACKNOWLEDGMENTS

This book derives from research done for my doctoral dissertation (Department of Anthropology, Cornell University, 1987) and from subsequent research in Brazil (1988) and Puerto Rico (1989). The three members of my doctoral committee—committee chair James Boon, Thomas Holloway, and David Holmberg—all provided a great deal of support, patience, and good critical feedback at all stages. Several persons provided helpful comments on earlier drafts of the manuscript: the historians Carlos Alvarado and Donald Warren, the anthropologist Patric Giesler, and several reviewers whose names I do not know. The late Ann Bates showed initial interest in the manuscript, and another editor, Philip Winsor, patiently shepherded the manuscript through the review and publication process at Penn State Press. Copyeditor Charles Purrenhage did a helpful and thorough job. To my former teacher John Palmer I owe much of my background knowledge on parapsychology.

In Brazil, the anthropologist Robert DaMatta graciously agreed to sponsor the project through the Museu Nacional of the Universidade Federal do Rio de Janeiro, and he provided a sounding board for many of my ideas. Both he and the anthropologist Márcio Silva served as principals in my rite of transition from "individual" to "person" in the Brazilian academic arena, and they helped teach me to see Brazil from a Brazilian perspective. Many members of the Spiritist movement patiently explained their work and ideas to me, beginning with Hercílio Costa and his family, who generously welcomed me and introduced me to the Spiritist and Umbanda scene of action in Niterói. Among the Spiritists in Rio, São Paulo, and Curitiba who were helpful to me are the following: Jorge Andrea, João Bovino, Cleusa and Dora Colombo, Coronel Cícero and Dona Nadir, André Ramos da Costa, Krishnamurti de Carvalho Dias, Antônio Ferreira Filho, Regis Lang, Paulo Toledo Machado, Maldanato, Miriam, Freitas Nobre, Agenor de Melo Pegado, Ney Prieto Peres and Maria Júlia Peres, Cristina Rocha and Luciano

Rocha, Dona Regina, Alexandre Sech and Maderli Sech, Octávio Mel-chíades Ulysséa and Neida Ulysséa, Homero Pinto Valada, Lauro Valera, and especially Hernani Guimarães Andrade and his assistant, Suzuko Hashizume. Louis Lean and Dona Didi generously provided me with access to the private library of Canuto Abreu, and the librarians of the Brazilian Spiritist Federation were also very helpful. Claudia Coelho provided a great deal of help on a Portuguese translation that may someday find a publisher in Brazil. Others in Brazil who were helpful include André Percia de Carvalho, Osmard Andrade de Faria, Padre Edvino Friderichs, Gary Dale Richman, and Horta Santos.

Grants from the U.S. Department of Education (Fulbright-Hays) and the Social Science Research Council supported fieldwork in Rio de Janeiro, São Paulo, and other cities from September 1984 to March 1986, and the Social Science Research Council also provided write-up support. In 1985, Harold Midkiff and Marco Antônio of the Fulbright Commission in Brasília helped secure a much-appreciated visa renewal, allowing me to avoid the usual nightmare of Brazilian bureaucracy. In addition, the Latin American Studies Program (funded by the Scott Paper Foundation) and the Center for International Studies of Cornell University provided funding for a preliminary field trip to Brazil during the summer of 1983, and Colgate University's program of Major Faculty Grants provided an opportunity for follow-up research in 1988. My 1989 trip to Puerto Rico was self-funded; Xavier Figueiroa and Teresita Martínez helped me make affordable arrangements in San Juan, and Carlos Alvarado directed me to appropriate sources and contacts. An earlier and condensed version of Chapter 5 appeared in *Religião e Sociedade* (1987a), one of Chapter 7 likewise appeared in *Cultural Anthropology* (1989a), and Appendix 3 was originally presented as a paper at the 1989 meetings of the American Anthropological Association. If there are any royalties on the book *Spirits and Scientists*, they will be donated to the charitable activities of one or more Spiritist centers in Brazil.

Finally, I wish to recognize my friends, colleagues, and relatives, both at home and in Brazil, who made my time in Brazil not just endurable but enjoyable: Kitty Broadbent, Claudia Coelho, Bill Fisher, Patric Giesler, Roberto Machado, Flávio Marega, Diane Marting, Monique Sessler, Márcio Silva and his family, Neila Soares and her family (especially Dona Lygia), Dana Wheeler, and my father, mother, brother, and sister.

ABBREVIATIONS AND CONVENTIONS

Abbreviations

The following abbreviations for organizations are used throughout this book:

ABRAP   Brazilian Association of Parapsychology (Associação Brasileira de Parapsicologia)

AEPR   Spiritist Association of Puerto Rico (Asociación Espiritista de Puerto Rico)

AMESP   Spiritist Medical Association of São Paulo (Associação Médico-Espírita de São Paulo)

CLAP   Latin American Center of Parapsychology (Centro Latin-Americano de Parapsicologia)

FEB   Brazilian Spiritist Federation (Federação Espírita Brasileira)

FEERJ   Spiritist Federation of the State of Rio de Janeiro (Federação Espírita do Estado do Rio de Janeiro)

FEESP   Spiritist Federation of the State of São Paulo (Federação Espírita do Estado de São Paulo)

IBPP   Brazilian Institute of Psychobiophysical Research (Instituto Brasileiro de Pesquisas Psicobiofísicas)

ICEB   Institute of Brazilian Spiritist Culture (Instituto de Cultura Espírita do Brasil)

UNICAMP   The State University of São Paulo, Campinas (Universidade Estadual de Campinas, São Paulo)

USE   Union of Spiritist Societies of the State of São Paulo (União das Sociedades Espíritas do Estado de São Paulo)

Translations and Other Conventions

Unless otherwise noted, all translations are my own. In some cases, I had to use the old Portuguese orthography—for example, in the spelling of "Adolpho" in the title of Abreu 1950—and I use the Portuguese convention "Quevedo" rather than the Spanish "González Quevedo" for Padre

Pedro Oscar González Quevedo. In Portuguese the word *espírita* is both a noun and an adjective (both masculine and feminine) that means "Spiritist," whereas the word *espírito* means "spirit." I have translated AMESP as "Spiritist Medical Association of São Paulo" rather than "The Association of Spiritist Doctors of São Paulo," because the members of the association are not all doctors. I have also used the technically correct term "psychical research" rather than the more common "psychic research"; this and many other unfamiliar terms are defined in the Glossary.

It has not always been possible to check nineteenth-century sources and names, and the closing of the library of the Brazilian Spiritist Association (Federação Espírita Brasileira) in 1988 made it impossible to check some sources (such as Casella 1961, 1961–62, 1962; Faria 1961–62; and Imbassahy 1961, 1962a–d). In many cases, books do not include a publication date, so I have used a "c." (for "circa") to give my best estimate of the publication date.

INTRODUCTION

In February 1985, the elegant Maksoud Plaza in São Paulo hosted the First International Congress on Alternative Therapies. The flyer announced the purpose of the meeting as follows:

> To promote a meeting of researchers and professionals (such as doctors, psychologists, therapists, healers, etc.) from different parts of the world, whose work is directed toward a more comprehensive and integrated view of the human being and who take into consideration the relationship between body-mind-spirit and its implications in the prevention, maintenance, and/or recovery of health.

The conference was proclaimed as a positive response to a meeting in 1977 of the World Health Organization, which had called for the study of alternative treatments and therapies that take into consideration the social, cultural, and economic factors of each country. At the First International Congress on Alternative Therapies, Brazilians joined with invited guests from other countries to deliver papers on topics as diverse as the laying-on of hands and spiritual *passes*, past-lives therapy, disobsession and exorcism therapies, transpersonal psychology, acupuncture, chromotherapy, yoga therapy, iridology, psychotrance therapy, homeopathy, parapsychological cures, and psychic surgery.

If Brazil is known as one of the world's richest laboratories of religious syncretism—the meeting and mingling of Catholic saints and West African *orixás*—this conference involved another kind of syncretism, a "modern" or even "postmodern" syncretism that not only brought together different worldviews and healing traditions from Western and non-Western cultures, but also articulated them in terms of Western science, biomedicine, and various contemporary political ideologies. Yet, to describe the juxtaposition of ideas and actors under the rubric of "syncretism" might mean underplaying an implicit order,[1] and an eye and ear attuned to the world of alternative Brazilian religion, science, and medicine—a Brazilian New Age which makes that of California seem bland in comparison—could detect the order behind an apparent pastiche of alternative therapies. As a Spiritist psychiatrist pointed out to me during the conference, "This has ended up being a Spiritist congress"; although the official sponsors of the conference included a diverse group of alternative organizations from several countries, the most influential were the Spiritist leaders, doctors, and intellectuals from São Paulo.

Spiritists form a highly visible and numerically important social movement in Brazil, one that has already attracted the attention of historians, sociologists, and anthropologists.[2] Sometimes called "Kardecists," or *kardecistas*, Spiritists define their doctrine as a synthesis of science, philosophy, and Christian morality. Although their intellectual father, Allan Kardec, was a Frenchman rooted in both the rationalism and romanticism of nineteenth-century Europe, his synthesis of diverse religious and philosophical currents has won a wide following in contemporary Brazil, a nation known for its multicultural eclecticism. Kardec's doctrine includes beliefs that have historical origins in hermetic and esoteric traditions (the astral body, vital fluids, and spirit communication through mediums), Indic philosophy (reincarnation and karma), highly reformed Protestant theology (a unitarian doctrine and the interpretation of heaven and hell as psychological states), Catholicism (the emphasis on spiritual hierarchies and the mediating role of an extrabiblical doctrine), social reformism (the emphasis on equality, progress, freedom of thought, and education), as well as modern science (what Kardec called the "experimental" side of Spiritism, which later became known as psychical research and still later as parapsychology).

The last aspect of Kardec's doctrine has especially interested the intellectuals of the Spiritist movement in Brazil; they have developed an elaborate system of science and medicine that is the topic of this book. Although the medical profession and university scientists generally frown on Spiritist "pseudoscience," it plays a key role in mediating between elite science and medicine on one side and popular religion and healing on the other. The work of Brazilian Spiritist intellectuals therefore provides a good case study of what anthropologists encounter with greater and greater frequency: an international world in which the non-Western and traditional are entering into increasing dialogue with the Western and "modern," and a world in which local movements and communities have an increasingly sophisticated and even critical view of cosmopolitan science, medicine, religion, and political ideology. In a sense, this is the anthropology of the future. By using the work of Spiritist intellectuals as a case study, *Spirits and Scientists* provides one way of challenging the walls that many sociological and anthropological studies build around local systems of religion, medicine, or science as distinct "fields" or "systems"; instead, the following pages develop a methodology for the study of such systems as part of a broader, cosmopolitan ideological arena. As a result, the theoretical problem of how to understand religious syncretism, complexity, or interpenetration—a problem which continues to occupy the attention of students of religion—is now dissolved and recontextualized with respect to this broader framework.

The French sociologist/ethnologist Roger Bastide has provided the most important sociological interpretation of Spiritist scientific thought, and his ideas continue to influence students of Brazilian religion today. Bastide (1967) situated Spiritist intellectuals' scientific thought within a triadic scheme of class stratification among spirit-mediumship religions: on the bottom he placed the working class (especially mulattoes and blacks), drawn to Umbanda;[3] in the middle was the white middle class, which formed the heart of the evangelical side of the Spiritist movement; and at the top were the professional groups of the upper class who were more interested in psychical research (*metapsíquica*), or the scientific side of Spiritism.[4] In *The African Religions of Brazil*, Bastide described Spiritist scientific thought as follows:

One type of [S]piritism is that of the intellectuals, doctors, engineers, civil servants, and even members of the teaching profession—the type that claims to be scientific. Yet behind their experimentation with parapsychology, one senses a predilection for the mysterious, the restlessness of a soul in search of miracles, Saint Thomas wanting to reach out and touch the miracle. ([1960] 1978: 314)

Bastide apparently liked this vignette enough to repeat it in a somewhat more refined statement written seven years later:

One finds the [S]piritism of the upper class among the group of plantation owners, or the high bourgeoisie, industrialists, [and] merchants, and among the group of intellectuals, teachers, lawyers, and above all doctors. But one speaks less of [S]piritism than of *métapsychie* [parapsychology or psychical research], which is to say that [S]piritism is only accepted to the extent that it transforms itself into science. Nevertheless, the success of certain mediums . . . shows that they do not make much of a distinction between charlatanism and controlled experiments, and behind the *métapsychie* one senses a certain taste for the miraculous: an experimental miracle reveals itself. (1967: 5)

It is worth considering for a moment the implicit sociological assumptions of these passages. Bastide's interpretation of Spiritist scientific thought represents a kind of Veblenesque "snob" theory: the upper segments of the social pyramid in Brazil may be as mystical as the rest of the population, but they like to clothe their mysticism in a scientific language. It is true that this theory has a certain amount of explanatory power: it tells us why an intellectual, scientific Spiritist discourse has emerged in the first place and which segments of society ensure its continued survival. However, it does not help very much when one tries to comprehend the meaning of the tremendous body of books, articles, speeches, and lectures that Spiritist intellectuals have produced.

To understand the meaning of Spiritist intellectual discourse, one needs context, and this context must be broader than the one Bastide supplies: the class and status divisions among spirit-mediumship religions. In *The Gods of the People* (1980), Carlos Rodrigues Brandão adopts as his unit of analysis the Brazilian religious system as a whole, which he subdivides into three main "areas": the spirit-mediumship religions, Protestantism, and Catholicism. Within each area, he distinguishes a "popular domain," a "domain of mediation," and an "erudite domain," the latter occupied by Spiritism, Presbyterianism and Baptism, and the Catholic church (1980: 114ff.).[5] Brandão's work has the advantage of adopting the entire religious system as the unit of analysis, and at one point he provides a brief discussion of the crucially important interactions between categories such as Catholicism and Spiritism (pp. 104–8); nevertheless, even the entire religious system is too limited a framework for understanding the thought of a group of intellectuals who are deeply involved in the currents of contemporary science, medicine, social science, and politics, and one must instead situate the notion of "religion" in a broader arena of ideological dialogue, debate, and discourse.

By extending the scope of analysis to a broader framework of actors and ideologies, it becomes clear that the scientific and medical thought of Spiritist intellectuals is considerably more complicated than Bastide had envisioned. Rather than representing the upper end of a limited field of spirit-mediumship religions, Spiritist thought instead occupies a mediating position between the popular religions below it in the social pyramid and those ideologies and groups which have more prestige and/or power, such as official Catholicism, orthodox science, state ideology, Northern Hemisphere heterodox science, and even the social sciences.

Much of the current research in Brazilian studies is beginning to examine religion in terms of this broader context, and what I say here only makes this tendency and theoretical position more explicit.[6] I think of this broader confluence of social and cultural systems as a historically and culturally situated "ideological arena" that includes religion, science, medicine, social science, and political ideology, at both the national and the international level. This framework combines the approaches of Geertz (1973) and Bourdieu (1982) and adds to them an emphasis on the relations among the various "ideologies" or discourses. Despite their radical differences, both these social theorists interpret religion, political ideology, science and so on as relatively differentiated "cultural systems" or autonomous "fields." In contrast, the framework here is closer to what the anthropologist James Boon described as that part of the functionalist monograph which ethnographers tended to leave out: "chapters on relations between a particular culture and others and on that culture's own sense of others" (1982: 15). In the condition that the anthropologists George Marcus and Michael Fischer (1986) refer to as a world of "posts"—postcolonialism, postmodernism, and the like—what one might have previously viewed as relatively discrete or autonomous fields of discourse are instead seen here as dialogically related to each other in a broader ideological arena.[7]

An important aspect of the ideological arena is the relationship between the dominant institutions of society, those which represent the various kinds of orthodoxy (religious, scientific, medical, political, etc.), and the more popular groups which attempt to appropriate the language of orthodoxy, as occurs when popular religious, philosophical, and occult groups discuss their thought in a scientific idiom. Scientists and other representatives of orthodoxy may respond by engaging in what the sociologist Thomas Gieryn (1983) calls "boundary-work," which often includes explaining why the claims of heterodox scientists are not, from the orthodox perspective, scientifically valid.[8] *Spirits and Scientists* expands on Gieryn's concept of "boundary-work" by recognizing that, for example, Umbandists look down on Macumba magicians, Spiritists on Umbandists, Spiritist intellectuals on other Spiritists, and so on in a hierarchical and recursive structure. Thus, there are multiple boundaries that collapse and are redrawn according to context. In addition, as the case of Brazilian Spiritism shows, boundary-work involves more than just intellectual arguments that defend social interests and that challenge or preserve social hierarchies; boundary-work is also a kind of cultural or social drama (V. Turner 1974) in which broader values and worldviews clash and articulate themselves (see also Hess 1991d and Downey 1988).

An intellectually honest discussion of these processes must eventually come to terms with the fact that the social sciences are also part of this same dialogue. In other words, we, too, are engaged in our own forms of boundary-work. This level of complexity allows for a reflexive critical portrayal of the social sciences within the ideological arena. For example, if one looks again at Bastide's statement about Spiritist intellectuals, it is evident that he manages to describe Spiritist intellectuals as snobs in a way that itself can only be described as condescending. In other words, his description assumes that his own perspective, ostensibly that of a neutral social scientist (a neutrality which this study will question), is somehow superior to that of the Spiritist: Bastide inscribes one sort of hierarchy even as he describes another. *Spirits and Scientists* addresses this problem in more detail in Chapter 7, which provides, in the phrase of Marcus and Fischer (1986), a "cultural critique" of the ideological dimension of social scientists' theories about Brazilian religion.[9]

The choice to write reflexively about the discourse of the social sciences is related to my methodological decision to violate one of the taboos of anthropological writing: the textual taboo. If I had chosen to focus on sex, for example, in a study of prostitutes or college undergraduates, it is unlikely that the anthropological community would even blink. In a similar way, in *Spirits and Scientists* I have chosen to emphasize Spiritists' texts, or "public discourse"—that is, their books, articles, pamphlets, conference speeches, lectures, tape-recorded interviews with me, and so on. However, as I have become painfully aware in the past few years, some anthropologists maintain a rather strong taboo on the use of texts—a kind of disciplinary boundary-work that prohibits healthy exogamous relations with other fields, such as literary criticism—and consequently it is necessary to justify a choice that, in a world of interdisciplinary experiments and "blurred genres" (Geertz 1983: ch. 1), should not need justification at all.

One argument for using texts as my organizing device is that it becomes easier to juxtapose Spiritists' discourse with that of their Others, especially social scientists: "textual equality" reinforces the idea that both are part of the same arena of ideological debate and dialogue, rather than related as observer/observed or subject/object. A more important justification comes from the Spiritists themselves: the primary activity of Spiritist intellectuals is, as with most other intellectuals, to write, lecture, grant interviews, or, more generally, produce texts. Furthermore, because the "tribe" of Spiritist intellectuals is scattered across huge cities throughout one of the largest countries in the world, their sense of community derives largely from their textual relations—their exchanges of books, articles, newspapers, and so on. Even when their relations are not mediated by "texts," such as when they get together at meetings and conferences, what they do is lecture and give talks; that is to say, they produce a highly textualized form of public discourse. Finally, after I interviewed or talked informally with Spiritist intellectuals (and many of their critics), they often ended the dialogue by giving me books and telling me to go home and read them. "Study the doctrine," Spiritists admonished me, and in a sense this is what I do in *Spirits and Scientists*.

The choice to emphasize texts, therefore, does not indicate an underlying allegiance to the seamless semiotics of the "world as a text" (see the critique in Clifford 1983). Instead, such a choice provides a way of getting at the issues of rhetoric, ideology, cultural values, and institutional legitimation that are involved in the boundary-work of the ideological arena. Just as Spiritist intellectuals do not see their texts as ends in themselves, in *Spirits and Scientists* I use their texts as the windows on or gateways to the question of ideology, of how ideas are related to the diacritics and dialectics of social structures and cultural meanings.

To read texts in terms of their social, cultural, and historical context inevitably leads to the society, culture, and history in which they are embedded. Consequently, the Spiritists' texts are discussed in terms of a great deal of ethnographic description and historical contextualization: rituals, conferences, legal conflicts, educational programs, interviews, conversations, gossip, and so on. Meetings and conferences, of course, provided an opportunity for participant-observation; but field research in this context meant not only conventional methods—spending time talking with Spiritists (and their critics), attending their conferences, observing the sessions of Spiritist centers, listening to lectures (even giving a few), interviewing them, and teaching a course in their college—it also meant studying their history in their libraries and reading and interpreting the many books and articles they gave me. My method and discourse are therefore syncretic and interdisciplinary, like the work of the Spiritist intellectuals themselves.[10]

Syncretic and interdisciplinary, but, I hope, comprehensible and well organized as well. Part One provides frameworks for understanding the Spiritist movement and the role of the Spiritist intellectuals. The first chapter adopts some of the categories of the holistic ethnographic monograph and describes the position of Spiritism in the Brazilian religious system as well as Spiritist beliefs, practices, social organization, and representations of the otherworld. Chapter 2 situates the Spiritist intellectuals in the broader ideological arena of contemporary Brazil; it also examines the cultural context of Spiritist science and medicine.

Part Two presents contextualized case studies of Spiritist philosophical, scientific, medical, and sociological thought. The first two chapters of this section are historical: Chapter 3 examines Kardec's doctrine in the context of nineteenth-century French ideology, and Chapter 4 moves on to some of the social and cultural forces behind its Brazilianization at the turn of the century. The remaining chapters examine contemporary relations between Spiritism and the parasciences, official and alternative medicine, and the social sciences. Throughout Part Two, each chapter begins with a "reference text" that serves as an organizing device and as an example of a specific kind of discipline (Spiritist doctrine, parascience, medicine, social theory) or "genre" (see Appendix 1) of Spiritist scientific and philosophical thought.[11] Because the theoretical argument of this book is that the narrow class and status dynamics of the spirit-mediumship religions cannot provide an adequate context for understanding Spiritist doctrine, medicine, and science, chapters begin with this context but then move out to the broader religious, scientific/medical, and political contexts. These include other texts, historical events, overheard gossip, observed rituals, and whatever else is relevant to the fullest possible understanding of Spiritist thought in the context of the ideological arena.

PART ONE

AN INTRODUCTION
TO SPIRITISM IN BRAZIL

CHAPTER ONE

THE ELEMENTS OF SPIRITISM IN BRAZIL

"To understand Spiritism," a Spiritist once admonished me, "you must begin with the fact that Brazil is an Afro-Latino country." I take this suggestion seriously and begin with the two poles of Brazil's religious system: one African, dominated by Yoruba religion; the other Christian, dominated by Roman Catholicism. Brazilian religion is therefore substantially different from that of most parts of Latin America, where the non-Western pole of the religious system is rooted in native American cultures. Native American religions do exist in Brazil, and one finds both African-Amerindian syncretism in the north and Northeast and native American spirits in the Umbanda pantheon in southern Brazil, but the indigenous religions play a much less important role in Brazil than in the Andes, Mexico, and Central America. The Brazilian religious system is therefore closest to those of other New World countries of the African diaspora, such as Haiti, Cuba, and even parts of the American South.

Although about 90 percent of all Brazilians declare themselves Catholic in the national census, most of them are only nominally Catholic. In
part this reflects the relatively weak institutionalization of the Catholic
church prior to the twentieth century, when the priest was subservient to
the plantation owner and his Catholicism was absorbed by the latifundia
culture. This historical legacy left a dynamic system of popular Catholicism that includes religious healers, festivals, and pilgrimages as well as a
rich exchange of promises made to saints and miracles that the saints
return to their devoted (Zaluar 1983). Popular Catholicism is not just a
rural phenomenon of the past; it flourishes today even in the largest and
most modern cities (Queiroz 1977). In addition to Catholicism, about 5
to 10 percent of the Brazilian population is Protestant. Presbyterians,
Baptists, and Lutherans lead the list of traditional Protestant churches,
and the Lutherans are well represented among the descendants of German immigrants in the South. Although the traditional Protestant sects
are growing, the most rapidly growing sector of Protestantism is Pentecostalism. In 1930 Pentecostalism constituted only 10 percent of all Protestants, but by 1964 that figure had grown to 73 percent (Bruneau 1974:
63).

At the African end of the religious system, the Yoruba religions
brought by African slaves have had the greatest influence. Yoruba-
derived religions involve spirit mediumship, and the mediums, known as
"mothers of the saints" (babalorixás), receive Yoruba deities called orixás.
These religions are most firmly established in the Northeast; in Bahia
they are known as Candomblé Nagô and in Recife as Xangô (Bastide
[1960] 1978: 191). However, Yoruba culture is not the only strand in
Afro-Brazilian religion. For example, in Maranhão, one finds Dahomey-
influenced religion, and in earlier parts of this century, one could find
another kind of African religion in Rio known as "Macumba." Macumba
emerged from practices that survived among Bantu slaves; however, this
religion has lost most of its original African features, and much of its
early history appears to be irretrievably lost (Hess 1991e).

Umbanda, a Brazilian religion that emerged in the twentieth century, is
sometimes classified as an Afro-Brazilian religion; however, the heavy
participation of the middle classes (Brown 1986; Ortiz 1978), as well as its
incorporation of Catholic and Spiritist elements, makes such a classification problematic. Umbandists recognize the saints of the Catholic church,
the orixás of Candomblé, and the intellectual spirits of Spiritism, but they
also have their own pantheon of spirits which includes slave spirits, or "old
blacks" (pretos velhos), native American spirits (caboclos), trickster Yoruba

spirits (*exús*), and other figures, frequently derived from Brazilian popular culture. Umbanda varies widely from center to center (these centers are sometimes called temples, or *terreiros*), ranging from those which study the doctrine of Allan Kardec to those which appear quite close to Candomblé.

The ecumenical or syncretic spirit of Umbanda is perhaps the most characteristically Brazilian feature of Brazilian popular religion; it provides a parallel in the religious system to the tremendous number of interstitial categories between black and white in the racial system. However, Umbanda is not the only religion that mediates between the Yoruba and Christian religions.[1] Because Spiritism and those Pentecostal sects which receive the Holy Spirit not only practice spirit mediumship/spiritual healing but also embrace the values of Christian morality, they also mediate between popular religious beliefs and orthodox Christianity. The parallel can be overdrawn, however. Unlike the reformist Spiritists and Pentecostalists, Umbandists have an ecumenical outlook toward Catholicism and the Afro-Brazilian religions. For example, Umbandists can also be Catholics, but this is not true for Spiritists or Pentecostalists. Likewise, Umbandists do not have a central, unifying doctrine, whereas Spiritists and Pentecostalists do (respectively, Kardec's works and the Bible). Still, the religious ecumenism of Umbanda, in contrast with the reformist attitude of Spiritism, does not imply that Spiritism might be ecumenical or eclectic in relation to some other system of thought. In fact, the reformist tendency of Spiritists with respect to the religious system contrasts with their ecumenical approach to many alternative therapies and sciences.

Spiritist Doctrine

For Spiritists, the doctrine of Kardec ties together the diverse tendencies within their movement. Allan Kardec is the nom de plume of the French educator Hippolyte Léon Denizard Rivail (1804–69), who had already published widely on pedagogy when he began to study spirit mediumship in the 1850s. As a result of his studies, Kardec became convinced of the scientific validity of reincarnation, the "perispirit" (roughly, the astral body), and spirit communication through mediums, three of the cornerstones of Spiritist doctrine. Spiritists today may be intellectual or evangelical, Roustaingist or Ubaldist,[2] doctrine-oriented or practice-oriented, but they all accept the basic principles of Allan Kardec's first two books, *The Book of the Spirits* (1st ed. 1857) and *The Book of the Mediums* (1859). In addition to these first two books, which employ a relatively scientific discourse, Kardec's doctrine includes *The Gospel According to Spiritism* (1864) and *Heaven and Hell* (1865), which employ a relatively moral-religious discourse, as well as his *Genesis* (1868) and *Posthumous Writings* (1890), the latter meaning "posthumous" in the conventional sense.

Reincarnation distinguishes Spiritism from its Anglo-Saxon sibling, Spiritualism, for which reincarnation is a controversial tenet.[3] As an official National Spiritualist Association of Churches publication states, "Reincarnation is a debatable subject—while organized Spiritualism as a whole has not, as yet, accepted it as part of its belief, it is nevertheless believed to be true by thousands of Spiritualists in America and other countries."[4] For Kardec, reincarnation is closely related to two other principles: the "law of cause and effect," which governs the accumulation of karma according to the goodness of one's deeds, and the importance of free will and choice in the spiritual evolution of each human being across various incarnations. This nexus of principles appears to represent a wedding of nineteenth-century liberalism with Indic doctrines; however, as a unit the relationship between free will and the accumulation of karma also resembles the Augustinian doctrine regarding the relationship between free will and the attainment of grace. Reincarnation thus forms part of a nexus of values in Spiritist doctrine that strikes a resonant chord in Brazil's predominantly Catholic culture.

The corollaries of reincarnation—free will and the law of cause and effect—are among what Kardec terms "the philosophical and moral principles" that derive from the facts of spirit mediumship. As Brazilian Spiritists frequently explain to novices, Kardec's doctrine is "based on science with philosophical implications and moral consequences." For Kardec, these three different aspects of Spiritist doctrine result in different categories of Spiritists:

> Spiritism presents three different aspects, viz., the facts of spirit-manifestation, the philosophic and moral principles deducible from those facts, and the practical applications of which those principles are susceptible; hence three classes into which its adherents are naturally divided, or rather, three degrees of advancement by which they are distinguished, first, those who believe in the reality and genuineness of the spirit manifestations, but confine themselves to the attestation of these, for whom Spiritism is

merely an experimental science; second, those who comprehend
its moral [consequences]; and third, those who put into practice,
or at least endeavor to put into practice, the system of morality
which it is the mission of Spiritism to establish. ([1860] 1875: 420–
21; [1860] 1983: 408)

Consequently, the social divisions of the Spiritist movement into various
groups that are more "scientific" or more "evangelical" are already to
some extent prefigured by the semantic divisions discussed in Kardec's
doctrine.

In addition to reincarnation and its corollaries, the philosophical implications of Kardec's doctrine include the rejection of a number of basic
Christian tenets, among them the divinity of Christ, the trinitarian concept of God, the divine nature of miracles (which Spiritists believe to be
natural, psychic phenomena), the existence of angels and demons (only
more or less highly evolved spirits), and the physical reality of heaven
and hell. As a man of reason, science, and progress, Kardec rejected
these ideas as outmoded superstitions. In the case of heaven and hell, he
even went further and forged an alternative, psychological interpretation: "It was reserved for Spiritism to give, in regard to all these points,
an explanation which is at once, and in the highest degree, rational,
sublime, and consoling, by showing us that we have *in ourselves* our 'hell'
and our 'heaven,' and that we find our 'purgatory' in *the state of incarna-
tion, in our successive corporeal or physical lives*" ([1860] 1875: 408, #1017;
[1860] 1983: #1016). Despite Kardec's rejection of a number of key
Christian dogmas—which is crucial to understanding the hostility that
the Catholic and Protestant churches subsequently harbored against
Spiritism—his doctrine does embrace Christian morality. This appears
most clearly in his *Gospel According to Spiritism* ([1864] 1944c), but even
The Book of Spirits includes maxims that draw on Christian morality. For
example, Kardec writes, "Selfishness is the source of all the vices, as
charity is the source of all of the virtues" ([1860] 1875: 357). Furthermore, along more Protestant lines, Kardec believed that it was not
enough to practice Christian charity; one should also internalize Christian values. This inward embracing of Christian morality is the source of
true happiness, a joy that is completely fulfilled only in the spirit world:
"Man enjoys the first fruits of this felicity upon the earth when he meets
with those with whom he can enter into cordial and noble union. In a life
of greater purity than that of the earth, this felicity becomes ineffable
and unbounded, because their inhabitants meet only with sympathetic

souls whose affection will not be chilled by selfishness" ([1860] 1875: 389, #980).

If Kardec's doctrine represents an attempt to bridge the gap between "is" and "ought," or scientific knowledge and religious morality, this intellectual gap returns in contemporary Brazil as a social difference between two categories of Spiritists: the intellectuals and the nonintellectuals, who are sometimes termed "evangelical Spiritists" or even "Christian Spiritists." Although the division is a noticeable one and one that is evident and important to many Spiritists, it is also fuzzy, and the term for the nonintellectuals is problematic. Following Cavalcanti (1983: 27), "evangelist" seems most appropriate, since even the intellectuals are Christian in the sense of accepting Christian moral teachings. However, the term "evangelista" in Portuguese generally means Protestant, so the English term "evangelist" should be taken to be the equivalent of the Portuguese term "espírita evangélico" (evangelical Spiritist), or someone who follows more the "parte evangélica" (evangelical part) of Kardec's doctrine.

The term "evangelist" has the additional benefit of describing well the air of proselytism that one frequently finds among these Spiritists, and it also corresponds to the Portuguese word in the title of Kardec's *Gospel According to Spiritism* (*O Evangelho Segundo Espiritismo*). One of the key distinguishing features between intellectuals and evangelists is that the intellectuals tend to take more interest in *The Book of the Spirits* or *The Book of the Mediums* than in *The Gospel According to Spiritism*. Spiritist intellectuals frequently complain that the evangelical Spiritists do not pay enough attention to Kardec's more philosophical and scientific texts, *The Book of the Spirits* and *The Book of the Mediums*. They also complain about the evangelists' tendency to view Kardec's writings as quasi-sacred texts marking the "third revelation" (after those of Moses and Christ), whereas the intellectuals see these texts as the sometimes flawed but generally true writings of a brilliant nineteenth-century thinker. For this reason, some Spiritist intellectuals have told me they do not like to be called "Kardecists"; to them, this term suggests an uncritical attitude toward the codifier's texts.[5] Instead, they use the term "Kardecist" only when there is a danger of their being confused with Umbandists; when such a danger is absent, they prefer to use the term "Spiritist" to signify their nondogmatic attitude toward the Kardecian corpus.

Nevertheless, all Spiritists, intellectual and evangelical alike, place a great value on Kardec's doctrine as their basic source of orientation and as the distinguishing feature that separates Spiritism from other spirit-mediumship religions in Brazil (as well as from Anglo-Saxon Spiritual-ism). They call the doctrine "the basis" (*a base*), meaning that it is the starting point for the study of Spiritist doctrine—before one examines Spiritist writings of a second and third echelon, such as the works of the spirits André Luiz and Emmanuel, who communicate in the automatic writing of the medium Francisco Cândido "Chico" Xavier.[6] The term "basis" also has a meaning with respect to the social organization of the Spiritist movement: Spiritist doctrine functions as a kind of cement that provides the "basis" for unity among the diverse tendencies of the movement.[7]

Spiritist Practice

Although one might describe Spiritism in terms of "ritual" (in the sense of secular rituals as described by Leach [1968] and Moore and Myerhoff [1977]), when I have used the term, Spiritists have corrected me and have denied that their movement has any rituals. They associate the term "ritual" with Catholicism, Protestantism, Umbanda, Candomblé, and "religion" in general, a domain they distinguish from their more scientific and philosophical "practice." Another feature that distinguishes Spiritist practice from religious services is that Spiritists do not charge for any of their sessions, services, or charitable activities (except for patients in their psychiatric hospitals). They proudly explain how they are different from Catholics and Protestants, who pass around an offering plate, and Umbanda and Candomblé priests and priestesses, who sometimes charge a fee for their services and for materials or sacrificial animals sometimes used during their rituals. Likewise, North American Spiritualists not only pass the offering plate but usually charge for private psychic readings and séances, and Spiritists frequently told me how they did not like the mercenary tendency of many of their siblings to the north, whom they saw as succumbing to the "materialistic" values of North American culture.

Spiritists recognize several major categories of "sessions" or "meetings," among them doctrinal study, development of mediumship, works of charity, and deobsession or disobsession (*desobsessão*).[8] In the study and development sessions, Spiritists generally read and discuss Kardec or another Spiritist writer, sometimes both. The study and development sessions that I attended usually began and ended with a kind of laying-on of hands called *passes,* and in some cases we drank "fluidified" water that had been spiritually cleansed with *passes*. During the study session itself, we read a passage from Kardec or Xavier and then discussed it in a seminar-like format. In some cases, students were encouraged to relate the passage to problems in their everyday life, not unlike the procedure of Bible study groups. In the mediumistic development sessions, we turned out the lights and concentrated, and some of the mediums-in-development received spirits; others were not successful.

A second major type of Spiritist practice is charitable work, which strikes a resonant chord in a culture imbued with the principle of justification by good works rather than by faith. Spiritist charity includes a wide array of social services that are offered to the working class and the poor, such as nursery services for workers and orphanages for unwanted and homeless children. I would classify most of the Spiritists involved in these services as more "evangelical" than "intellectual," but again these categories are fuzzy. One center that I visited also sponsored a "kilo campaign," and I have heard from other Spiritists about similar campaigns in other centers. In the kilo campaign, each of the more fortunate, middle-class Spiritists who are affiliated with the center donates one kilogram of basic staples every week to the poor, who come once a week to listen to Spiritist doctrine and to receive their groceries.

Spiritists are also committed to providing medical services for the poor. In some large centers, doctors and dentists volunteer their services for the local population, and this work may tie in to the spiritual services of disobsession and *passes*. In Rio, one also tends to find *receitista* mediums, who provide homeopathic prescriptions with the help of spirit guides. Spiritists also own and operate dozens of psychiatric hospitals, of which some are private and others are part of the national medical system. In most of these hospitals, Spiritists control the administration, while the treatment rests in the hands of professional psychiatrists and psychologists, who are the employees. Frequently, next to the hospital, one finds a Spiritist center where mediums receive and "disobsess" the spirits who they believe are causing the mental illness of some of the patients.

In a few hospitals, Spiritist psychiatrists and psychologists also control the day-to-day treatment and operations, and in these cases one finds some alternative therapies of a Spiritist orientation. Such is the case at the Spiritist Hospital of Good Rest (Hospital Espírita de Bom Retiro), led by a psychologist, Maderli Sech, and her husband, Alexandre Sech, a psychiatrist. Both of the Sechs are Spiritists, and since taking over the day-to-day treatment and operations of the hospital, they have gradually changed its therapeutic orientation to include alternative therapies that are more compatible with Spiritist principles. For instance, the Sechs have increased occupational therapy and psychotherapy, cut down the use of drug therapies, introduced Spiritist *passes* and homeopathy, and made plans for yoga therapy. Disobsession still takes place outside the Spiritist hospital in a nearby Spiritist center; generally, patients remain in the hospital while Spiritists take the names of the patients of participating families to the center, where mediums receive and enlighten the obsessing spirits. Alexandre Sech has also instituted a program of evaluation that employs Kirlian photography (see Glossary), and he has publicized this program in talks throughout Brazil. According to Alexandre Sech, some of the ten doctors on the hospital staff left after the changes he and Maderli instituted, but most decided to stay.

Perhaps the primary type of Spiritist therapy in Spiritist centers is "fluidotherapy." Spiritists believe that physical illness and obsessing spirits have a negative influence on the perispirit (roughly equivalent to the astral body) and that *passes* both discharge the negative energies and infuse the perispirit with positive energies. Mediums give *passes* at almost any kind of session, and in the big centers and Spiritist federations, there are often long lines of "frequenters," nonmembers who attend irregularly and receive such therapy from mediums. This is usually a private practice that occurs in a small room off to the side of the central room or lecture hall. To perform a *passe*, a medium waves his or her arms over the body of a client and thus provides a transfer of energies to the client. The source of the energies may be the medium (in the magnetic type of *passe*) or the spiritual world (in the spiritual type) or both (in the mixed type).[9] Figure 1 shows one exposition of the different sources of energy for *passes;* drawn by a Spiritist engineer, its flowchart format also expresses how Spiritists construct their practice in scientific terms.

Although disobsession may be viewed as a kind of therapy for the living, intellectuals tend to see it more in terms of education and counseling for the spirits. Spiritists prefer the term "disobsession" to "exorcism" because they do not believe in demons and think that possession represents only an extreme case of the more general problem of spirit obsession, or the ability of certain perturbing or earthbound spirits to influence the thoughts and health of the incarnate "obsessed" (*obsediados*). Spirit obsession may occur for a variety of reasons, but Spiritists believe that a large number of the frequenters who come to their centers for disobsession treatment are victims of black magic. Many Spiritists (but less so among the intellectuals) do not distinguish among Umbanda,

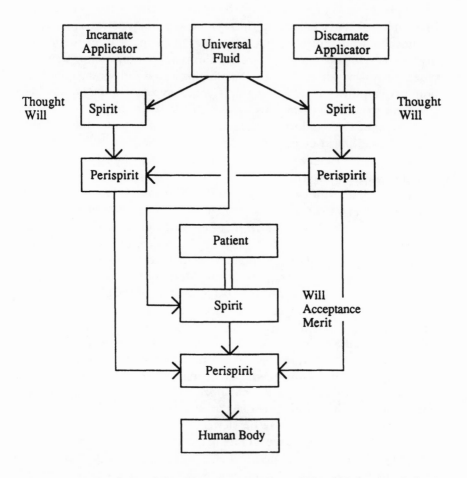

Figure 1. Mechanisms of the *Passe*. (SOURCE: Peres 1984: 238, by permission.)

Macumba, Quimbanda, Candomblé, Xangô, and other varieties of more or less Afro-Brazilian religions; to them, it is all "black magic" (*magia negra*). For these Spiritists, "black" has associations of both evil and African, and in performing disobsession on victims of "black" magic, these Spiritists are implicitly "disobsessing" Brazil of its African heritage, which to them represents a burden holding Brazil back from science, progress, enlightenment, and development.

However, Spiritists do not blame the Afro-Brazilian religions as the only source of obsessing spirits. I have also seen the spirits of Catholics, Protestants, atheist intellectuals, gamblers, and sex maniacs appear in disobsession sessions. Blame also rests with the victim, because the baser thoughts of the living—desire, envy, greed, and so on—attract obsessing spirits. Therefore, disobsession and the *passe* are only spiritual bandages, which can alleviate the symptoms but not the cause of the spirit obsession (M. Peres 1985). In order to eliminate the cause and prevent further obsessions, the frequenter must study Spiritist doctrine and put into practice its moral consequences. Thus, disobsession involves evangelizing not only spirits but the afflicted, a process that Spiritists refer to as "indoctrination" (*doutrinação*).

In some centers, frequenters stay in the same room and watch the "mediums of incorporation" (*médiuns de incorporação*), who sit at the table and receive the earthbound spirits, while other members, the "mediums of clarification" (*médiuns de esclarecimento,* who do not "receive" or "incorporate" spirits), sit at the table and "indoctrinate" or enlighten these spirits. In other centers, frequenters will stay in one room and listen to an evangelical message while the mediums perform disobsession behind closed doors in another room. Spiritist intellectuals generally prefer that the client not be present during the disobsession session; if the client were present, they believe, the obsessing spirit might be tempted to attack him or her (W. F. Melo 1984: 21). The client might also become hysterical, an event that I witnessed during several sessions in which clients were present. In both kinds of disobsession (i.e., with and without the presence of clients), higher-level "spirits of light" (*espíritos de luz*) help the mediums; and at some points, usually after the evening's work has been finished, a medium may receive a spirit of light, who conveys a message for the members. The message of the spirit of light usually emphasizes the evangelical and Christian side of Spiritist doctrine and practice.

Although there are standardized rules for holding disobsession meetings (e.g., Xavier 1964), in practice there is quite a variety among centers, and it is worth comparing two very different Spiritist centers, one located in São Paulo and associated with the Spiritist intellectuals of that city, the other located in Niterói and headed by a Roustaingist medium. In the São Paulo center, Spiritists do not allow the afflicted to attend the disobsession meeting; instead, the afflicted must either wait or attend an evangelization session, during which they listen to a member of the center who talks about Christian morality and Spiritist doctrine. This is very different from the practice in the Niterói center, where the frequenters sat in rows of chairs and faced the table where the mediums sat and performed the disobsession.

In the Paulista center, the disobsession meeting began with a lecture that was part of a course on Spiritist doctrine. After the lecture and discussion, the mediums broke up into groups of four, seated together in a circle, and one of the mediums turned off the lights and turned on the classical music, signifying the transition from the this-worldly to the otherworldly part of the session. Each group of four mediums had a stack of green cards filled out by those clients who suffered from spirit obsession. The cards bear only the name and address of the client, not a description of the affliction. Spirit guides ("spirits of light") use these cards to summon the obsessing spirits, but the guides who summon the spirits do not always send the obsessing spirit who is associated with the name on the green card. This does not represent a problem, however, because the Spiritists know that the real cure for spirit obsession is the afflicted person's decision to make an inner change. In other words, in this relatively intellectual Spiritist center, the work of disobsession is more that of a therapy or educational session for the spirits than for the frequenters.

Each group of mediums received three to six spirits during the session. There were various types, including spirits of priests, intellectuals, and doctors, but the largest category was victims of black magic. The members of the group took turns receiving spirits. While a medium of incorporation received a spirit, another member of the center (or medium of clarification) spoke with it, and the other two members generally remained silent and joined hands with the former two in order to donate positive energy to the spiritual chain they formed with their hands.

Usually the medium of clarification was able to persuade the spirit that he or she had really died and was lost, and the spirit then agreed to let a guiding spirit escort it to a higher plane. More recalcitrant spirits were taken by the guiding spirits to a spiritual hospital to receive treatment. In some particularly difficult cases, the leader of the center intervened. For example, in one case of black magic, the leader had to send spiritual energy charges into the medium's feet; then she took off seven invisible capes and seven invisible collars, which symbolized the bonds of black magic. In another case, the spirit was a woman who could not forget an evil deed she had performed. After an attempt to persuade the spirit that "to forgive is to forget" did not work, the leader regressed the spirit back to the traumatic event, which led to a teary recall and a release from the memory. At the close of the session, the leader received one of her guiding spirits, who offered some words of wisdom to the group, and then the session ended.

According to my informant for this center, the mediums use a great deal of hypnosis, and they sometimes have to regress spirits who suffer from traumatic memories, a practice that they had followed long before past-lives therapy had become the vogue. In other cases, the leader gave the spirit a kind of shock treatment by putting her hands over the medium's "chakras"—centers of energy in the spiritual body—and sending energy into them. On another occasion, during a talk that was perhaps "para inglês ver" (for the gringo's sake), the leader of this center also emphasized that in some cases mediums were not really receiving spirits. She said that, in such cases, disobsession functions as a "group therapy" that supports the spiritual and psychological development of the medium.

In contrast to the ambience of the Paulista center, that of the Niterói center was much less like a school or counseling center than a Pentecostalist church. For example, the mediums used a microphone in the manner of television evangelists and sermonized to the frequenters as we sat and waited for our turn to come. The session opened with a reading from Spiritist doctrine; then one of the mediums gave an evangelical talk in which she invited the members of the audience to open their hearts to Jesus. After this, the leader of the center made a few informal comments, then an assistant turned down the lights. The mediums and mediums-in-development left their seats among the frequenters and took their places at the two tables at the front of the room. A group of three mediums gave *passes* to the frequenters, who left the audience one by one and took a seat at the front of the room. Among the frequenters was a woman who had brought her mentally retarded son to receive *passes;* immediately after he had been attended to, the pair left.

After everyone received their *passes,* the leader of the center separated out about half a dozen people with problems, directing them to receive treatment one at a time. Clients took a seat at the foot of the table and placed their hands on the tabletop. The mediums sat at the table with their hands on the surface, and then one or more of the mediums of incorporation received a spirit. The remaining mediums of clarification then talked in low, hushed voices and "indoctrinated" the spirit; that is, they reoriented the spirit according to Spiritist doctrine. When this process ended, a new client took the seat at the foot of the table, and the process was repeated. On this evening, I witnessed a particularly violent case of a woman who did not want to sit down, and she ended up standing on the chair off to the side where the people receive *passes*. Several mediums made awful animal noises as they received the spirit, which, according to my informant, probably meant that they had received one of the "baser" spirits of Umbanda or Quimbanda (black magic). Eventually the mediums were successful, and the woman left calmly; the leader and his wife returned to the table. After other episodes of disobsession, the meeting ended with two prayers, one by the leader's wife and the other by the leader through his spirit guide, a Spanish doctor who had been his brother in a past life.

To summarize, a major difference between the two centers was the emphasis on education in the first center, where the session began with a class that was part of a course on Spiritism. The second center had a more evangelical approach and appeared to incorporate Umbanda spirits and a Pentecostalist preaching style into its "ritual." Another difference was that the Paulista center viewed disobsession primarily as a means for helping to reorient lost or errant spirits, and it was only peripherally connected with healing and the problems of the living, which were treated separately in a session of study or "indoctrination." In contrast, the second center linked disobsession to the ailments of the living. Of course, the two processes of helping the quick and the dead do go together, but as this comparison shows, there are important differences of emphasis from center to center.

Social Space and Social Organization

The spatial arrangement of the Niterói center is much more common than that of the Paulista center—so much so that Spiritism is sometimes called "Spiritism of the table" to distinguish it from Umbanda. In this center, an opposition emerged between the members of the center (the mediums of incorporation and/or clarification), who sit together at a table at the front of the social space, and the frequenters, who sit in rows of chairs and who sometimes come as clients for disobsession. The anthropologist Roberto DaMatta notes that in Brazil the table may serve as a symbol of personal ties among the people who "compose" the table (1981: 251). In contrast, the rows of chairs, where the frequenters sit, represent the outside of the social space, the place for those who are beyond the personal ties of the table. During the disobsession meetings, the categories of "member" and "frequenter" within the Spiritist center collapse with respect to the obsessing spirits, who now become the outsiders. Spiritists will often say to the spirits, "You are in the house of God," and Spiritists sometimes refer to the Spiritist center as a "home" (lar).[10]

Thus, two important divisions mark the social space of the Spiritist center: (1) table and row; (2) the center, or house of God, and the outside space of the obsessing spirits. These spatial divisions correspond to the more general spatial categories of Brazilian culture that DaMatta describes in A Casa e a Rua (The House and the Street, 1985). In the house, one is a "person" (pessoa)—or, better, an "insider"—that is, someone who is related by particularistic ties of kinship and friendship networks, whereas in the street, one is an "outsider" (indivíduo) with respect to these networks.[11] For DaMatta, the Latin American ethic of "personalism" represents a point midway between Western individualism and Indic holism as discussed by Louis Dumont (1980). DaMatta argues that Brazil is not just a personalistic culture; it is characterized by traditional, personalistic values as well as by modern, universalistic values, and these two types of values confront each other in a unique way that he calls "the Brazilian dilemma" (1978). This conflict of values and its relationship to Spiritism will be described using a terminology that blends DaMatta's and Parsons's categories.[12]

The values and structures of the Spiritist center become clearer when one contrasts the social space of the Spiritist center with that of Spiritualist and Protestant churches in the United States. Although it is also common in the United States to refer to the church as the "house of the Lord," the values instituted in the Spiritualists' "house of the Lord" differ strikingly from those of their siblings in Brazil. In North American Spiritualist and Protestant churches, a dialogue takes place between the congregation and the minister, who speaks alone and from the pulpit or lectern rather than with a group of members seated at the table. The logic of a Spiritualist minister speaking from a pulpit is that of an individual speaking to the congregation assembled as a community, which is viewed in Anglo-Saxon culture as an assemblage of equal individuals brought together under a social contract or covenant; that is, under a system of universalistic values. This contrasts with the polarity of insider/ outsider in the Spiritist center, in which a member of the center sits or stands at the table and speaks to the frequenters assembled as outsiders; that is, as actors whose only relationship to one another is their status of being outside the personal network of kin and friendship ties of the Spiritist center or "home."

The values that one sees reflected in the spatial organization of Spiritist centers are also reflected in the social organization of Spiritist centers and federations, which tend to be personalistic, hierarchical, and authoritarian. Spiritist centers often are built up around a single, charismatic medium or around a small number of people who provide the funding, labor, and leadership of the center. Likewise, the Brazilian Spiritist Federation (FEB), the leading national federalizing body, has an authoritarian structure. Although each state federation has a voice in the FEB's National Federative Council, ultimate power in the selection of the president lies with the FEB, a self-perpetuating, collegiate body that in effect controls the National Federative Council.

Despite the charismatic organization of many Spiritist centers and the authoritarian structure of the FEB, some Spiritists have articulated alternative, democratic visions that call for a change in the top-down organization of the FEB, which some refer to pejoratively as "the Vatican." In 1984 and 1985, for example, the Niterói-based Spiritist Federation of the State of Rio de Janeiro (FEERJ) and some other state federations called for a democratization of the National Federative Council.[13] As I talked to more Spiritists, I also heard that the large and powerful Spiritist Federation of the State of São Paulo (FEESP)—probably the largest in Brazil, and much larger than the FEB itself—had broken all ties with the FEB, a move that some Spiritists told me represented a big step toward democratizing the FEB or that was perhaps even the beginning of a schism in the Spiritist movement. Yet, when I interviewed the president of the FEESP about this "schism," he downplayed differences and explained relations between the FEB and the FEESP by introducing a third, mediating federation:

> So you asked whether the FEESP does not belong to the FEB. It's not that the FEESP doesn't belong to the FEB. It's just that we [the FEESP] created a department here in São Paulo in order to represent the FEESP [to the FEB's National Federative Council]. We created USE, the Union of Spiritist Societies of the State of São Paulo, and this is what is enrolled there [with the FEB]. It was

created in order to make the fusion. USE was created precisely as a branch of the FEESP, but they understood it differently. . . . USE was supposed to be a part of us [the FEESP], but contrary and perturbed elements—those who thought they were the lords of the situation—thought that the FEESP was below them, and so on. . . . [Instead, USE] is an appendage that has become autonomous. . . . But another thing: we and those from USE, the board of directors of today, are like this—closely tied. We go there; they come here. We have meetings here; we also go to their meetings there. . . .[14]

Rather than dwell on the details of these rather labyrinthine interfederation relations, details that seemed to change with each person's version of the story, one might instead examine the values articulated. The introduction of a third federation that mediates relations between the FEESP and the FEB is inscribed in a narrative that reveals a strong concern with hierarchy: who is "part of" whom and who is "below" whom. Furthermore, the dissident elements of USE are even described as "perturbed" elements, a loaded word in the Spiritist idiom that resonates with the idea of "perturbing spirits" (*espíritos perturbadores*). For example, one Spiritist in Niterói told me that when she disagreed with her superior in a Spiritist organization, the latter told her she was suffering from obsessing or perturbing spirits and needed to undergo disobsession: from dissent to disobsession. A second example of the articulation of traditional Brazilian values in this narrative is the ethos of personalism: while the president downplays conflicts by locating them in the past, he describes the current relations between USE and the FEESP as mediated by friendly, personal ties. Thus, while there is a hint of a move toward more democratic structures within the Spiritist movement, even someone who is in a position to question the authority of the FEB still reveals a discourse that is preoccupied with hierarchy and personalism.

Of course, such an interpretation should not negate the fact that the FEESP provides a great many badly needed services to the poor; but, to paraphrase Bastide (1967: 14), who saw in Spiritism a continuation of the traditional Brazilian virtue of charity rather than a concern for social justice, these services come wrapped in an ethic that teaches the poor to be hard workers and morally upright citizens rather than to seek political and social empowerment. Yet, the president also sees his work as having a political impact, if only in a more indirect sense: "We work for the doctrine. We found schools; we strive to teach; we strive to make students; we strive to make workers. We strive to make a moral movement in order for this whole situation to change. And this is what we are working for. . . . We work with Christ, and we strive to serve Christ."

The Spirit World

The dramatic oppositions of this-worldly Spiritism—intellectual and evangelical, democratic and authoritarian, medium and frequenter—are to some extent ameliorated in representations of the other world, which one can view as a kind of utopian blueprint for this-worldly Brazil. To begin to understand the complexities of the other world, one must first note what one does *not* find there. The other world is inhabited by spirits, which are human or extraterrestrial but not supernatural: Spiritists do not believe in the existence of Candomblé *orixás* or Catholic and Protestant angels and demons. Instead, they think that these categories represent either "mystifications" or inadequate descriptions of what are merely discarnate human spirits.

From the Spiritists' point of view, Umbandists at least do not misunderstand this fundamental point, and in this sense they are not so backward as Catholics or Protestants. However, Spiritists generally believe that the low social status of Umbanda spirits—which are often slaves and Indians—reflects on the Umbanda mediums' "low level" of spiritual development: both Umbanda and Candomblé mediums lack Spiritist doctrine, and as a result they tend to attract less-developed spirits. This in turn can cause the mediums to attract malevolent spirits and even to become obsessed by these spirits, and this, in some Spiritists' eyes, makes these religions "asylums" of the obsessed.

It is true that the mediums of the large Spiritist Federation of the State of São Paulo (the FEESP) receive spirits of Indian chiefs, but to the Paulista mediums these noble savages are a long way from the backward *caboclo* spirits of Umbanda sessions. Theoretically, the Catholic saints, *caboclos*, and black slaves of Umbanda could appear within the Spiritist session, since they are all spirits of former humans; the only time I have seen Umbanda spirits appear in Spiritist sessions, however, they appeared as lost or obsessing spirits, as in the case of the above-noted disobsession in which the woman got up on the chair. From this perspective, the conflict between the spirits of light, who aid and oversee disobsession, and these wayward and lost spirits, whom the mediums receive for indoctrination, corresponds to the social confrontation between the Spiritist movement and other religions, particularly Umbanda and Candomblé.

The spirit guides of Spiritist mediums often represent professions or historical figures of great distinction. They may be highly developed spiritual figures, such as Ramatís (an Asian wise man) or Emmanuel (sometimes associated with the Roman Senator Publius Lentulus and the Jesuit leader Manuel da Nóbrega); physicians, such as Dr. Fritz or André Luiz (the latter is sometimes associated with the scientist-doctor Carlos Chagas, and the German doctor is a respected category); great writers, such as Irmão X (Humberto de Campos) and Victor Hugo; or important figures in the history of the Spiritist movement in Brazil, such as Bezerra de Menezes. In all of these cases, the spirits represent what Spiritists believe to be the most exemplary aspects of human civilization: spirituality, science and medicine, and literature.

Spiritist representations of the spirit world are not limited to categories of spirits; there is a rich literature, dictated by spirits through mediums, which describes in detail what life is like on the other side. Of the otherworldly Spiritist travelogues, perhaps *Nosso Lar* (*Our Home*, 1944), psychographed by the medium Chico Xavier, is the best known. At the time I was doing my field research, Xavier was a retired civil servant of lower-middle-class background who lived in Uberaba, a city in the interior state of Minas Gerais. Spiritists believe that his humble background and minimal formal education support their conclusion that the highly erudite spirits he receives could not possibly be products of his unconscious mind. The book *Nosso Lar* is the first in a series of the same name that the spirit doctor André Luiz wrote through the medium Xavier, and almost all Spiritists are familiar with the work. One can therefore speak with some assurance of the representations of the otherworld in *Nosso Lar* as characteristic of Brazilian Spiritism.

Nosso Lar is the name of the celestial colony reserved for Brazilians. It has been in existence since the sixteenth century, when the first Portuguese who died in Brazil founded it (Xavier 1984: 32, 69), but it is still in the development stage (*trabalho de realização*), a situation that many Brazilians would liken to their terrestrial homeland. This rather low position in the celestial hierarchy is reminiscent of Brazilians' perception of their country's place in the this-worldly, international hierarchy. Still, Nosso Lar is located directly above Rio de Janeiro, and for Brazilians it is, even literally, "our home." The analysis that follows will provide one interpretation of why that is so. This interpretation will not present a detailed reading of the text of *Nosso Lar;* instead, its goal is to situate the colony Nosso Lar in the broader context of Brazilian culture.

The book *Nosso Lar* contains an evangelical preface written by the spirit Emmanuel, but the principal author is the spirit André Luiz, who was a doctor in this life and who is associated by some Spiritists with the famous Brazilian medical scientist Carlos Chagas. The opposition between Emmanuel and André Luiz corresponds to the difference in the Spiritist movement between the evangelists and the intellectuals, and it marks *Nosso Lar* as a relatively "intellectual" book. Indeed, the central dilemma that Luiz attempts to resolve in this book is the relationship between the intellectual and the emotional, or the scientific and the religious, sides of his psyche.

Nosso Lar opens with André Luiz tossing about in the *Umbral,* a threshold zone between earth and heaven where he has spent an unknown amount of time being chased by one terrifying image after another:

> I had the impression of having lost my sense of time. The notion of space also evaporated.
>
> I was convinced that I no longer numbered among the living of this world. My lungs gulped in huge breaths.
>
> Since when had I become the missile of irresistible forces? It was impossible to know.
>
> In truth, I felt bitterly dwarfed by the obscure grids of horror. My hair bristled, my heart skipped beats, and a terrible fear engulfed me. Many times I yelled like a madman, asking for forgiveness and crying out against the sad depression that subjugated my spirit, but when the implacable silence did not absorb me, a booming voice with cries even more moving than my own was the only answer my cries received. (Xavier 1944: 17)

Luiz calls out, but no one answers; he hears only silence or the voice of someone more isolated than he.

Finally, after what seems like an eternity of suffering, the celestial powers send Clarêncio, a highly evolved spirit, to rescue Luiz and to become his patron: "A friendly old man smiled at me paternally. He leaned toward me and stared at me with his big, lucid eyes and said, 'Courage, my son! The Lord has not abandoned you' " (Xavier 1944: 24). Luiz later learns that he was rescued only after his mother descended from higher planes to Nosso Lar in order to *dar um jeitinho* (intervene to bend some rules) on her son's behalf (pp. 47–48). After her prodding, the celestial bureaucracy sends Clarêncio. The double intervention—the mother in the bureaucracy and the bureaucracy in the threshold zone of *Umbral*—has the underlying structure of the transformation of outsider into insider, of street into house.

Umbral is literally a "threshold," that which in DaMatta's terms divides house and street. One might map this division of house/street onto the opposition of celestial Nosso Lar/terrestrial Brazil, or one might interpret *Umbral* itself as a social space like the street, where one is an outsider with respect to the personal ties of Nosso Lar and Brazil. In either case, Nosso Lar is—as the name suggests—structurally a "home." Furthermore, like the dwellers of terrestrial Brazilian homes, its inhabitants are constantly preoccupied with maintaining the boundary between itself and the outside zones, where other spirits—like terrestrial thieves and gangs—lurk and threaten to invade.

André Luiz feels at home in Nosso Lar, and it is not very difficult for him to adapt to life there. After a short period of recuperation, he decides to work for the Ministry of Aid and its hospital. A doctor during his earthly existence, Luiz characterizes his identity as a unity of "the friend, the doctor, and the researcher" (Xavier 1944: 74). In this triangle of roles, the figure of the doctor appears between the other two terms— in other words, between roles governed respectively by particularistic and universalistic principles. The dilemma represented by these two options preoccupies and troubles Luiz, and before he goes to work in the Ministry of Aid, an elderly, maternal woman named Laura offers him advice on the nature of his work there:

> Don't try to be a moth and go from lamp to lamp. I know that the spirit of intellectual research is very strong in you. Being a studious doctor and passionately interested in novelties and enigmas, it will be very easy for you to fit into your new position. But don't forget that you will be able to obtain insights more precious than the simple analysis of things. Curiosity, even when wise, is a very interesting mental zone, but it is sometimes dangerous. . . . Learn to construct your circle of sympathies, and don't forget that the spirit of investigation should manifest itself after the spirit of service. (Xavier 1944: 137–38)

Laura, female and charitable, speaks to André, male and intellectual, and advises him that in the work of healing he can find unity between these opposing tendencies. Like the ideal Spiritist, the ideal doctor combines knowledge and compassion.

Thus, neither head nor heart dominates André Luiz, and he is likewise neither completely friend nor researcher. The dilemmas that the spirit Luiz faces and resolves suggest why it is that Spiritist mediums have an elective affinity for doctor spirits: the role of the doctor mediates between important clusters of values for which Spiritist doctrine and the Spiritist movement as a whole also mediate. For Spiritists, the movement is a synthesis both of moral-religious values (heart) and of scientific thought (head), ideological divisions that correspond to the social divisions between evangelical and intellectual Spiritists and between the mystical masses and the scientific elites. André Luiz's dilemma therefore corresponds to the larger dilemma of the Spiritist movement in Brazilian culture and society: it mediates between elite thought, represented here by science and the head, and popular thought, represented here by religion and the heart.

A similar process occurs in the representation of the government of Nosso Lar. The anthropologist Luiz Soares (1979: 139) suggests a close similarity between Xavier's thought and integralism,[15] and while this point may be controversial, it is true that the government of Nosso Lar has a hierarchical structure reminiscent of that of the Estado Novo, the authoritarian state of the Getúlio Vargas regime, which dominated Brazil when *Nosso Lar* was written. In Nosso Lar, there are no elections; instead, the government is a dictatorship run by spirits from higher planes who descend to Nosso Lar to perform their functions as charity work, not unlike the charitable practices that middle-class Spiritists perform in the centers for the working class and the poor. The social organization of Nosso Lar is based on six government ministries and reconstructs the Latin American political structure of bureaucracies that surround strong leaders.[16] Luiz's colleague Lísias explains the social organization of Nosso Lar as follows:

Didn't you see, during the prayer, our Spiritual Governor surrounded by seventy-two collaborators? Those are the ministers of Nosso Lar. The colony, which is essentially still in the development stage, is divided into six ministries. We have the Ministries of Regeneration, Aid, Communication, Enlightenment, Elevation, and Divine Union. Given that our city is in a zone of transition, the first four connect us with the terrestrial spheres, and the last two link us with the superior plane. The lowest services are localized in the

Ministry of Regeneration, and the most sublime in that of Divine Union. Clarêncio, our friend and boss, is one of the ministers of Aid. (Xavier 1944: 51)

The government of Nosso Lar is therefore a huge bureaucracy run by a friendly dictator, a semideveloped colony in the intercolonial celestial scheme. Like the government of contemporary Brazil, it claims to be effective and compassionate, and it is in theory houselike, but it still requires some lobbying or the *jeitinho*, as when André Luiz's mother intervenes to rescue him from the *Umbral:* on earth as it is in heaven.

Still, the spirit world of Nosso Lar is not a simple reflection of Brazilian society, not even the Brazilian society of the Estado Novo. Although both share a hierarchical and authoritarian political structure, in Nosso Lar the dictatorship is benevolent and the *jeitinho* works for common people such as André Luiz. In contrast to this-worldly Brazil, in Nosso Lar the governor does not need to use authoritarian police measures to deal with dissidence; instead, he merely explains to the troublemakers their mistakes, which they readily see (Xavier 1944: 55). If the governor of Nosso Lar is a kind of Brazilian *coronel*, he is a modified one, for he does not need to call on hired thugs (*jagunços*). Furthermore, the substantive concerns of the ministries of Nosso Lar differ from those of the terrestrial Brazilian ministries: only a madman would choose the Orwellian National Intelligence Service (SNI) of this world over the Ministry of Aid of the otherworld. Thus, the possibility of reading *Nosso Lar* as a critique of the Estado Novo exists alongside that of reading it as an integralist text: on earth as it is not in heaven.

Representations of otherworldly politics and social organization are by no means static, and upon moving on to the 1950s and the medium Hercílio Maes's (1965) description of life among the more spiritual Martian race, one finds a somewhat more democratic political organization with a greater role for women that corresponds to the democratic interlude in Brazilian politics during the 1950s and early 1960s. Likewise, by the 1980s, Zíbia Gasparetto's description of the otherworld includes political demonstrations against the higher spiritual levels and a thoroughly democratic rhetoric that is more in tune with the "diretas já!" (direct elections now!) prodemocracy movement of the early 1980s (Hess 1989b).

My argument here, as throughout this book, is to question the prevailing social science representation of Spiritism (particularly Spiritist-intellectual thought) as a middle-class, elite, or bourgeois ideology and to show instead how closer inspection reveals a more complex process of mediation between elite and popular ideology, authoritarian and democratic values. This argument draws considerable support from the Spiritists' self-representations, which are replete with images of mediation. Spiritists—from Kardec's description of his doctrine as a synthesis of science, philosophy, and religion; to the mediums' bridging of this world and the other world; to the value dilemmas of André Luiz and the sociopolitical structures of Nosso Lar—represent themselves as mediators. The message is the medium.

CHAPTER TWO

SPIRITIST INTELLECTUALS
AND THEIR WORK

Unlike the majority of Spiritists, the intellectuals generally have college educations and belong to one of the professions. They also have their own specialized institutes and associations whose activities are distinct from the day-to-day work of Spiritist centers. However, intellectuals sometimes assist in the charitable and evangelical work of the centers, and it may therefore be useful to make a distinction between the Spiritist intellectual as an actor and as a role. The latter involves researching, teaching, and writing about the scientific and philosophical aspects of Spiritism.[1]

The Spiritist Medical Association of São Paulo (AMESP) and the Campus Universitário "Dr. Bezerra de Menezes" (Brazil's Spiritist college) in Curitiba are the largest of the Spiritist-intellectual institutions. Other organizations associated with the intellectuals—such as the Brazilian Institute of Psychobiophysical Research (IBPP) in São Paulo and the Institute of Brazilian Spiritist Culture (ICEB) in Rio—are little more than

small offices, yet their influence within the Spiritist movement is dispro-
portionately much greater than their size. The IBPP, for example, is the
organization of Hernani Guimarães Andrade, whose work has set the
standard throughout Brazil for a Spiritist vision of scientific research.
There are now institutes of psychobiophysical research in several cities
across the country, and Hernani Andrade designed much of the curriculum for the parapsychology program of the Spiritist college in Curitiba.
Likewise, the ICEB—which is only an office in the Rio de Janeiro–based
state Spiritist union[2]—has, like Hernani Andrade's institute, an influence disproportionate to its size. Among its activities, the ICEB runs a
well-attended lecture series, and its leaders have argued in favor of a
more scientific and philosophical interpretation of Spiritist doctrine
(Dias 1985).

The Campus Universitário "Dr. Bezerra de Menezes" is a small college
on the outskirts of Curitiba. The college has three faculties, two short of
the number necessary for becoming a university (which would bring with
it both a gain in status and a loss of control). The college's success is
largely the work of Octávio Melchíades Ulysséa and his wife Neida. Despite the importance of these two charismatic leaders, the college is quite
institutionalized and has a sizable faculty and staff that allow it to offer
undergraduate degrees in a number of areas. Most important for the
development of Spiritist science is the parapsychology program, which in
the 1980s was an undergraduate program for which there were plans to
expand to the graduate level. This program was built around the National Institute of Psychobiophysical Research, led in the mid-1980s by
Cristina and Luciano Rocha, two protégés of Hernani Andrade.

By far the most active of the Spiritist-intellectual organizations is the
AMESP. Although the AMESP is technically a São Paulo medical organization, it attracts members from outside the health professions and outside São Paulo. Its members meet on Saturday mornings to hear a guest
speaker, frequently a non-Spiritist psychologist, doctor, or scientist but
sometimes also a member of the Spiritist movement. In addition to providing a guest lecture series, the AMESP has pioneered the introduction
of neurolinguistic programming and past-lives hypnotherapy into Brazil, and it cosponsored the First International Conference on Alternative
Therapies. Its members are especially interested in the past-lives therapy
because it provides a link between psychotherapy and the Spiritist principle of reincarnation.

Some other organizations and groups might be included among the

Spiritist intellectuals, but I chose not to research them in detail. There is a group of Rosicrucians with some Spiritists at UNICAMP (the State University of São Paulo at Campinas), but they are not closely integrated with the organizations mentioned above. The Campinas group has held several conferences on "mind-matter interaction," and they were hoping to establish an Institute for the Study of Mind-Matter Interaction at this prestigious state university. In July 1985 they held the First International Conference on Mind-Matter Interaction, which included celebrity alternative physicists and philosophers from North America, Europe, and elsewhere. At this conference, the Spiritist voice was just one among many, reflecting the multiple constituencies of the Campinas group.

Two other groups in Rio might be confused with the Spiritist intellectuals. The Society of Medicine and Spiritism of Rio de Janeiro includes some doctors among its members, but it focuses on disobsessing its clients rather than on producing an elite, scientific discourse. Although the second Carioca organization, the Brazilian Association of Parapsychology (ABRAP), has informal ties with Spiritist intellectuals, and although several of its members believe in the existence of spirits, technically the organization has a secular, non-Spiritist and non-Catholic orientation, and the president who assumed office after the Spiritist Mário Machado retired, Horta Santos, is not a Spiritist. Nevertheless, among rival Catholic parapsychologists there appears to be a perception that the ABRAP is a Spiritist organization, and one ABRAP leader informed me that the organization has encountered difficulties in its efforts to gain educational accreditation—a problem which he believes is due to Jesuit influence in the Federal Department of Education.

Although I visited all of these organizations, I had more prolonged contact with Dr. Hernani; with the AMESP, whose meetings and conferences I attended in 1985 and where I gave two guest lectures; with the Bezerra de Menezes College, where I gave an introductory anthropology course; and with the ICEB, where I gave two guest lectures. By attending conferences and meetings and by giving invited lectures and teaching classes, I became acquainted with many of the leading Spiritist intellectuals and developed an understanding of how their thought fits into what I am calling the "ideological arena." Likewise, at the same time, I developed some understanding of how their thought and style of interaction expresses some of the deeper values and structures of Brazilian culture.

Spiritist Intellectuals in the Brazilian Ideological Arena

Spiritist intellectuals help the Spiritist movement to position itself in the complex arena of competing ideologies, sciences, medical systems, and religions. In so doing, they rely on Kardec's doctrine for guidance in their efforts to reinterpret parapsychology, to propose alternatives to official medicine, and to contribute their own social theory of Brazilian religious syncretism and healing. The multiple domains of Spiritist scientific theory mean that Spiritist intellectuals have relations with several other actors in the ideological arena. Within the religious system proper, the most salient Others are evangelical Spiritists, Umbandists, Candomblé adepts, and laypeople who do not belong to any of the above groups (generally nominal Catholics). Within the broader ideological arena, there is also a dialogue between Spiritists and representatives of the state (e.g., New Republic legislators and judges), Catholic parapsychologists, natural scientists, social scientists, medical professionals, parapsychologists from other countries (especially Western Europe and the United States), and a variety of occult or New Age groups (ufologists, astrologists, Rosicrucians, etc.).[3] Since it is better to introduce these Others in the specific contexts discussed in Part Two of this book, I shall restrict my comments to only a few more contextual remarks.

In Brazil there is no secular, academic organization of parapsychologists such as the Parapsychological Association, whose members come principally from North America, Australia, Japan, and Western Europe. With the exception of one doctoral dissertation (Lessa 1975) and a pair of articles on the psychoanalysis of telepathic dreams (Levy Júnior 1970), the secular university environment has fostered no empirical research which could be compared to that of the Parapsychological Association. When I reviewed the major Brazilian psychology, psychiatry, and psychoanalysis journals for the 1960s and 1970s, I found only a few articles that provided cursory descriptions of Northern Hemisphere parapsychology (e.g., Passos 1964; Ribas 1966), and two of the authors of this group were a Catholic parapsychologist (Quevedo 1962) and a Theosophist/Spiritist psychiatrist (Lyra 1976a, 1976b). A medical doctor and hypnotist, Osmard Andrade Faria, has shown some interest in the topic and has written a textbook of parapsychology (1981), but his work is rather isolated from his colleagues in the medical profession. Although orthodox scientists and doctors in Brazil are probably slightly less skeptical of parapsychology than those in Western Europe and North America, it is still a heterodox science in Brazil. As the psychiatry professor Darcy de Mendonça Uchôa summarized, "The Brazilian university environment has shown itself to be adverse to this material" (1976: 107; see also 1981).

Because there is no academic, secular community of parapsychologists (Hess 1987c), Spiritists tend to situate their alternative theories of science and medicine within a triple field that includes orthodox Brazilian medicine, the parapsychology of North America and Western Europe, and Catholic parapsychology. Probably the most important of the disciplines against which Spiritist intellectuals define their own theories and ideas is Catholic parapsychology. Until recently, the leading Catholic parapsychological institution was the Latin American Center of Parapsychology (CLAP, located in São Paulo), led by Padre Oscar González Quevedo, S.J. (known in Brazil according to the Portuguese convention as Padre Quevedo, not González Quevedo). In addition to doing research and education, the center maintained a clinic and published the *Revista de Parapsicologia*. However, the center was closed in the early 1980s, and at around the same time the Catholic church hierarchy censured Quevedo for his view that diabolic possession is always a psychological or parapsychological process. In 1985–86, the Jesuit parapsychologist was under prohibition to give lectures or to speak in public.[4] Nevertheless, he has educated a generation of priests and laity in Brazil and throughout Latin America, and his ideas (except for those on demonic possession) are highly influential within the Catholic church. When I talked with Quevedo's superior, who would speak to me only briefly, he informed me that the church was planning to continue disseminating Quevedo's line of parapsychology (presumably with a more orthodox interpretation of diabolic intervention).

In addition to Quevedo, two other intellectuals have made significant contributions to defining Catholic parapsychology in Brazil. The Franciscan bishop in Bahia, Boaventura Kloppenburg, has published several books of pastoral orientation that discuss parapsychology. Although Kloppenburg was less involved in these issues after Vatican II, when he lived outside of Brazil, since his return he has been preparing a new edition of his 1960 book about (against) Spiritism, and in the future his ideas might well return to prominence.[5] More ecumenical was Frei Albino Aresi (now deceased), who ran a series of clinics in which he practiced alternative therapies of a "spiritual" nature (see Bibliography). His assistants also gave lecture courses on parapsychology and semioccult topics, and although Aresi had distanced himself somewhat from Catholic parapsychology and had become more of a popularizer, he still maintained a broadly Catholic orientation.

Spiritist parapsychology also provides a general framework for the alternative therapies of a Spiritist orientation, but because such therapies may violate some legal statues, such as the *curandeirismo* law, Spiritist intellectuals are drawn into the political arena. Because Spiritist intellectuals defend proposed changes in the *curandeirismo* law, they present a theory of spiritual or religious healing as a form of "alternative" medicine, an approach to medical pluralism that social scientists have also defended under the rubric of "parallel" (Loyola 1984) or "complementary" (Milner 1980) medical systems. Although Spiritists attempt to distinguish their own spiritual healing from that of Umbanda, Candomblé, and popular Catholicism, in fact their program of political reform and ideas about alternative medicine might help legitimate these other religious healing practices. The political and social discourse of Spiritist intellectuals, then, positions them between popular healing traditions and the orthodox medicine and political ideologies that defend the status quo.

The Spiritist intellectuals' mediating position between popular healing and orthodox medicine is similar to that of many social scientists in Brazil. Since Bastide, many social scientists have criticized any attempt by the medical profession to define the spirit-mediumship religions in terms of psychopathology, and as a result social scientists sometimes play the role of advocates of spirit-mediumship religions without being members of them. This elite/popular mediation is also parallel to some of the work of the New Republic ideologues, who mediate between popular demands for reform and elite demands for maintaining the status quo. In some cases, Spiritists have turned to social science and the ideology of the New Republic as sources of support for their ideas, a point that will be discussed in more detail in subsequent chapters.

Others in the ideological arena are therefore not always competing or rival ideologies and actors. On some issues Spiritist intellectuals may converge with the medical profession or with Catholic parapsychologists—as in their common opposition to *curandeirismo*—just as on other issues the Spiritist position may favor some aspects of popular healing practices or popular beliefs concerning spirits and spiritual forces. This complexity allows Spiritist scientific thought to play a mediating role in the ideological arena.

Spirits and *Brasilidade*

The question of legitimation and interests in the ideological arena provides one axis for a sociocultural understanding of the thought of Spiritist intellectuals, but this should be balanced with a second axis, that of cultural values. To a North American, the ubiquity of the belief in spirits is a surprising and foreign aspect of Brazilian culture. Puritanism and Anglo-Saxon "common sense" have left a relatively more skeptical culture with respect to belief in spirits; such skepticism is less prevalent in Brazil, even among the most highly educated. In the right context, many educated Brazilians will confess that they believe in spirits or at least admit that in the centers and *terreiros* things happen that they cannot explain. Frequently one hears the expression "Não acredito, mas tenho respeito" (I don't believe in it, but I respect it), but this kind of respect might entail visiting a center to help an ailing relative or to seek advice from a medium when a lover is being unfaithful. And certainly few Brazilians are foolhardy enough to kick over the Macumba offerings that one frequently encounters on street corners and beaches.

Belief in spirits and spiritual forces, therefore, cuts across class and educational lines in Brazil to a much greater extent than it does in the United States. Roberto DaMatta notes: "Long before being aware that death means nonbeing or nothingness, I think that the majority of Brazilians become aware of the dead of their family, house, neighborhood, community, nation, and century" (1985: 119). And if the children of white, middle-class Brazilians do not learn about the dead from their parents, they are likely to learn about them from their maids and nannies, who in much of Brazil, but especially in Rio and to the north, tend to be Afro-Brazilians. Spirits are therefore part of *brasilidade*, or "Brazilianness"—that elusive amalgam of symbols and feelings which constitutes national identity, is now converted into a commodity in the culture and tourist industries, and helps sell Brazil as the land of carnival and Candomblé.

Belief in spirits also cuts across sectarian divisions among popular religions. For example, the cult of the saints of popular Catholicism involves a structure of relations between the living and intermediary, otherworldly beings which is very similar to that of Spiritism, Umbanda, and Candomblé. The Spiritist's relations with the spirit world, therefore, mark a continuity, in a more rationalized and secular form, with the cult of the saints (DaMatta 1986: 115ff.) as well as with Umbanda and

Candomblé. This pattern even extends to the Holy Ghost of Pentecostalism, which Spiritists think of as another form of popular "spirit-mediumship religion" (religião mediúnica). In all of these religions, Brazilians establish personal ties with an intermediary, otherworldly being that is somewhere between God and this world.

The logic of this system is an inclusive one: the otherworldly patrons of opposing religions are not mutually exclusive alternatives, and seeking favors from otherworldly patrons does not even exclude recourse to this-worldly patrons. For example, when one gets sick in Brazil, it is deemed best to cover all the bases, from orthodox medicine to a bottle of rum to homeopathy and other alternative therapies to the help of "God, saints, and spirits," as Milner (1980) calls these religious therapies. If this tactic involves the mixing of many remedies and therapies, so be it, for in a country in which nothing seems to work anyway, the rationale is an instrumental and syncretic one—what Bastide ([1960] 1978) described as "magical accumulation"—rather than the moralistic and reformist one of the Enlightenment or the Protestant ethic. The more therapies one has recourse to, and the more patrons one can turn to, the greater one's options and chances for escape from illness and bad luck.

The belief in spirits is therefore part of the broader cultural pattern that crosscuts otherworldly and this-worldly Brazil, a pattern that Bertram Hutchinson described as the "patron-dependent" ethic (1966) and that DaMatta (1981) has discussed in terms of hierarchy and personalism.[6] Saints, spirits, and the Holy Ghost serve as otherworldly patrons or godfathers who, in return for respect and homage, perform services for their clients. Brazilians approach these intermediary beings as benefactors who intervene in otherworldly processes, just as their this-worldly patrons and godfathers intervene and provide the jeitinho in this-worldly bureaucracies. The forces of the otherworld, like those of this world, are just too big and too powerful to heed the pleas of the common man or woman. Of course, this does not mean that this-worldly and otherworldly patrons are identical. One key distinction is that the two types of patrons provide different (but generally complementary) services. Whereas the this-worldly patron may provide protection from the law, find work for the client, and help educate the client's children, the otherworldly patron is more likely to heal illnesses, to resolve lovers' quarrels, and perhaps to relay messages to "discarnate" relatives.

In short, situating the belief in spirits within the Brazilian context inevitably leads back to this structure of patron-client relations in a hierarchical social system, a structure one can follow as an Ariadne's thread that runs through the labyrinth of traditional Brazilian culture. The structure of otherworldly Brazil, with its hierarchies of pure and impure spirits, angels and demons, *Oxalás* and *Exús*, is therefore not so different from that of this-worldly Brazil.

Nevertheless, one must be careful not to reduce the otherworld to a mere reflection of this world; as in the case of André Luiz, the *jeitinho* works for him, whereas it does not work for many Brazilians who often lack the same kind of connections, and Nosso Lar is by no means a copy of the Estado Novo. The otherworld represents both the dilemmas of and the alternatives to this world. In this sense, one might paraphrase Claude Lévi-Strauss and say that spirits are good to think. Or, better, since a particular kind of thinking is at stake here, spirits are good to mediate. The hierarchical relationship of patron and client is not just a relationship in which the powerful dominate the weak. It also provides possibilities, in DaMatta's terms, for the weak to pull the strings of *jeitinho* and to maneuver their way around the rules as clever *malandros* (rogues). In contrast to the representation of evangelical Protestants in the United States, who point to the heavens and say "one way," in Brazil intercourse with the otherworld is a two-way street.

Spiritist Scientific Thought and Brazilian Culture

In an implicit and largely unconscious manner, the same structures of traditional Brazilian culture are at work in the way the Spiritist intellectuals go about doing their science. Just as the otherworldly patron-client tie is a reciprocal one, so the science of the Spiritist intellectuals runs from elite, modern, scientific thought to popular, traditional, religious thought and vice versa. The tensions of this two-way street play themselves out in multiple ways: in the content of the representations, in the methodologies at stake, and in the social forms taken by Spiritist science.

Looking first at the content of representations, there are complex implications involved in the fundamental assumption behind Spiritist scientific discourse: the idea that there can be a "science of the spirits." This idea implies a "reification" of the spirit world, in the sense that spirits are made scientifically real, and this reification in turn has two consequences. By making the spirit world into an object of scientific study, Spiritist intellectuals desacralize the spirit world by treating it as an extended part of the natural world. But this reification works in another way: it represents an alternative interpretation of orthodox scientific thought; in other words, it makes real a discourse of the spirit world that orthodox science would label "pseudoscientific." In this case, to reify spirits and the spiritual enhances their value by making them worthy of study as scientifically validated phenomena.[7]

A similar tension occurs in the Spiritist intellectuals' attitude toward Kardec's doctrine. They oscillate between treating it as a revealed truth and as a source of empirically testable hypotheses. Depending on which direction they take, Spiritist intellectuals will find new empirical research either more or less compelling. Those who view Kardec's doctrine as a source of hypotheses, rather than as a revealed truth, are more likely to engage in empirical research. But empirical research—in other words, research based on direct observation, experiments, or firsthand reports— is extremely rare among Spiritist intellectuals. (The great exception is the work of Hernani Guimarães Andrade, and although many Spiritists have praised his empirical approach, few have emulated him.) Instead, most Spiritist intellectuals base their scientific research on the texts of the old masters of psychical research. The Spiritists' reverential attitude toward psychical research contrasts strikingly with the opinion of post-Rhinean parapsychologists in Europe and North America, who suspect the methodology of the psychical researchers and think of them as representing an earlier, less scientific phase of parapsychology. Unlike these Northern Hemisphere parapsychologists, who do new research either in laboratories or in field settings, most Spiritist intellectuals ground their scientific truth on the authority of the old texts of psychical research and make the locus of their research the library.

The noblesse oblige attitudes of traditional Brazilian culture dovetail with the tendency among Spiritist intellectuals to avoid doing new empirical research. Spiritist intellectuals have sometimes said to me that their tendency to rehash old research is determined by the economic hardships of doing research in a Third World country. Yet, it must be said, they are generally well-to-do and seem to have no trouble organizing and funding expensive international conferences that include paid tickets for invited guests from foreign countries. More likely, they view empirical research as "work" or, better, "travail," which they associate with manual labor and the lower classes.[8] One Spiritist made a telling comment to me when he said that Brazilian Spiritist intellectuals like to let North American and European parapsychologists do the empirical research while they sit back and speculate on what it all means. The hierarchy of patron and client resonates with this hierarchy of theoretical and empirical research, an attitude that Spiritists share with other Brazilian intellectuals, such as social scientists. The theoretical, library-research style of most Spiritist intellectuals is reminiscent of the patron's negative attitude toward the nitty-gritty of manual labor (empirical research) and his more favorable attitude toward thinking and creative endeavors (theoretical work). Thus, traditional Brazilian values about work inform the low priority that Spiritist intellectuals place on empirical research.

Perhaps more important, the differing attitudes toward empirical and theoretical research among Spiritist intellectuals are related to the differing attitudes toward Kardec's doctrine mentioned above. Theoretical work usually involves articulating some branch of scientific knowledge in terms of Kardecian doctrine, and in general Spiritist intellectuals use that doctrine as an encompassing theoretical framework for the empirical results of parapsychological research completed in foreign countries. This occurs most clearly in the case of polemical replies to Jesuit parapsychologists, but it also occurs in Spiritists' expository descriptions of parapsychology (see Appendix 1 on the different genres of Spiritist science writing). At the other extreme, the few examples of empirical research may invert this relationship by encompassing the tenets of Spiritist doctrine as empirical theories; as a result, empirical texts can challenge and reform Spiritist doctrine. Thus, for example, by turning the issues of past-lives memories or the statements of spirit communicators into problems of empirical investigation, Spiritist intellectuals can transform Spiritist doctrine from a revealed truth into a body of empirical hypotheses and theories.

Spiritist intellectuals, therefore, experience in a unique way what DaMatta (1978) calls "the Brazilian dilemma." Caught between a personal loyalty to the principles of Spiritist doctrine and the universalistic rules of scientific empiricism, they must negotiate between two desirable value systems. In turn, these two alternatives correspond to different groups in the social pyramid: the universalistic rules of modern empirical science represent the perspectives of the orthodox medical profession, social scientists, and Northern Hemisphere parapsychologists, all of whom generally have more prestige and power than Spiritist intellectuals, just as allegiance to Spiritist doctrine represents the Spiritist intellectuals' ties to the rank and file of their movement, people who are generally below them in the class structure and status hierarchy. The class conflict between elite and popular ideology, therefore, links up with the dilemmas of empirical and theoretical research styles and of modern and traditional values. More specifically, the empirical preference involves a framework in which scientific methods may be used to encompass Spiritist doctrine (thus, an elite perspective encompasses popular thought), and the theoretical preference tends to operate in the opposite direction.

In addition to questions of content and methodology, the two-way street in Spiritist scientific thought also makes itself visible at the level of social action—specifically, the tension between Spiritist intellectuals' allegiance, on the one hand, to traditional Brazilian social forms and, on the other hand, to the social forms of orthodox Western science. Like most Brazilians, Spiritist intellectuals prefer face-to-face, oral modes of communication over written modes, and they really seem to enjoy holding conferences. Yet, despite the label of "parapsychology conferences," the conferences of Brazilian Spiritist intellectuals have little in common with those of North American and European academic parapsychology, where the social forms of science come closer to enacting Mertonian "norms."[9]

To begin to understand this complex relationship between the social style of the conference and its ideology, one must first understand one implication of the preference for oral communication: Spiritist intellectuals rarely print or circulate their conference talks beforehand for peer review, as is the practice in the conferences of the Parapsychological Association. (On the oral character of Brazilian conferences, see Lima 1985: 40–41.) In fact, the peer-review process never takes place among Spiritist intellectuals, an extension of a phenomenon generally seen in Brazil (where, for example, my own discipline, anthropology, shows a similar lack of interest in anonymous peer review). The tendency to shy away from anonymous peer review may be because, like other Brazilian intellectuals, Spiritists find it rude to criticize their colleagues since criticism is usually interpreted to be personally motivated; on a more practical note, anonymity is difficult to maintain in a culture of personalism. In Brazil, the purpose of the conference is less to debate different ideas and theories than to find a common ground, and personalistic social relations dovetail with the ideological relations of comparison and syncretism rather than with those of contrast and diacritics. This ties back into the tendency toward theoretical speculation and away from empirical research: refuge in abstract concepts makes similarities easier to find, just as reference to the "facts" and to methodologies makes differences more difficult to overlook.

The emphasis on oral communication also drives Spiritist science away from formal journal articles and written correspondence (with the one exception of the AMESP's *Boletim Médico-Espírita,* which was just beginning to be published in the 1980s). This means that Spiritist intellectuals tend to publish their ideas in popular books or in the periodicals of the Spiritist movement. These forums in turn drive Spiritist scientific thought toward polemical and expository genres of writing and away from the empirical genre (again, see Appendix 1), and consequently they tend to be drawn back into the issue of how science is related to Spiritist doctrine rather than how Spiritist doctrine can provide a source of hypotheses for testing.

Thus, in different ways, the preference for oral communication dovetails with the tendency for religious and scientific values to "interpenetrate," if I may borrow the term used by Bastide to describe Afro-Catholic syncretism ([1960] 1978). Osmard Andrade Faria, a medical doctor and hypnotist who has written a major textbook on parapsychology, believes that this interpenetration of religious and scientific values makes it difficult for anything approximating a scientific discourse to emerge in Brazilian parapsychology:

> Spiritists have every right to hold their conferences . . . where Spiritists can talk *(discutir)* with Spiritists. Catholics have their right to hold their own conferences. That's normal. But let the scientists have their right as well. Let each have their own conference, but don't let them come spoiling the others. . . . What I found was the following: they take advantage of the popularity of parapsychology in order to infiltrate it with their doctrine. . . . Everything is completely contaminated by these ideas of mysticism. And this holds everything back and makes things difficult. I even found that [the North Americans who came to Brazilian parapsychology conferences] felt irritated . . . not because they aren't religious. North Americans are all very religious. The religious sentiment among the North Americans runs very deep. But this is one thing and that is another. The hour of religion is the hour of religion, and the hour of science is the hour of science. And you can't mix them. (Interview, August 5, 1985)

Faria would like to reform Brazilian parapsychology so that it conforms more with the secular pattern of North America and Western Europe, where even if parapsychologists have religious preferences, they tend to separate their religious and parapsychological discourse. In Parsonian terms, Faria would make more "specific" the "diffuse" relations that one finds in Brazil between an intellectual's role as a member of a religious movement and his or her role as a parapsychologist.

In the conferences of the "cosmopolitan" Parapsychological Association (the international organization that meets in Europe and North America), universalistic values are more evident in both ideology and social relations. In addition to the relative lack of the interpenetration of religious and scientific values, there is also a strong tradition of mutual criticism, and frequently a question-and-answer period follows a major paper, which will have been printed up and distributed before the conference. During question-and-answer periods, the conference participants often ask hard questions which show that they distinguish between the paper and the person who gives it (or at least that this is the ideology according to which they judge themselves). In the setting of the Parapsychological Association, the community of parapsychologists is instituted through a society of dissenting individuals with their opinions, theories, and data, all of which is regulated by the rules, the agreed-upon methods, that form the universalistic standard upon which all research may be judged (see Lima 1985: 42). These parapsychologists celebrate their tradition of mutual dissent, pointing to it as a sign that their discipline is genuinely scientific and not pseudoscientific.[10] The standards of methodology and the disinterested nature of mutual criticism makes possible the debate, and self-motivated attacks by scientists who speak for personal reasons (and who in the process distort these conventions) bring about the disapproval of the community (Lima 1985: 23).

The Brazilian anthropologist Roberto Kant de Lima finds many of these same structures in his comparative study of the North American and Brazilian anthropology communities. He also notes that in the Anglo-Saxon context "questions and answers were frequently quite aggressive, but their apparent 'objectivity' made the discussion appear to be without personal character" (1985:23). The distinction between "personally motivated" and "objective" criticism corresponds to the one between particularistic and universalistic values, with scientists considering legitimate only universalistic, "objective" criticism. As a result of having a clearer methodological division—which is more blurred in Brazil (especially in heterodox science conferences)—Anglo-Saxon criticism can reach sharper and more heated levels of disagreement without necessarily threatening personal friendships and professional ties, in contrast to what would likely happen in Brazil.

Because, in the Brazilian context, there is a more diffuse relationship between scientific persons and their ideas—the conflation of papers and persons that is reflected in the transformation of the paper from a written to a spoken form of discourse (Lima 1985: 23)—in contrast to the role specificity of the "scientific citizen," a problem emerges when debate occurs. Debate can become aggressive or even violent because there is no standard of criticism that allows the distinction between proper and improper, neutral and personal. When this kind of anarchy threatens to destabilize personal relationships and conference proceedings, the authority of Spiritist doctrine may help restore the disorder. On a similar point, Talcott Parsons writes that in Latin American societies "there is no inherent objection to authority so long as it does not interfere too much with expressive freedom; indeed, it may be welcomed as a factor of stability" (1951: 199).

One therefore can begin to see the extent to which Spiritism in Brazil is Brazilian. Spiritists have sometimes corrected me when I used the phrase "Brazilian Spiritism," arguing that there is only one Spiritism and thus "Brazilian Spiritism" is an impossibility: there can only be a "Spiritism in Brazil." Still, some Spiritists are Brazilians, and as with other Brazilians, even other scientists and intellectuals, the personalistic social forms of traditional culture tend to encompass the relatively universalistic social forms of open debate and anonymous peer review that are more characteristic of scientific debate in North America. In Brazil, one sometimes feels that the content, the logic, and the truth of what is said all matter less than whether it fits into the ongoing web of ideas that represent personal ties. Brazilians' concern not to offend their friends and colleagues, not to upset the warm glow of domestic caring (carinho), mutes debate. One argues only with one's enemies; to argue (discutir) is not to invoke the rules, the social contract, but to revoke the personal ties. In other words, to argue in Anglo-Saxon scientific cultures is to initiate the ritual that marks the passage from individual rights to communal obligations; to argue in Brazilian scientific cultures is to initiate the ritual that marks the passage from, again in DaMatta's terms, the insider (pessoa) to the outsider (indivíduo).

The "Debates e Perguntas" (literally, "Debates and Questions")[11] section of the First Brazilian Symposium on Parapsychology, Medicine, and Spiritism dramatizes this point. Organized by the AMESP Spiritists of São Paulo and held in São Paulo on October 26, 1985, this one-day conference included several of the leading intellectuals of Brazilian Spiritism. In what probably was at least partially a long reply to a conference of parapsychologists, ufologists, and natural medicine specialists held in Brasília earlier in the year, several of the speakers criticized non-Spiritist approaches to parapsychology and medicine as well as some popularizing or "mystifying" tendencies within their own movement. At the Brasília conference (discussed in more detail in Chapter 5), a wide variety of Brazilian occultists and New Agers used the term "parapsychology" to mean almost any kind of occult study, and in this conference the Spiritist intellectuals sharply criticized the popularization of parapsychology and exhorted the members of their own movement to adopt a more scientific approach to both parapsychology and Spiritism. As the Spiritist intellectual Dr. Ary Lex noted, in most Spiritist centers it is almost impossible to do any research or even to ask research-oriented questions: "Communications are not analyzed; there are no debates; there are no questions."

However, although intellectuals like Lex called for critical questioning in the study of mediumistic communications in Spiritist centers, no one seemed willing to analyze, debate, or question the long lectures of this conference. (For a discussion of this as a general Brazilian phenomenon, see DaMatta 1978: 152.) In the "Debates e Perguntas" periods following each group of talks, members of the audience or other Spiritist intellectuals generally preferred to ask questions of clarification rather than to issue critical commentaries. In Brazil, one really debates only with outsiders or with a faceless Other; to criticize, question, or debate with someone in a face-to-face, public situation is considered uncomfortable and impolite. Unless such criticism is framed in the form of a brief aside in a long comment filled with what is otherwise glowing praise, it will mark a transition of the relationship between speakers from insider to outsider.

Questions therefore stayed within the parameters of clarification, and debates were nonexistent; during their lectures, though, Spiritist intellectuals made some very polemical statements regarding the relationship between Spiritism and parapsychology. This instance of "boundary-work" shows how Gieryn's (1983) concept applies not only to discussions between orthodox and heterodox scientific groups but also to those among various heterodox sciences. For example, Valter da Rosa Borges argued against the way many Brazilians—presumably including Spiritists as well as Jesuits and occultists—have appropriated parapsychological discourse by claiming that it confirms or proves religious values:

> Parapsychology is an extensively interdisciplinary science, and for this reason it is urgently necessary to clarify its boundaries in order to avoid individual colonizations and epistemological transgressions. . . . In the epistemological space of parapsychology, the

Spiritist hypothesis, with the psi agency, is absolutely unnecessary. Parapsychology neither denies nor supports the extraphysical existence of man and, consequently, his possible postmortem survival. [Postmortem] survival may constitute material for parapsychological speculation if one day Spiritism acquires the status of an established science that would have interdisciplinary relations between parapsychology and Spiritist doctrine. Parapsychology shares boundaries not only with religion, notably and especially with Spiritism, but also with physics, biology, psychology, and others. (My transcription of his speech, October 26, 1985)

Thus Borges articulated a vision of secular space for Brazilian parapsychology, a space in which religious and scientific values could be related but would not interpenetrate. However, this secular space was defined in different terms from that of the cosmopolitan parapsychology of North America and Europe:

Parapsychology investigates paranormal phenomena, in other words the paranormality of those exotic phenomena which can be produced by man, and Spiritism in turn is interested in those mediumistic phenomena (that is, those exotic phenomena) which can be attributed to spirits. From the Spiritists' viewpoint, parapsychology studies only the so-called animistic phenomena [*fenômenos anímicos;* i.e., caused by the living rather than by spirits]. . . . If all exotic phenomena, even if they be of a mediumistic type, are one day able to be produced voluntarily by man, then they will pass over to the category of "paranormal" and be included within the boundaries of parapsychology. However . . . the general rule is that almost all paranormal phenomena emerge independently of human will. . . .
I want to make my own position very clear. I am a Spiritist. I am only making an epistemological division of fields, in order that there be no superimposition of research. Hence the emphasis of parapsychology is to investigate animistic phenomena, and one cannot extrapolate from this field in order to make one's project the problem of [postmortem] survival, because this is the object of Spiritism itself, and in fact this would imply the epistemological colonization of parapsychology. (My transcription of his speech, October 26, 1985)

If Borges's boundary-work on Spiritism and parapsychology may be interpreted as a move to articulate a secular discourse like that of North American and West European parapsychology, it should also be made clear that within the latter field of discourse postmortem survival is considered to be only a hypothesis. Furthermore, this hypothesis is generally less accepted than what is called the "super-psi" hypothesis (or what might be called in Borges's terms the "animistic" hypothesis): the idea that the category of paranormal phenomena believed to be suggestive of postmortem survival—mediumship, reincarnation, ghosts, and so on—can be explained as unconscious products of the living. In other words, unlike Brazilian Spiritists, cosmopolitan parapsychologists do not divide ostensibly paranormal phenomena into the "animistic" and the "spiritic"; instead, they compare the "super-psi" (animistic) and the "survival" (spiritic) hypotheses as two competing explanations. For Borges, however, the "animistic" and "spiritic" are less rival explanations of the same phenomena than terms that refer to two different types of phenomena. Thus, Borges transforms cosmopolitan parapsychology's tension between two competing and distinct hypotheses (resonating with the values of equality, competition, and individualism) into a Brazilian solution of two related fields of inquiry, each of which has its own object of inquiry. Furthermore, since Borges also claims that "almost all paranormal phenomena emerge independently of human will," he is articulating a relationship between these two disciplines that makes Spiritism the more important or "encompassing" science. As Brazilians say, there is "a place for everything and everything in its place," a phrase that DaMatta (1982) finds indicative of hierarchical and relational values. As he says, hierarchy unites the different (in this case, spiritic phenomena and their encompassed others, animistic phenomena), just as equality divides the similar (the super-psi hypothesis and its rival other, the survival hypothesis).

To avoid misunderstanding the preceding analysis (and to prevent its appropriation by anti-Spiritist groups), it is worth pointing out that my argument is *not* that because Spiritist scientific discourse incorporates popular thought or the values of traditional Brazilian culture, it is somehow less scientific than either the heterodox sciences of the Northern Hemisphere or the orthodox sciences of Brazil. I am making no claim that one or another of the discourses discussed here is more or less scientific than any other, nor even that phenomena labeled "paranormal" have obtained the status of scientific facts; instead, I put in brackets the question of the scientific status of Spiritist thought as "true" or "false," and I use the claims and categories of scientificity (or lack thereof) in order to get at issues of cultural values and ideological meaning. The point here is to show how Spiritist scientific thought fits into its cultural and ideological context, a context which is more easily understood when contrasted with that of its origins: nineteenth-century France.

PART TWO

CASE STUDIES OF
SPIRITIST SCIENTIFIC THOUGHT

CHAPTER THREE

KARDEC'S *BOOK OF THE SPIRITS*
Spiritism in Nineteenth-Century France

In *Spiritualism and Society,* the sociologist Geoffrey Nelson argues that nineteenth-century British Spiritualism was divided between the upper classes of London and the lower middle and working classes of the provinces (1969: 265). In turn, this class division corresponded to ideological differences: "In the north they were beginning to hold regular religious services in addition to meetings for the study and production of phenomena, whereas in London in the [1870s] the approach was more scientific, and it was not until much later that the religious approach became popular in the south" (1969: 265).

This division, between an upper or middle class with a preference for a scientific idiom and a lower or working class with more evangelical tendencies, is probably typical of Spiritist and Spiritualist movements throughout the Western world. This was even true of French Spiritism, which was much more centralized than Anglo-Saxon Spiritualism and which soon became dominated by Allan Kardec and his Spiritist doctrine, constituting itself around a popelike figure and a churchlike doctrine. Still, the French movement soon became characterized by a class and ideological division similar to that discussed by Geoffrey Nelson for nineteenth-century British Spiritualism and by Roger Bastide for twentieth-century Brazilian Spiritism. This framework of class and ideological divisions can therefore serve as a sound starting point for a contextualized reading of the principal text of French Spiritism, Kardec's *Book of the Spirits;* nevertheless, although the framework of class divisions as suggested by Bastide and Nelson provides key insights into Kardec's thought, a broader framework involving the entire ideological arena will provide a more balanced reading of Kardec's most important text.

The Book of the Spirits collates more than a thousand answers to questions directed by its author to the spirits. Kardec catechized spirits in a way that inverts the pattern of the Catholic church, whose priests pose questions to the laity. Instead, the representative of the this-worldly, Kardec, questioned the otherworldly spirits, who in turn communicated through mediums and answered his questions in the form of enlightened exegeses. The French intellectual then cross-examined the spirits and sorted out their accounts into what he viewed as the "correct" picture. In the tradition of the Napoleonic Code, Kardec describes the result, *The Book of the Spirits*, as a "codification" of answers that he received from many different spirits.

Kardec organizes his confluence of spirits and topics into four main sections: "Of Primary Causes," which discusses God, the general elements of the universe, and the vital principle; "Of the Spirit World or the World of the Spirits," which discusses types of spirits, their interaction with the living, and the role of the spirits in psychological phenomena such as dreams, somnambulism, and the like; "Of Moral Laws," which outlines the twelve moral laws that govern the universe; and "Of Hopes and Consolations," which discusses celestial and terrestrial pain and pleasure. In the course of constructing his book of Spiritist doctrine, Kardec enlisted the help of many spirits, including John the Baptist, St. Augustine, St. Vincent de Paul, St. Louis, the Spirit of Truth (sometimes said to be Jesus), Socrates, Plato, Fénelon, Ben Franklin, and Emanuel Swedenborg (Kardec [1860] 1875: l; [1860] 1983: 44). Despite this diverse array of otherworldly informants, Kardec emphasized that their messages were fundamentally similar:

> The conformity of the teachings transmitted, notwithstanding the diversity of the sources from which they have emanated, is a fact

of great importance in relation to the establishment of Spiritist doctrine. Our correspondence shows us, moreover, that communications, identical (in substance, if not in form) with those embodied in the present work, have been obtained in various quarters and even, in some instances, previously to the publication of *The Book of the Spirits*, which has served to systematize and to confirm them. ([1860] 1875: 23–24)

For Kardec, this doctrine was a systematic and scientific account of the spirit world—what we might call today an otherworldly ethnography—made possible by the rediscovery of mediumship. Yet, in addition to describing the other world, the spirits prescribed a set of guidelines for action in this world, and these moral principles followed the central tenets of Christian morality. Like other intellectuals of the nineteenth century, Kardec was concerned that advances in scientific knowledge were eroding religious spirituality and Christian morality. Discoveries in geology, astronomy, and biology—especially Darwin's theory of evolution, which was published one year after the first edition of *The Book of the Spirits*—challenged traditional Christian cosmology and chronology, and findings in history and archaeology made difficult a literal reading of the biblical narrative. Kardec viewed his doctrine as a kind of empirical science of the spirit world, but a science that bridged the gap between "is" and "ought" by taking what he interpreted as the facts of spirit communication and transforming them into the moral principles of Spiritist doctrine.

Today, many evangelical Spiritists in Brazil identify as "religion" what Kardec called the "moral" principles of Spiritist doctrine. They refer to Spiritist doctrine as the "third revelation," the culmination of the revelations of Moses and Christ. Kardec's own words lend some support to their interpretation: "Jesus came to show men the road to true goodness. Since God sent Him to recall to men's minds the divine law they had forgotten, why should He not send spirits to recall it to their memory once again, and with still greater precision, now that they are forgetting it in their devotion to pride and to material gain?" ([1860] 1875: 424; [1860] 1983: 410) For Kardec, Spiritism bridged the gap between science and religion, provided a rational basis for faith, linked social progress to spiritual progress, and equilibrated natural laws with moral laws. His doctrine spanned the gulf in ideology just as the spirit medium bridged the gap between this world and the other world.

Despite this vision of synthesis, Kardec's Spiritist movement soon faced internal social divisions for which the religion-versus-science issue was a key ideological marker. To the side of religion, the writings of Jean-Baptiste Roustaing restored crucial elements of Catholic cosmology, and to the side of science what Kardec called the "experimental" side of Spiritism soon became the independent science of psychical research. In his writings, Kardec dealt with these internal divisions in somewhat different terms. Although he wrote originally for the Parisian middle class, which he called the "head" of the Spiritist movement, his tremendous success during the 1860s is rooted in the charismatic appeal he had among the working classes of southern France, especially in Lyons, which he referred to as the "heart" of the movement.[1] In 1858 and again in 1860, Kardec claimed that most Spiritists came from the upper ranks of society, but after his visit to Lyons in 1861 he noted that Spiritism was "propagated with the most rapidity among the working class,"[2] and their interest is probably what accounted for the rapid growth of the movement.[3] The enthusiasm of the Lyonnais Spiritists for their charismatic leader was so great that in 1862 Kardec pleaded that they not spend a great deal of money on a lavish banquet for him, as they had done the year before.[4]

If Kardec's greatest support came from the working classes of the South, it is not surprising that this was also the cradle of his challengers.[5] In 1866, a member of the Spiritist Society of Bordeaux named Jean-Baptiste Roustaing published *The Four Gospels: The Revelation of the Revelation,* a Spiritist tract based on communications through the French medium Madame Collignon. In this text, the authors of the Gospels communicated new and corrected versions of their biblical accounts. Among the changes, they reasserted key Catholic dogmas such as the virgin birth and the trinitarian doctrine, and they also embraced the docetic doctrine that Christ materialized on earth and had a completely fluidic, or "perispiritual," body. Kardec—who, even in *The Gospel According to Spiritism* ([1864] 1944b), viewed Spiritism as a philosophy with a Christian morality but not as a Christian religion (Dias 1985)—did not accept Roustaing's ideas, and he criticized them in the *Revue Spirite* and in his book *Genesis.*[6] Although Roustaing was poorly received in France, his ideas became an important means for the expression of factional divisions throughout the history of Spiritism in Brazil.

It is likely that Kardec's popular following also brought with it an interest in combining spirit mediumship with popular religious healing, either of the Catholic or the Mesmeric type. Kardec distanced himself from the former by rejecting supernatural beings and miracles as the explanation of spiritual healing, and he distanced himself from the latter by emphasizing the importance of the moral state of the healer. Once he had divorced the spirit medium from the language of religious miracles and Mesmeric healing, Kardec did not oppose using the medium for curative purposes.[7] Thus, one spirit defends the reality of the laying-on of hands, a practice that Spiritists later developed into spiritual *passes:*

556. Do some persons really possess the gift of healing by merely touching the sick?
The Mesmeric power may act to that extent when it is seconded by purity of intention and an ardent desire to do good, for, in such a case, good spirits come to the aid of the Mesmerizer. But you must be on your guard against the way in which facts are exaggerated when recounted by persons who, being too credulous or too enthusiastic, are disposed to discover something marvelous in the simplest and most natural occurrences. ([1860] 1875: #556)

Here Kardec accepts the possibility of spiritual healing, but he does so by focusing attention on its moral preconditions. In general, Kardec preferred using the spirit medium to educate and provide moral guidance rather than to heal.

When Kardec discussed Spiritism and healing, he focused on how Spiritism might help treat cases of possession as a kind of mental illness. For example, in 1862 and 1863 the Spiritist leader devoted a series of articles in the *Revue Spirite* to the "possessed" in the asylum of Morzines, and he concluded that the cause was spirit obsession.[8] Thus Kardec attempted to situate Spiritist healing in the context of elite medicine, a move that contrasts with what happened to Spiritist healing in Brazil, where, as the historian Donald Warren has argued (1984), the spirit medium became deeply intertwined with popular healing and homeopathic medicine.

Ultimately more subversive to the Spiritist movement were the scientists and intellectuals, some of whom accepted some Spiritist and Spiritualist phenomena as paranormal but who believed them to be the result of the medium's unconscious powers rather than the work of spirits. In Britain, these scientists and intellectuals eventually organized themselves into psychical research societies, beginning with the founding of the London Dialectical Society in 1869, the year in which Kardec died, and with the research of William Crookes in the years that followed.[9] In 1882, a group of British Spiritualists, scientists, and scholars formed the

Society for Psychical Research; but the Spiritualists soon left, protesting against what they thought was the overly skeptical attitude of the scientists and scholars.

In France, psychical research (*métapsychique*) emerged in an institutional form somewhat later, when the *Annales des Sciences Psychiques* was founded in 1890.[10] In Paris in 1918, the industrialist and Spiritist Jean Meyer founded the Institut Métapsychique International, which shortly thereafter began to publish the *Revue Métapsychique*, a journal devoted to the study of telepathy, clairvoyance, and phenomena of spirit mediumship. This differentiation—*métapsychique* from Spiritism in France and psychical research from Spiritualism in the English-speaking countries—did not occur in Brazil, where the Spiritist intellectuals carried the banner of psychical research.

If there is considerable evidence that in nineteenth-century France the tension between science and religion came to signify a class and regional conflict within the Spiritist movement, this division by itself is not sufficient for a detailed, contextualized understanding of Kardec's doctrine. The split between science and religion also aligned with a split between the Spiritist movement as a whole and social categories outside it. Just as Spiritism threatened to destabilize an ideological boundary between two institutional representatives of science and religion—namely, the medical profession and the Catholic church—these institutions in turn attempted to destabilize and marginalize the Spiritist movement.

Furthermore, Kardec's rivals also included an entire field of heterodox philosophies and reform movements that presented similar schemes of spiritual, social, scientific, and religious reform—all of which, to varying degrees, attempted to synthesize popular and elite ideology. Kardec may have been modest regarding his personal role in writing *The Book of the Spirits*, but that modesty obscures how much he was aware of these other movements. The Spiritist codifier asked leading questions, injected lengthy recapitulations of the spirits' replies, selected carefully which statements to include and where, and was probably quite aware of how Spiritist doctrine was distinguishing itself from rival ideologies and cosmologies. Among them were Pestalozzian education, positivism, Mesmerism, Fourierism, and Swedenborgianism, not to mention the Catholic church, official science and medicine, and the factions within the Spiritist movement. Table 1 shows how Spiritist doctrine differentiated itself from these other ideas according to various distinctive features, and the remainder of this chapter explores how Spiritist doctrine and the Spiritist movement differentiated themselves from similar hetero-

Table 1. Characteristics of Spiritism and Other Ideologies in Nineteenth-Century France

Ideology	Dominant Imagery	Healing or Morality Emphasized	Type of Reform Emphasized (Social/Spiritual)
Christianity	Religious	Morality	Spiritual
Fourierism	Religious	Morality	Social
Mesmerism	Mixed	Healing	Neither
Natural science and orthodox medicine	Scientific	Healing	Neither
Pestalozzian education	Scientific	Morality	Social
Popular Catholicism	Religious	Healing	Spiritual
Positivism	Scientific	Morality	Social
Spiritism	Mixed	Morality	Both
Swedenborgianism	Religious	Morality	Spiritual

doxies as well as from the orthodoxies of the Catholic church and the medical profession.

The Church and Its Reformers

Several of the spirits who appear in *The Book of the Spirits* were important figures in the Catholic church, and this suggests that the complicated relationship between Catholicism and Spiritism is a good starting point for our journey through the world of nineteenth-century French ideology. Kardec's nineteenth-century English translator Anna Blackwell writes: "Born in a Catholic country, but educated in a Protestant one, [Kardec] began, while yet a mere boy, to meditate on the means of bringing about a unity of belief among the various Christian sects" (Blackwell 1875: 10).[11] Whatever the biographical reality of that statement, Kardec sought the common denominator among the Christian sects, and he found it in Christian morality: "The moral teaching of the higher spirits may be summed up, like that of Christ, in the gospel maxim, 'Do unto others as you would that others should do unto you'; that is to say, do good to all and wrong to no one. This principle of action furnishes mankind with a rule of conduct of universal application, from the smallest matters to the greatest" ([1860] 1875: xviii; [1860] 1983: 22). In addition to invoking the golden rule as the badge of Christian unity,

Kardec also forged unity by quoting Catholic spirits who had Protestant messages. A case in point is the spirit of Fénelon, the Catholic archbishop who tutored the Duke of Burgundy before falling from royal and church favor. The spirit Fénelon appears as one of the authors of the spirit communication of the prolegomenon and again in the chapter on moral perfection. In the latter, the spirit argues that selfishness is the root of all evil:

> Man is often rendered selfish by his experience of the selfishness of others, which makes him feel the need of defending himself against them. Seeing that others think of themselves and not of him, he is led to think of himself rather than of others. But let the principle of charity and fraternity become the basis of social institutions, of the *legal* relations between nation and nation and between man and man, and each individual will think less of his own personal interests, because he will see that these have been thought of by others; he will experience the moralizing influence of example and of contact. Amidst the present overflow of selfishness, much virtue is needed to enable a man to sacrifice his own interests for the sake of others, who often feel but little gratitude for such abnegation; but it is above all to those who possess this virtue that the Kingdom of Heaven is opened, and the happiness of the elect assured; while, at the day of the judgment, whoever has thought only of himself will be set aside, and left to suffer from his loneliness. ([1860] 1875: #917)

Manuel and Manuel describe the terrestrial Fénelon as an agrarian utopianist (1966: 69–80; 1979: 386–91), but the spirit Fénelon combines a utopianism of social reform with a Calvinistic warning about the fate of the preterit. In the introduction to *The Book of the Spirits,* Kardec writes, "And, after all, what does it matter whether a spirit really be Fénelon or not, if all that he says is excellent, and such as Fénelon himself is likely to say?" ([1860] 1875: xxxii).

The piety and self-abnegation of the spirit Fénelon are reminiscent of the beliefs of Jansenism, a Catholic reform movement that bore some doctrinal similarities to Calvinism.[12] Kardec also appeared to see in Jansenism a kind of model for his own movement: he had plans to build a Spiritist community, which he described as "the Port-Royal of Spiritism, but without the monastic character" (Kardec [1890] 1944f: 339–443; Wantuil and Thiesen 1980: 232–33). Port-Royal was a seventeenth-century French convent that was persecuted for propagating Jansenism; however, by pointing to Port-Royal as a model for his Spiritist movement, Kardec probably was not implying that he accepted Jansenist principles. Rather, it is likely that he wished to emulate the "Solitaires," a group of austere men who were affiliated with Port-Royal and who organized Les Petites-Écoles, where experimental pedagogical methods were used to teach small children (Escholier 1968: 66). Again, as with Fénelon (who had advocated educational reforms that anticipated the ideas of Rousseau), what is important is less the specific doctrinal principles than the general principles of piety and self-abnegation.

Another Catholic reformer who appears as a spirit in *The Book of the Spirits*, St. Vincent de Paul, was known for having initiated new methods of sacerdotal training in addition to having sponsored numerous charitable activities. Although in this respect the work of St. Vincent brings to mind aspects of Jansenism, he, like Fénelon, was critical of Jansenism. Thus, two Catholic reformers and a Catholic reform movement, which the two reformers had opposed during their terrestrial lives, all appear without contradiction in *The Book of the Spirits*. Kardec seems more interested in their similarities than in their differences: all represent reformist and heterodox positions with respect to the Catholic church, and all linked the value of spiritual purity to that of educational reform. In addition, Kardec probably saw himself, like Fénelon and the Port-Royal group, as a well-intentioned reformer who drew unjust criticism and persecution from the Catholic church.

Whereas Kardec stressed similarities between his doctrine and aspects of Catholicism, the church hierarchy did not see his doctrine from the same ecumenical point of view. Like the Catholic reform ideologies, the Spiritist doctrine and movement drew harsh criticism from the Catholic church. By the 1860s, numerous Catholic publications had branded Spiritism a primitive superstition or form of demonolatry. For example, in 1864, the dean of the Faculty of Theology of Lyons began public-education courses against Mesmerism and Spiritism, a strategy similar to that of Catholic parapsychologists in Brazil today.[13] The Catholic church also adopted more traditional tactics, such as papal prohibitions: in 1856, during the term of Pope Pius IX, the Holy Office prohibited necromancy, clairvoyance, and "other analogous superstitions" as "heretical, scandalous, and contrary to the honesty of customs"; and in 1864 the Vatican put the Spiritist canon on the Index.[14] For Catholic theologians, Spiritism was worse than Protestantism, because Spiritism denied key dogmas such as the Trinity and the reality of heaven and hell, and it supported beliefs such as reincarnation and communication with the dead, which to Catholic theologians meant a return to pagan superstition if not a dangerous flirtation with the devil.

Perhaps the most striking instance of the Catholic church's hostile response was the auto-da-fé that the bishop of Barcelona ordered on October 9, 1861, for some three hundred Spiritist books written mainly by Kardec. The auto-da-fé undoubtedly stirred up French nationalism—one of the burned books was *L'Histoire de Jeanne d'Arc,* dictated by the saint through a French medium—and it helped to create a following in both France and Spain. Kardec's popularity could only have increased when the bishop died nine months after the auto-da-fé and his repentant spirit appeared through French mediums and begged for Kardec's forgiveness, which the Spiritist leader graciously granted. This drama undoubtedly contributed to Kardec's charisma, and he was reportedly "stupefied" by the tremendous growth of adherents when he toured Lyons and Bordeaux in 1862.[15]

Despite the negative reception that the Catholic church hierarchy gave to Kardec's doctrine and movement, Catholic cosmology deeply influenced key parts of Spiritist doctrine. Thomas H. Huxley's famous epithet for Comtean positivism—Catholicism without the church—could also apply to Kardecian Spiritism. Kardec, for example, secularizes the Catholic pantheon of demons and angels by making them spirits of "discarnate" humans, but his discussion of the various gradations and levels of spirits preserves the principle of an otherworldly hierarchy. Furthermore, the mechanism of reincarnation allows Kardec to maintain the crucial mediating term of purgatory (Le Goff 1984) by transforming it into this-worldly existence. Instead of going to an otherworldly purgatory, human beings simply return for another life on earth. One's status in this world depends on the karma accumulated from violations of the divine law in past lives; as a result, punishment balances redemption in the Kardecian cosmology. Kardec writes: "When we undergo the consequences of such violations, we have only ourselves to thank for it" ([1860] 1875: #964).

Still, Kardec's doctrine transforms key Catholic beliefs even as it embraces them. For example, in Kardec's scheme, punishment is not absolute, as it is in the Catholic concept of hell. The spirit of Augustine comments that "justice does not exclude kindness, and God would not be kind if he condemned the greater number of his creatures to horrible and unending punishment" ([1860] 1875: #1009). If God condemns the spirits who refuse to attempt self-purification, it is only to a hell of their own making; for Kardec, hell is the "moral fires" of one's conscience. Like the great Protestant thinkers of the Reformation and the reformers within the Catholic church, Kardec both conserves and subverts Catholicism.

Enlightened Teachers and Their Pupils

Although Kardec was baptized a Catholic, the formative intellectual influence was his schooling under Johann Heinrich Pestalozzi, the well-known educational reformer whose school was located in Protestant Switzerland. As a student, Pestalozzi had been a member of the Helvetic Society, a youth movement dedicated to elevating the country's moral standards to those of the Enlightenment and influenced by Montesquieu and Rousseau. Gradually the Swiss student's ideals of political and social reform became routinized as the "Pestalozzi method," a pedagogical philosophy that drew heavily on Rousseau's *Émile*. In contrast to the rote memorization and disciplinarian style of most elementary schools of the day, Pestalozzi emphasized developing the child's ability to learn. During the first decade of the nineteenth century, his Yverdon school garnered international fame and attracted the children of elite families throughout Europe and the United States. Among these families were the Rivails of Lyons, who, according to the translator Anna Blackwell, "had been for many generations honorably distinguished in the magistracy and at the bar" (1875: 9).

At age ten, schoolboy Hippolyte Léon Denizard Rivail (Kardec) arrived at Pestalozzi's Yverdon school, to stay for what was most likely a decade. Rivail emerged a fervent disciple of Pestalozzi, despite the general demise and internecine quarrels that plagued the institute during this period.[16] In 1815 Frau Pestalozzi died, and with the loss of her pacifying influence a whole series of long-standing, simmering disputes erupted. At the heart of the disputes were the figures of Johannes Niederer, the theoretician who helped present Pestalozzi's ideas to the public, and Joseph Schmid, the domineering but practical administrator and Pestalozzi's favorite. In the spring of 1816, sixteen masters resigned in protest of Schmid's authoritarian regime; in 1817, Niederer left. As a result of this sudden loss of talent, Pestalozzi assigned senior pupils some of the teaching assignments and had coffee with them during his midday meal. Kardec's Spiritist biographers mention that he was a precocious student and that he taught his classmates at an early age; perhaps this crisis was the occasion for his first teaching experience. The young Rivail probably supported the Schmid faction, and it is likely that Schmid, who had developed a highly successful way of teaching mathematics, provided a source of ideas for Rivail's first textbook, which was on arithmetic.

By the end of 1817, there were three other institutes in the tiny town of Yverdon, two of which were led by former teachers in Pestalozzi's school. In 1818, Pestalozzi opened a school in nearby Clindy in order to train needy children to become teachers of other poor children; under Schmid's direction, however, the school became a source of badly needed staff for the main institute. The main institute declined even further in this period, and after a polemical pamphlet published by Niederer called "How Herr Schmid Manages the Pestalozzi Institute" and a series of court battles, Schmid was expelled from the Canton of Vaud in 1824. Pestalozzi left with him, going to Neuhof to open a new school for needy children. Many of his teachers, who by now were highly qualified, did not follow the master into this new venture and instead sought better positions at other schools. It is likely that Rivail was one of these teachers, and the rather shadowy story of the demise of the Yverdon Institute possibly explains the gaps in Rivail's biographies regarding his activities between 1818 and 1824.[17]

Rivail's work with Pestalozzi and his assistants provided the kind of experience necessary for leading the Spiritist movement. From Schmid, Rivail probably learned the art of practical administration, which allowed him to found and maintain control of an international movement; and from Niederer he may have learned the art of presenting new ideas to a skeptical public. More important, though, Spiritist doctrine borrows heavily from the Pestalozzian educational philosophy. Pestalozzi's emphasis on teaching needy children is reminiscent of Kardec's emphasis on charitable activities, which today in Brazil one sees expressed in the numerous orphanages, hospitals, nurseries, and welfare programs that the Spiritist movement supports.

In many respects, *The Book of the Spirits* is like a Pestalozzian textbook, and its introduction even compares spirits with professors:

> Whoever would acquire any science must make it the object of methodical study, must begin at the beginning, and follow out the sequence and development of the ideas involved in it. If one who is ignorant of the most elementary facts of science should ask a question in regard to it of the most learned of professors, could the professor, however excellent his goodwill, give him any satisfactory

answer? . . . It is exactly the same in regard to the relations we establish with the spirits. If we would learn in their school, we must go through a complete course of teaching with them; but as among ourselves, we must select our teachers and work on with steadiness and assiduity. (Kardec [1860] 1875: xxiv; [1860] 1944d: 31)

Thus, Kardec's work can be likened to a textbook dictated by the spirits for those students who "would learn in their school." Furthermore, in Kardec's world, every pupil has his or her own teacher, the spirit guide, as one spirit describes: "Every man has a spirit who watches over him; but missions are always proportional to their object. You do not give a professor of philosophy to a child who is only learning to read. The advancement of the familiar spirit is always proportioned to that of the spirit he protects" (Kardec [1860] 1875: #509). The spirit protector is like "a father who watches over his child" (#510), and both are like a Pestalozzian teacher. Pestalozzi, who always referred to his staff and students as his children, made one of the hallmarks of his system the doctrine that what is taught should vary by what the student needs to learn. Thus, needy children should learn skills that will be valuable to them as factory workers, whereas upper-class children should learn subjects appropriate to their station in life. Not only is *The Book of the Spirits* a Pestalozzian textbook, but Kardec's world is a Pestalozzian school.

The idea of teaching students the skills appropriate to their social class did not have the conservative overtones that it might have for today's readers; instead, as a disciple of Pestalozzi, Rivail saw education as the key to harmonizing the relations between rich and poor. When Rivail arrived in Paris in 1824 or shortly thereafter, he must have been full of youthful zeal for social change by means of educational reform.[18] He soon opened a Pestalozzi school in Paris, and in 1828 he submitted to the French legislature "A Plan for the Improvement of Public Instruction," in which he developed the ideas of the Pestalozzi system, defended education as an exact science like medicine (as he would defend Spiritism later), and proposed an École Théorique et Pratique de Pédagogie. In 1831 the Royal Academy of Arras awarded him a prize for a similar essay.

However, Rivail soon encountered major setbacks. A huge gambling debt acquired by his uncle forced the educational reformer to close down his school in 1835, and the French legislature extolled but ignored his plan for the School of Pedagogy. Although Rivail had earned sufficient recognition that the Lycée Polymathique asked him to give courses, his subsequent works reveal his new role in the university system: in 1848 (the year of Spiritualism's birth in Hydesville, New York), Rivail published *A Manual for the Use of Candidates for Examination in the Public Schools,* and in 1849 he published *Normal Dictations for the Examinations of the Hôtel de Ville and the Sorbonne.* These publications bear the mark of middle age: his youthful dreams of vast educational and social reform had led only to a position as a minor government bureaucrat who wrote examination manuals. In 1852 and 1853, a few years before Rivail converted to Spiritism and adopted the name "Allan Kardec," he even appears to have moonlighted as a bookkeeper or manager of a theater that featured a stage magician.[19]

Thus, attention to his years as an educator reveals a continuity between Rivail and Kardec rather than a break. If from one angle of the prism of historical context, *The Book of the Spirits* appears to be a reformist Catholic text, from another angle it appears to be a reformist Enlightenment textbook. A second voice, that of the educational reformer, speaks through Kardec's text, and the question-and-answer format now appears to resemble more the curious student questioning the model teacher than it does a Catholic priest catechizing the layperson. Indeed, Pestalozzi castigated catechism as the "parrot-like repetition of unintelligible sounds" (a phrase that today reverberates with the voice of the Brazilian educational reformer Paulo Freire), and the Swiss teacher may not even have considered himself a Christian (Downs 1975: 103, 105). Like Kardec, Pestalozzi embraced Christian morality without accepting Christian theology; both men transplanted Christian morality into the rich soil of Enlightenment ideology. Yet, even the two voices of Christian morality and Enlightenment ideology do not exhaust the plenitude of *The Book of the Spirits;* still other voices speak through the text.

Romantic Undercurrents

Despite Kardec's identification with Enlightenment ideals of progress and social reform via educational change, many of his ideas stand out more sharply when compared with hermetic traditions and their eighteenth- and nineteenth-century progenies such as Mesmerism, Fourierism, and Swedenborgianism. Mesmerism provides the principal link between Kardec's Spiritism of the nineteenth century and the hermetic ideas of earlier centuries.[20] Prior to the French Revolution, Kardec's hometown of

Lyons was a hotbed of Mesmerist and hermetic ideas, and the historian Robert Darnton describes the Lyons Mesmerist society, "La Concorde," as a caldron of "Rosicrucians, Swedenborgians, alchemists, cabalists, and assorted theosophists recruited largely from the masonic Ordre des Chevaliers Bienfaisants de la Cité Sainte" (1968: 68). Darnton goes on to note that in the Lyons of prerevolutionary France, many of these masons also belonged to "a spiritualist secret society which prepared to propagate the true, primitive religion from hieroglyphic messages received from God by its founder, J.-B. Willermoz. God was also speaking to Willermoz through the somnambules of Concorde . . ." (1968: 68).[21] Spiritic and mystical systems permeated prerevolutionary France, and by 1781 even the Parisian Mesmerist Society was interested in spirit communication (Darnton 1968: 70).

The French Revolution opened a chasm between Kardec's lifetime and the wilder schemes of Lyonnais mysticism. Nevertheless, it is among the shattered fragments of early-nineteenth-century Mesmerism that one finds many of the elements of Kardec's Spiritist doctrine. Kardec writes that "magnetism prepared the way for Spiritism," and he adds that he accepted magnetism for decades before becoming a Spiritist.[22] At first, many postrevolutionary Mesmerists avoided the spiritic interpretation of the somnambule, the interpretation that had been popular during the 1780s. By the 1830s, however, the spiritic interpretation was gaining currency again in Mesmerist circles. The return of spiritic ideas in Mesmerist circles received its fullest expression in 1848, when Alphonse Cahagnet published his *Arcanes de la vie future dévoilés,* which discussed spirit communications received through his somnambules and which prefigured Kardec's Spiritism (Podmore 1902: 82). Moreover, Kardec's entry into Spiritism apparently began with his observations of the "somnambules" of a magnetizer (Mesmerist) named Fortier: the first Spiritist mediums.

In the introduction to his *Book of the Spirits,* Kardec sided with the spiritic Mesmerists by rejecting the theory that a mediumistic trance is only "waking somnambulism"; that is, a kind of lucid trance state achieved by magnetism. Yet, *The Book of the Spirits* does more than transform the Mesmerists' somnambule into the spirit medium; it also reinterprets key Mesmerist ideas. For example, Kardec expands the Mesmerists' "magnetic fluid" by equating it with the "vital principle" and the "universal fluid" ([1860] 1875: iv; [1860] 1983: 10–11).[23] A spirit explains to Kardec: "What you call the electric fluid, the magnetic fluid, etc. are modifications of the universal fluid, which, properly speaking, is only a matter of a more perfect and subtle kind, and that may be considered as having an independent existence of its own" ([1860] 1875: #27). In a later chapter, titled "The Vital Principle" ([1860] 1875: ch. 4), Kardec notes that the vital principle or universal fluid links spirit and matter, permeates all life, endows plants and animals with vitality, and separates them from inanimate objects. The spirits also teach Kardec that the universal fluid is the basic material for the perispirit, or astral body. The idea of a subtle body, which is one of the cornerstones of Kardec's doctrine, marks the transition from a fluidic, Mesmeric world to a spirit world.[24]

Several other ideas in *The Book of the Spirits* have hermetic resonances that recall the ideas of Charles Fourier. Kardec attributes the origins of his doctrine of reincarnation—as noted, one of the major features that distinguish Latin American Spiritism from Anglo-Saxon Spiritualism— to Pythagoras, who in turn "borrowed it from the philosophers of Hindoostan [*sic*] and Egypt, by whom it was held since time immemorial" ([1860] 1875: 91, #223). In 1862, however, an anonymous Fourierist wrote to Kardec and expressed his surprise that the Spiritist codifier had not recognized Fourier as a precursor with respect to his doctrine of reincarnation, and Kardec later recognized Fourier's influence.[25] At another point, Kardec's otherworldly ethnography sounds clearly hermetic themes[26] that may have also derived from Fourier:

> According to the statements of the spirits, the earth, as regards the physical and moral qualities of its inhabitants, is one of the least advanced globes of our solar system. Mars is stated to be at a point even lower than that of the earth in every respect.[27] The sun is not a world inhabited by corporeal beings, but is a place of meeting for the spirits of a higher order who, from thence, send out radiations of their thought towards the other worlds of our solar system. . . . The size of the planets, and their distance from the sun, have no necessary relation with their degree of advancement; for Venus is said to be more advanced than the earth, and Saturn is declared to be less advanced than Jupiter. (Kardec [1860] 1875: #188)

On this hermetic theme, the historian Nicholas Riasanovsky notes, "Fourier hoped that sufficiently powerful telescopes would enable men to observe the system of Harmony as practiced by the Solarians or inhabitants of Jupiter" (1967: 216; see also 1969: 86–100).

Kardec was probably more aware of the points of contact between his doctrine and that of Swedenborg. Swedenborgian ideas were current in Mesmerist circles in France, and Cahagnet's *Arcanes de la vie future dévoilés* contained post-Swedenborgian descriptions of the spirit world.[28] At the end of *The Book of the Spirits*, Kardec's discussion bears some similarities to Swedenborgian philosophy. Thus Kardec writes that heaven and hell are, in the words of one spirit, "only symbols":

> You ask [the spirits] which heaven they inhabit, because you have the idea of several heavens, placed one above the other, like stories of a house, and they therefore answer you according to your own ideas; but, for them, the words "third," "fourth," or "fifth" heaven, express different degrees of purification, and consequently of happiness. It is the same when you ask a spirit whether he is in hell; if he is unhappy, he will say "yes," because for him, *hell* is synonymous with *suffering;* but he knows very well that it is not a furnace. ([1860] 1875: #1017)[29]

Kardec's grand synthesis, his wedding of Protestantism and Catholicism, of science and mysticism, closes with this hermetic theme: the entire cosmology is just a symbol of the development or purification of the soul. This theme is very similar to Swedenborg's ideas on spiritual development, and it is not a coincidence that Kardec later expanded his hermetic, otherworldly ethnography of the fourth book of *The Book of the Spirits* into a separate book called *Heaven and Hell*. In Swedenborg's book of the same title, he also describes "what is meant by the fires of hell and by the gnashing of teeth": it is "the love of the self and the world" (Swedenborg 1867: 326–28).

Despite the similarities between Spiritist doctrine and Mesmerism, Swedenborgianism, Fourierism, and other hermetic-influenced systems of thought, Kardec could hardly be called a hermetic philosopher. He was most likely unaware of any hermetic connection outside of the links to Mesmer, Swedenborg, and Fourier; like a third-generation North American or Brazilian, he spoke a different language than his grandparents spoke, although a few traces of the old stock remained. For Kardec, hermetic ideas on spiritual development were just part of a philosophy that wedded spiritual and social reform, science and religion, natural and moral laws. Thus, Kardec incorporated hermetic ideas into a doctrine that was uniquely Kardecian, transforming the hermetic emphasis on personal purification into a reformism with an almost millenarian sense of social progress.

Kardec's reformism bears some similarities to that of another utopianist, one who was both a contemporary and a compatriot: Auguste
Comte. In nineteenth-century Brazil, positivism had a rich if bizarre
historical development that culminated in a Positivist church, and the
parallel success of positivism and Spiritism has led some scholars, such as
the anthropologist Diana Brown (1986: 23) and the Spiritist intellectual
J. Herculano Pires (1964: 155), to wonder about the connections between
these two French exports.[30] Pires argues that when Kardec proposed a
"psychological period" in an article in the *Revue Spirite* (1858: 93–94), he
was adding a new phase onto Comte's evolutionary scheme. Yet, neither
this article nor Kardec's doctrine in general contains any explicit discussion of Comtean positivism, and this rather weak connection appears to
have developed into an antagonism in nineteenth-century Brazil.[31]

The connection between Spiritism and positivism becomes less problematic when one abandons the question of influence and instead examines how both doctrines are expressions of the utopian expectations that
science raised in the middle of the nineteenth century. Kardec's ideas are
similar to those of the late Comte—about which Pires seems to have been
unaware—notably the ideas of *The Catechism of Positive Religion* ([1852]
1858: 182). In this text, Comte developed a seventh science that he called
"moral science," or the "science of the individual man," the chief concern
of which was "forming conceptions of moral subjects which shall be at
once real and useful" (p. 183). Like Comte and other thinkers of the
middle and second half of the nineteenth century—Marx, Droysen, and
Spencer—Kardec drew an "ought" (a prescriptive philosophical doctrine) from an "is" (a descriptive science). Thus, the subtitle of *The Book of
the Spirits* uses the phrase "Spiritualist Philosophy" and not "Spiritualist
Science"; for Kardec, the former encompasses the latter. In the terminology of the twentieth century, there is both a Spiritist science, which
consists of the empirical study of spirit manifestations and statements,
and a "metascience"—a philosophy of Spiritist science. The entire third
part of *The Book of the Spirits* is dedicated to a discussion of "moral laws"
such as the Law of Progress and the Law of Equality, which are both
descriptive and prescriptive laws. Like the positivism of the late Comte,
Kardec's rationalized philosophy performed for his epoch what Geertz
(1973: 126ff.) describes as the work of religions everywhere: to synthesize ethos and worldview, "ought" and "is."

Kardec differed from Comte and the utopian socialists (Fourier,
Owen, and Saint-Simon) because he focused his utopian ideas on otherworldly existence, but once one ignores this difference, the similarities

are striking. Comte discussed a sexless utopia devoted to spiritual love, and Fourier developed plans for harmonious phalansteries based on the balance of passions (Manuel and Manuel 1966: 8; 1979: 659). Likewise, Kardec described a spirit world in which spirits do not have gender "as you understand" it, and in which their relations are based on "a similarity of sentiments" that leads to "love and sympathy" ([1860] 1875: #200). However, Kardec differed from his positivist and utopian socialist contemporaries by not engaging in this-worldly schemes for a secular church, scientist-philosopher-kings, or phalansteries. Instead, his political ideas on progress and equality bear closer resemblance to the liberalism of such contemporaries as John Stuart Mill. Nevertheless, like Comte and the utopian socialists, Kardec attempted to reinvigorate Christian morality by distilling it from Christian theology; he interpreted social reform as contingent upon inward psychological or spiritual reform; and he emphasized education as the proper means of reform.

Before their divergence into revolutionary socialism and religious communalism, most early-nineteenth-century reformists bound together their political and spiritual programs through the common means of educational reform. The New Harmony commune—whose leader, Robert Owen, looked favorably upon Spiritualism (Moore 1977: 97)—pioneered the Pestalozzi method in the United States (Silber 1960: 310ff.), and Fourier developed a revolutionary educational policy for his phalansteries (Manuel and Manuel 1979: 659). Even before the French Revolution, one can find figures like Nicolas Bergasse, a Mesmerist Rousseau who saw education as the means for restoring the harmony of primitive society (Darnton 1968: 118–19). Thus, the Enlightenment voice of outward educational reform merges with the hermetic voice of inward spiritual reform.

Medical Repression

Among the groups that Kardec hoped to educate was the medical profession, which he hoped might develop a more sophisticated understanding, through Spiritist doctrine, of mental illness. However, the medical profession's reaction to Spiritism was quite hostile. In 1859 Dr. Déchambre, a member of the Academy of Medicine, published a critique of Spiritism, and by 1863 reports were circulating about cases of insanity caused by Spiritism.[32] In addition, a report before the Academy of Sciences of Paris attributed spirit raps to knee-cracking, an idea that had already emerged in the United States with respect to the Fox sisters, whose mediumistic feats had helped launch the Spiritualist movement.[33]

Nevertheless, as the historian Henri Ellenberger argues, Spiritism was "an event of major importance as a source in the history of dynamic psychiatry" (1970: 115); and in the decades that followed, Spiritism exercised an important influence on the development of medical science. Ellenberger argues that Spiritism provided a new source of psychological phenomena for medicine to study, but there is also some evidence that the dynamic theories of the unconscious from the late nineteenth century were themselves at least partially a result of the translation of the doctrine of spirit communication into the language of orthodox medicine.[34] Spiritist doctrine—which presented a unified explanation of mediumship, hypnotism, dreams, and mental illness—had already formulated one explanation for a wide variety of psychological phenomena, and as a result the medical profession did not need to perform this synthesis again.

Furthermore, there is also some evidence that some variants of the theory of the unconscious were direct translations of the doctrine of spirit communication. This is most plausible for Myers's concept (1903) of the subliminal self, an idea that James ([1890] 1950; [1902] 1961) adopted in his later work and a tradition that Jung continued (Moore 1977: 150). Likewise, Pierre Janet was quite familiar with the doctrine of spirit communication, and he devoted part of his *L'Automatisme psychologique* ([1889] 1899) to a critique of Kardec's doctrine. If one accepts such a "repressed" origin of at least some variants of the theory of the unconscious as being in fact "dissociated" Spiritist or Spiritualist doctrine, then the hostility of the orthodox medical profession toward Spiritists and Spiritualists, as well as their tendency to interpret spirit mediumship as psychopathology, takes on a different meaning. Instead of representing merely an atavistic form of cultural evolution, as many doctors saw Spiritism and Spiritualism, these two movements were much more modern and potentially threatening than the medical profession admitted. In Brazil, the potential for Spiritist medicine to become a rival alternative medicine rather than a nonrival (at the level of ideas) "popular" medicine was even greater, for the medical profession (especially psychiatry) was much less firmly established in Brazil than in Europe.

Thus, when Kardec confronted the thorny issue of "possession" in *The Book of the Spirits*, he addressed it in terms that were not so different from those of the orthodox medical profession:

The word "possession," in its common acceptation, presupposes the existence of demons—that is to say, of a category of beings of a nature essentially evil, and the cohabitation of one of those beings with the soul of a man in the body of the latter. Since there are no such beings as demons *in the sense just defined,* and since two spirits cannot inhabit simultaneously the same body, there is no such thing as "possession" in the sense commonly attributed to that word. The word "possessed" should only be understood as expressing the state of absolute subjection to which a soul in flesh may be reduced by the imperfect spirits under whose domination it has fallen. ([1860] 1875 #474)

Like the orthodox medical profession, Kardec criticizes a supernatural interpretation of possession and counters belief in demons with skepticism. If one substitutes "unconscious" for imperfect spirits, one sees how close Kardec's discourse is to that of modern psychiatry.

Close, but perhaps not yet close enough to award it the proverbial Freudian cigar. Kardec's Spiritism occupies an interstitial space between the popular healing practices and the medical orthodoxies of the day (and, within them, the milder heterodoxies of the new dynamic psychiatries). "Interstitial" seems to be the appropriate term for Spiritist doctrine in general. Spiritism occupies the spaces between existing institutional and ideological boundaries, between popular healing and orthodox medicine, between Catholicism and Protestantism, and among the various reformist and utopian movements of the day. If one were to skip ahead to Brazil, the word "syncretic" would perhaps be a more appropriate adjective. Indeed, the ideological multiplicity and flexibility of Spiritist doctrine was clearly a factor behind its enormous success in this Afro-Latin country.

CHAPTER FOUR

MENEZES'
INSANITY THROUGH A NEW PRISM
The Brazilianization of Kardec's Doctrine

Spiritists sometimes refer to Adolfo Bezerra de Menezes Cavalcanti as the "Brazilian Kardec"; today, demand for the spirit of Menezes is so great that, as one Spiritist explained to me, he can appear simultaneously through different mediums, an ability shared by only a few other highly developed spirits. During his earthly life, Menezes was a political leader and medical doctor who, in 1886, dramatically announced his adherence to the Kardecian doctrine before a gathering of members of Carioca high society, a courageous act that apparently helped stir widespread interest in the movement (Renshaw 1969: 132; Abreu 1950: 37). Later, in 1890 and then again from 1895 until his death in 1900, he served as president of the Brazilian Spiritist Federation (FEB), and Spiritists honor him today as the "unifier," the man who brought together the diverse factions of the nascent Spiritist movement at the end of the nineteenth century.

Menezes' intellectual output includes his voluminous *Philosophical Stud-*

ies (1977) and the smaller *Insanity Through a New Prism* ([1897] 1939), and his writings are nearly as renowned as those of Allan Kardec and Chico Xavier. Of all of Menezes' writings, *Insanity Through a New Prism* probably has the widest readership today, and it will serve as a way into the position of Spiritism in the ideological arena of late-nineteenth-century Rio de Janeiro. The book is divided into three sections: a defense of spiritualism as opposed to materialism; an outline of Spiritist philosophy and cosmology; and a description of spirit obsession and its treatment. In his study, Menezes defends a simple and clear thesis: in cases of mental illness that show no sign of cerebral lesion, the cause is spiritual, which is to say spirit obsession.

Insanity Through the Old Prism

The approach outlined by Roger Bastide (1967: 5) would lead us to characterize Menezes' therapy for obsession as a way of dressing popular religion in the clothing of science or as a way of translating the idiom of popular healing into that of modern psychiatry. This view would maintain that just as Umbanda upgraded the Afro-Brazilian religions via Spiritism in the 1920s, so in the late nineteenth century Spiritism upgraded the practices of popular religious healing via science.

Although Bastide's framework provides a good point of departure for a contextualized reading of *Insanity Through a New Prism*, it is extremely difficult to apply or test his framework, for good descriptions of the popular healing of turn-of-the-century Rio are extremely rare. The research of anthropologist Yvonne Maggie (1988) on the police reports and legal records of the period brings out some descriptions of Afro-Brazilian rituals, and one hopes that someday she will publish these ritual descriptions in their fullest detail. Another source of ritual descriptions for the period is the book *Religions in Rio*, by the newspaper columnist Paulo Barreto, better known by his pen name João do Rio. In this book, Barreto offers a rare glimpse of "low Spiritism" ([1904] 1951: 199ff.), a value-laden term that Spiritists and the elites used then (and continue to use today) to refer both to the low social class of the participants and to the imputed moral quality of the practices: magical and healing-oriented rituals that were probably close to what was later called Macumba magic and that in some ways were the precursor of what is today called Umbanda and Quimbanda magic (Bastide 1978; Maggie 1988; Hess 1991e).

Barreto claims to have visited some fifty centers of "low Spiritism," many of which aroused his disgust because they charged for their services or engaged in activities of dubious morality. Unfortunately, Barreto's righteous indignation meant that he tended to focus on the ridiculous or offensive rather than on the rich syncretism between Spiritism and Afro-Brazilian religions that was probably occurring among the so-called low Spiritist groups. Still, *Religions in Rio* provides one description of a session of "low Spiritism," and this gives us a sense of the type of healing ritual against which Menezes was defining his disobsession therapy. In this session, a Portuguese woman consults a medium regarding her husband's drinking problem, which has led him to abuse her, and the medium receives the spirit of the woman's mother while another member of the group asks the spirit of the mother what her daughter should do. The spirit of the mother urges her daughter to have faith in God, then she attributes the cause of her son-in-law's problem to black magic performed by "a dark *mulata*" who is interested in him. The mother's spirit provides the recipe of countersorcery: "Give to him the medicine that I'm going to prescribe, and stick a knife in the pillow three nights in a row" (Barreto [1904] 1951: 203). Another member of the center gives some *passes* to the medium, and the spirit departs.

This case is interesting because it combines elements that seem to be purely Spiritist—receiving a guardian spirit (the mother), exhorting the client to have faith in God, and giving the *passes*—with a magical action (sticking a knife in the pillow) and a prescription of either homeopathic or herbal nature. This is evidently a very mild form of "low Spiritism"; Maggie (1988) shows through the police reports that "low Spiritism" more frequently implied complicated countersorcery rituals which often included animal or food sacrifices (see Hess 1991e for some descriptions of contemporary formulas). Still, even Barreto's mild form of "low Spiritism" differs a great deal from the Spiritist disobsession session, where instead of responding to sorcery with the idiom of countersorcery, the mediums receive the obsessing spirits, talk with them, "indoctrinate" them in Christian morality, and persuade them to leave the victim alone.[1]

In addition to replacing the idiom of countersorcery with that of Christian charity, Menezes' disobsession therapy differs sharply from the "low Spiritist" countersorcery rituals by emphasizing its basis in scientific thought. A few lines from the preface to *Insanity Through a New Prism* give a taste of the importance of science in Menezes' Spiritist psychiatry:

> Until today, science has known only about the kind of insanity that has a source in the brain and that permanently disrupts the thinking process.
>
> The causes and forms can vary, but the pathological state of the individual is always the same: insanity characterized by mental perturbation and rooted in the brain.
>
> For science, if the brain is not damaged, there can be no psychopathological phenomena of insanity.
>
> This is the current doctrine, the invariable law of science.
>
> However, the celebrated alienist Esquirol has observed cases of insanity without the minimal cerebral lesion. . . . ([1897] 1939: 11)

Menezes argues that spirit obsession causes this second type of insanity. The implied reader appears to be a non-Spiritist intellectual, perhaps a member of the medical profession, whom Menezes, himself a physician, addresses as a colleague. He cites Esquirol, does battle with Auguste Comte, and, in the first section of the book, demonstrates his erudition by discussing a long list of European philosophers, scientists, and psychical researchers.

In short, Menezes saw his "disobsession" treatment as scientific and therefore completely different from the countersorcery of "low Spiritism." For some outsiders, the shared spirit idiom may suggest that the two practices have more in common than Menezes would recognize, but for him the only relationship is one of difference. And it is a big difference—the difference between popular superstition and the cutting edge of modern psychiatry.

Yet, if Menezes' interest is to make his own discourse acceptable to the medical and scientific establishment of the day, one wonders why at the end of *Insanity Through a New Prism* he makes the puzzling move of quoting a letter that the spirit of Samuel Hahnemann, the founder of homeopathy, had sent to him:

> As we write these lines, which were intuitively suggested to us, we received in the mail a letter without signature, whose author sent to us the following communication, which, he said, was instantaneously given to him, and he graciously offered it to us:

"Two causes can concur to cause the fact of mental perturbation: one external, one internal. . . .

In the first case, when the images come from the cerebral apparatus and this is affected, there is a type of insanity that medicine can cure.

In the second case, when there is no cerebral lesion, and without perturbation of the reception of the images and of their reflection, there is what is now called obsession, for which there is only one therapy: the spiritual. . . .

Until later, good friend—Hahnemann." ([1897] 1939: 164–69)

The style and the line of argument are so similar to Menezes' that one cannot help wondering whether he wrote it himself. This long letter—it stretches for nearly five pages through the third section of the book—seems out of place in comparison with the rest of the text. If the implied reader of the text is a skeptical intellectual, doctor, or psychiatrist, that reader is likely to be even more skeptical after reading the passage from the spirit of Hahnemann. Menezes takes great pains to show that he has mastered much Western philosophy and medicine, so why does he invoke the authority of the homeopathic doctor Hahnemann, and why does he do so in the form of a mysterious spirit communication?

In order to answer this question, one must situate Menezes' ideas in relation to a second category of implied readers: the various factions of the Spiritist movement of the late nineteenth century. When Menezes was writing *Insanity Through a New Prism*, the Spiritist movement was a labyrinth of competing organizations and factions. This context is crucial for understanding his thought, but it is also true that both the complexity of the internecine quarrels and the unavailability of documents make the period relatively inaccessible.[2] Nevertheless, by comparing and contrasting the secondary sources (and using the few primary sources that are available), one can trace a series of schisms and transformations among Spiritist groups in Rio at the turn of the century, for which the divisive issue was always the orientation of the groups as relatively scientific or moral-religious (see Appendix 2). At one extreme were the intellectuals (sometimes called "scientists"), who were interested in psychical research and the Kardec of *The Book of the Spirits* or *The Book of the Mediums;* at the other were the Roustaingists (sometimes called "mystics"), who believed in the virginity of Mary, the Holy Birth, the preternatural nature of Jesus' flesh, and the divinity of Jesus (Abreu 1950: 72–73). In between were a variety of positions, including that of the evangelical Spiritists, who followed Kardec's *Gospel According to Spiritism* but did not accept Roustaing's works.[3]

It is difficult to characterize most of the organizations of the period in terms of these factional divisions, but it is safe to say that the leaders of the Brazilian Spiritist Federation (FEB) were generally Roustaingists. The FEB was founded in 1884, but it did not become the central unifying force of the Spiritist movement until the early 1890s, when Spiritists rallied under the federation umbrella in response to an article in the new penal code that banned *espiritismo* (Abreu 1950: 52). Although it appears that the law was directed more toward "low" Spiritism than toward the Kardecian/Roustaingian variety, Brazil's Spiritists felt sufficiently threatened to attempt (unsuccessfully) to change the law (Wantuil 1969: 547–48). The general ambience of positivism and political uncertainty that surrounded the birth of the Old Republic in 1889 militated against the religious side of the Spiritist movement and, as a result of the threat of repression, Spiritists began to redefine their movement as a scientific endeavor. According to one Spiritist historian (Abreu 1950: 57), the FEB and the Spiritist Fraternity Society joined the camp of the "scientific" Spiritists in 1893. In that year, the Spiritist Fraternity Society renamed itself the Psychological Fraternity Society (Abreu 1950: 57), and the FEB even appears to have stopped studying Kardec for a brief period (Aquarone 1982: 111). In short, in response to external pressure, Brazil's Spiritists redefined their philosophy in terms of psychical research (*metapsíquica*), and the intellectuals came to lead the FEB.

Within two years, however, the receding threat of political repression, the continued reign of the Spiritist intellectuals (always, it seems, a minority), and severe financial problems all combined to provoke a crisis of leadership within the FEB. It was during this crisis that the leaders called on Bezerra de Menezes to serve a second term as president, which he did from 1895 until his death in 1900. For many years he had worked for the unification of the Spiritist movement, and during his second term as president, in fact, Menezes achieved a certain degree of unity largely by reorienting the FEB in a more evangelical direction. This unity was, however, far from complete: a group of scientific Spiritists continued to belong to another Spiritist organization (the Center of the Union for the Divulgence of Spiritism in Brazil), and it appears that the "unifier" never managed to persuade them to return to the FEB fold. Still, the evangelical Spiritists and the Roustaingists appeared to have reconciled, in part because in 1895 they agreed to a reform of the FEB statutes that made

Roustaing's *Four Gospels* officially sanctioned reading (Dos Anjos, Apr. 1979: 3).[4] During these years, the subtitle of *O Reformador*, the federation's official publication, also changed—from *Evolutionist Organ* to *Religious Monthly of Christian Spiritism*—to reflect the new evangelical outlook (Renshaw 1969: 132).

Given this swirling context of internal disagreement, *Insanity Through a New Prism* may be read as an artfully forged position that could be accepted by the diverse factions of the growing but threatened Spiritist movement. By adopting the unconvinced skeptical intellectual as the implied reader, internecine quarrels paled in comparison. Even disagreements between Spiritists and the Catholic church dissolved when contrasted with the challenge presented by the materialists: "Owing to [Spiritist phenomena], materialists have no foundation for their building, even if one accepts the Catholic hypothesis: that they are the work of Satan" ([1897] 1939: 80). By devoting a great deal of his text to the critique of materialism and the defense of otherworldly beings, Menezes was able to sidestep factional divisions within the Spiritist movement. Furthermore, he carefully combined his erudite and scientific style with a conclusion that emphasized the importance of Christian morality in the disobsession therapy. These are relatively noncontroversial principles for all factions of the Spiritist movement.

Menezes' decision to center his argument on disobsession may have also represented a second, related mediation between two divisive projects: the school for mediums and the FEB's Service of Cures, which was run by *receitistas* or homeopathic mediums (Richard 1914: 6; on homeopathy, see Warren 1986). The available evidence suggests that the homeopathic mediums were associated with Roustaingism and that the school for mediums was linked to the Spiritist intellectuals. More than a mere struggle between two interest groups, these projects also represented a fundamental disagreement over whether Spiritism was an educational or a healing movement, and differences were sharp enough that they later erupted into open conflict. Early in the twentieth century, for example, the intellectual Spiritists formed the rival Spiritist League of Brazil, which adopted resolutions in favor of a school for mediums and against the use of mediumship for prescriptions.[5] Likewise, the homeopathic mediums of the FEB did not support the school for mediums; and when Menezes' successor, Leopoldo Cirne, managed to persuade the FEB to establish the school for mediums (ultimately an ill-fated project), he had to agree to include Roustaing in the curriculum.[6]

These clues from the rather sparse historical record provide a better sense of what Menezes' disobsession treatment meant for the Spiritists of fin-de-siècle Rio. The sources claim that Menezes supported both the school for mediums and the homeopathic mediums, a position that would have been one of mediation and reconciliation between the opposing factions.[7] Nevertheless, *Insanity Through a New Prism* presents disobsession, rather than the prescriptions of the homeopathic mediums, as the paradigm of Spiritist therapy. Thus, Menezes' move to include a spirit communication from Hahnemann in his text is probably an attempt to win support for his disobsession therapy from the homeopathic mediums. Furthermore, by positioning disobsession as a new kind of psychiatry and as a scientific practice, he could appeal to the Spiritist intellectuals. In other words, Menezes' disobsession therapy could occupy a relatively neutral position between the intellectuals and the Roustaingists, between the projects of the school for mediums and the homeopathic Service of Cures.

To summarize my argument to this point, approaching Menezes' text through the prism of Bastidean sociology reveals how the "unifier's" disobsession therapy is situated in a stratified mediumistic field—between "low Spiritism," associated with the lower classes; the Roustaingists and the evangelical Kardecists; and "scientific Spiritism," associated with the intellectuals. Such a framework provides a rich context that allows several insights into the meaning which *Insanity Through a New Prism* had for Spiritists of the period; however, the framework still suffers because it limits the context of interpretation to the spirit-mediumship religions. One must also examine the meaning of the text when viewed from other ideological angles, particularly from the perspectives of the Catholic church and the medical profession.

Catholicism and Nationalism

Like the Afro-Brazilian religions and other popular religions in Brazil, Spiritism has suffered from persecution by the Catholic church. Almost as soon as the French movement arrived in Brazil, it came under attack by the Catholic church and began to define itself in opposition to Brazilian Catholicism. In 1865, for example, Dr. Déchambre's critique of Spiritism (see Chapter 3) was translated and published in Bahia. Luís Olímpio Teles de Menezes (no known relationship to Bezerra de Menezes) and other Brazilian Spiritists quickly countered, and within two years a Brazilian archbishop had issued the first pastoral letter against Spiritism (U. Machado 1983: 99–100, 84ff.). These external pressures affected the definition of the nascent Brazilian Spiritist movement: in 1871, Teles de Menezes attempted to charter the Brazilian Spiritist Society, which Kardec officially recognized in the *Revue Spirite* (1865: 323–35). The proposal received civil approval, but the Catholic church blocked it and, as a result, the group reapplied as the Brazilian Spiritist Association, asserting that it was a scientific society and not a religious one.[8]

Paradoxically, a development in the Catholic church itself may have contributed to the rapid growth of the Spiritist movement during the Old Republic.[9] Partly as a response to the declared separation of church and state at the outset of the Old Republic, the Catholic church underwent a process known as "Romanization" (P. Oliveira 1985: 279–96). Prior to the Old Republic, argues the political scientist Thomas Bruneau, the Catholic church relied on the state as the chief means of exercising and maintaining influence (1974: 33). The separation of church and state in1890 left the Catholic church in an institutionally weak position, a problem that was compounded by the prevalence of Afro-Brazilian religions in the cities and of a non-Roman, "popular" Catholicism throughout much of rural Brazil, where there was little state or church influence. The Catholic church therefore began a program of Romanization, building up its bureaucracy by adding dioceses and archdioceses, a cardinalate, dozens of seminaries, and thousands of new priests, many of whom were foreign-born. Bruneau writes: "By 1930 the Church in Brazil resembled the large bureaucratic organization which most people visualize when reading about the Church" (1974: 34).

An important part of the process of Romanization entailed the suppression of religious thaumaturgy that threatened to escape central church control. The church of nineteenth-century Brazil had been a church of popular healing rituals more than of Roman masses; but during the Old Republic and the Romanization process, the church attempted to weed out thaumaturges within its own ranks, the case of Padre Cícero being only the best known (Della Cava 1970; Azzi 1977). Despite this pressure from above, popular demand for faith healers (*curandeiros* and *benzadores*) did not diminish; if anything, the Romanization process served only to create a shortage of supply.

Spiritists could meet this demand by replacing the Catholic folk healer's blessings and rituals of exorcism with their magnetic or spiritual *passes* and disobsession therapy. The Christian discourse that accompanied Spiritist sessions made this substitution all the more palatable and, at the same time, helped to distinguish intellectual Spiritists from the rival practitioners of Afro-Brazilian religions and "low Spiritism." An understanding of the Romanization process, therefore, leads by a different path back to the question of the relationship between disobsession and popular religious healing. Yet, if on the one hand Spiritists constructed disobsession in opposition to popular religions and folk practices, on the other hand they did so with respect to the exorcism rituals of the Catholic priest. Again, descriptions of Catholic exorcism rituals from this period are almost nonexistent, but the journalist João do Rio (P. Barreto [1904] 1951: 157ff.) provides one example of an exorcism ritual performed by Frei Piazza of Rio, who in 1903 exorcised more than three hundred demons. The Catholic exorcism ritual involves asking the demon to give its name and to tell when it entered the victim's body; the exorcist also makes signs of the cross over the possessed's body, a procedure that is similar to the *passes* which Spiritist disobsession mediums provide. In addition, the dialogue with the devil is similar to the dialogue that the disobsession medium has with the earthbound spirit.

Despite these similarities, for Spiritists there is a striking difference between the relationship of the exorcist and the demon and that of the disobsessor (or "clarifying medium") and the obsessing spirit. For the Spiritist, the latter is merely a lost or wayward spirit, not the epitome of evil as in the Catholic concept of Satan. According to Menezes, one "must work with loving care in the moralization of the obsessing spirit" ([1897] 1939: 181). The dialogue with the otherworldly in Spiritism is therefore a session of conversion, a kind of reproduction of the Spiritist's dialogue with other groups in society, whereas for the Catholic, an exorcism is similar to a session of excommunication from the church. In short, if Menezes' disobsession therapy Europeanized "low Spiritist" exorcism, it also Brazilianized European-style Catholic exorcism.

In *Insanity Through a New Prism*, Menezes was explicitly aware of how Spiritism was distinct from Catholicism, although he seemed less aware of how he was Brazilianizing the Catholic exorcism ritual than of how he was transforming church doctrine, for which he reserved some of his strongest criticism: "Now that we have liquidated the question of the impugners of the Spirit [the materialists], a new and more dreadful struggle emerges with the Roman [Catholic] Church over the relations of the Spirit" ([1897] 1939: 81). In a string of negatives, he opposed key Catholic dogmas:

There is no eternal punishment, since spirits have more than one corporeal life.

There is no hell, since there are no material and eternal punishments.

There are no personal demons, since there is no hell and no eternal punishment.

There are no specially created angels, since the tradition that some are fallen is evidently false. . . . ([1897] 1939: 133)

In the context of Menezes' opposition to Catholic dogma, Spiritism's affinity with the popular traditions of the people now receives greater emphasis:

In all times and countries, the popular masses have always held in their breasts the belief that the souls of the dead come to speak with the living. . . .

In the Bible, one finds authentic proofs of the manifestation of souls that have left this life.

These are authentic, because the authority of the sacred writer would not allow anyone to attribute to him the intention of wronging readers with false propositions. And they are above suspicion, because the patriarchy was adverse to these practices, even to the point of threatening with death those who provoked such communications. . . .

In Brazil and Portugal, with whose usages and customs we are more familiar, one finds throughout all levels of society the belief in souls from the otherworld, anchored in facts observed by respectable people. ([1897] 1939: 47–48)

Like the Protestants, then, Menezes grounds authority not in the church but in the Scriptures or in everyday experience, but he also makes it clear how Spiritism's ultimate authority is science: "However, just as science does not base itself on conjecture, we appeal to the facts that give life to popular belief" ([1897] 1939: 47).

If the authority of Spiritism is, according to Menezes, ultimately grounded in science, his vision of science itself quickly merges into the otherworldly:

[The astronomer and psychical researcher Camille] Flammarion established definitively the principle that it is not only the planet Earth which serves as the habitation of the human species, but all

> the stars spread out through space without end, and they are
> innumerable, to the billions. ([1897] 1939: 81)

A few pages later, Menezes describes how this scientific knowledge implies "two new principles: a plurality of worlds and a plurality of existences of the soul" (p. 83). These two principles combine to collapse the
Catholic categories of heaven, hell, and earth into one purgatory, consist-
ing of multiple worlds and multiple incarnations that traverse those
worlds. In a process of "slow" but "infallible" progress (p. 96), spirits
gradually improve from a backward state to highly developed purity.

The sociologist J. Parke Renshaw (1969: 182, 198ff.) noted that
Spiritism appealed to the bourgeois concerns of the emerging middle
sectors of Brazilian society, and one can extend this interpretation by
reading into Menezes' progressivism a metaphor of middle-class mobil-
ity. Certainly the planet Earth, like the middle sectors, falls somewhere
between the backward and the advanced worlds (Menezes [1897] 1939:
102).

However, the metaphor of bourgeois aspirations cannot clearly explain all of the images in Menezes' description of relations among
worlds. For example, Menezes writes that "evil is a mode of the evolution
of the spirit, just as heat is for the evolution of a planet" ([1897] 1939:
98). Because the Earth still has active volcanoes and disequilibrium in
surface temperature, Menezes argues, it has not yet reached its final
point of evolution. This idea suggests that Menezes may subscribe to
nineteenth-century theories that explained Brazil's backwardness as a
result of climate. On a similar point, he writes:

> One day, presumably, all the regions of the Earth will enjoy an
> invariable and agreeable temperature, [and] its surface will be
> naturally purged of all morbid elements and blessed with ele-
> ments favorable to the prolongation of the life of its inhabitants.
> Likewise, this world of pain and suffering will one day transform
> itself into a world of well-being and pleasure, where the spirits
> who are incarnated here will no longer progress with tears and
> thorns, but with smiles and flowers. ([1897] 1939: 99)

For an intellectual speaking from a poor (but not the poorest) tropical
country, such images—purification through heat, the dream of an
"agreeable" temperature, and the pain and suffering of the people coupled to the promise of progress—may resonate more with the reality of

Brazil as a nation than with that of Brazil's emerging middle sector. One might even take the idea that "one day . . . all the regions of the Earth will enjoy an invariable and agreeable temperature" as an expression of a Brazilian wish to enjoy the same level of economic development as the colonial center.

Thus when Menezes argues that instead of one world and one existence of the soul, there are many, and when he discusses the relations among these worlds in terms of evolutionary progress, he might also be read as opposing images of colonial centralism with those of peripheral pluralism and development. The Brazilian intellectual also associates this pluralistic vision with modernity and the future; he "illuminates" the survival of Roman Catholic cosmology with his Spiritist science, which is rational, experimental, and progressive (Menezes [1897] 1939: 91). Pluralism stands for a future that includes Brazil, centralism for a past that does not.

And yet, Menezes does not draw on indigenous symbols to back up his Spiritist cosmology. Although he celebrates the popular traditions as *vox populi vox Dei,* his examples of the popular tradition come from isolated reports of experiences such as crisis apparitions that have little relationship to Afro-Brazilian or indigenous religions. Not until the modernist movements of the 1920s did Brazilians search in earnest for native symbols and reject those of European colonialism: the rogue hero Macunaíma (M. Andrade [1928] 1975), the Modern Art Week of 1922, the Brazilian Communist party, and the birth of Umbanda all mark a new phase in the quest for Brazilianness that involved a rejection of cultural colonialism. In contrast, Menezes rejects indigenous symbols, and as a result he falls prey to Eurocentrism even as he appears to be rejecting aspects of it. *Insanity Through a New Prism* contains passages referring both to worlds inhabited by backward spirits and those inhabited by developed spirits, but unlike the modernists of the 1920s, Menezes does not question the injustice of this hierarchical universe. Instead, the temporal element of nineteenth-century evolutionism allows him to defer justice to a future time when the backward spirits (like the less-developed countries) will also be "purified" (developed).

To summarize: with respect to Catholicism, the key element of Menezes' disobsession therapy is the idea that the obsessing spirits are not demons but, rather, are wayward or lost spirits who need help, just as the "backward" side of Brazil is not so much savage as it is undeveloped. With respect to popular religiosity, Menezes still recognizes a world of spirits—which are neither demons nor cerebral lesions—and to some extent, therefore, he legitimates popular belief. In this sense, disobsession mediates between the European, Catholic practice of exorcism and the African-Amerindian practices of spells, counterspells, and mediating spirits.[10] Yet, disobsession mediates between these two traditions by rejecting them both and then setting up a hierarchy that ascends from the Afro-Brazilian religions and "low Spiritism" to Catholicism and on to Spiritism. In so doing, Spiritism apparently rejects everything that is Brazilian in favor of this rationalized, scientific philosophy.

Nevertheless, Menezes also Brazilianizes the Kardecian procedures of disobsession. Whereas Kardec stresses the role of prayer and *passes* in disobsession, Menezes emphasizes the importance of a medium receiving the spirit and of a Spiritist engaging in dialogue with the spirit: the French prayer becomes the Brazilian chat, the *bate-papo* (Kardec [1890] 1944f: 67–74; [1859] 1944e: ch. 23). Like Kardec's Spiritist doctrine, which situated itself in the interstices of French ideology, Menezes' disobsession therapy situates itself between "high" Catholicism and "low" Spiritism and between Brazilian traditionalism and French modernism.

Brazilian Freud

The historian Donald Warren (1984: 75ff.) compares Menezes' disobsession therapy to Mesmerist techniques which, he argues, are one possible source of Menezes' practice. My own interpretation complements Warren's approach by focusing less on the question of sources than on that of structure—in other words, the question of how Menezes' ideas and disobsession therapy fit into the ideological arena of turn-of-the-century Brazil. Besides the Catholic church, a key actor in the ideological arena was the orthodox medical profession, and this point of comparison immediately raises the question of the similarities between disobsession and the "talking cures" of Sigmund Freud and Pierre Janet.

Like those dynamic psychiatrists, Menezes bases his argument on the fact that "there are insane [patients] whose brains do not have any organic lesions" ([1897] 1939: 8). Thus, when Menezes offers his disobsession therapy as a method for treating that type of insanity, he is attempting to fill a gap in the knowledge and practice of his colleagues in the Brazilian medical profession, a move similar to that of his contemporaries in Paris and Vienna. Like Janet and Freud, Menezes believed he had discovered a new type of mental illness:

One must understand how important is the practice of differentiating one type [of insanity] from another, so as not to confuse them in the same treatment, since they have different natures. My plan is to determine the special nature of insanity without cerebral lesion, to establish the diagnostic basis for differentiating one type from the other, and to offer a means of cure for this unknown type of insanity. ([1897] 1939: 13)

The backward state of fin-de-siècle Brazilian medicine fueled Menezes' hope that his colleagues in medicine would listen to his new ideas. At the time, Brazil had only two medical schools and no universities. Outside the main cities, psychiatric treatment was rarely, if ever, available. This situation persisted well into the twentieth century; thus, the director of the Hospital Espírita de Marília, located in the interior of the state of São Paulo, informed me that when his hospital was founded in 1948 psychiatric treatment was available nowhere else in the area. Many of the first patients came from the local jails, and treatment of mental illness was reminiscent of that described by Michel Foucault (1973) with respect to the Europe of several centuries past. Coupled to this shortage of psychiatric care was the state of confusion and ferment in Brazilian psychiatry. Until 1902, when the psychiatrists Juliano Moreira and Afrânio Peixoto moved from Bahia to the National Hospital in Rio, psychiatry in the Brazilian capital was largely dominated by the neurology of João Carlos Teixeira Brandão and Antônio Austregesílio (Azevedo n.d.: 270; J. F. Costa 1976: 24–25).

Despite the fact that Menezes correctly perceived a vacuum in the orthodox Brazilian medicine of the day, his Spiritist ideas and new treatment faced nearly wholesale rejection and hostility.[11] One of the more strident opponents of Spiritism was Raimundo Nina Rodrigues, a professor of medicine at the medical school in Bahia. Rodrigues pioneered the new dynamic psychiatry of Janet in Brazil, using it to analyze trance episodes in the Afro-Brazilian religions of Bahia, and he interpreted Spiritist mediumship (along with Afro-Brazilian trance episodes and popular Catholic religiosity) as manifestations of "hysterical somnambulism" or collective insanity (Rodrigues 1901; [1896] 1935).

Rodrigues's view is strikingly similar to that of his and Menezes' contemporary Joaquim Maria Machado de Assis, the great Brazilian writer whose columns and fiction revealed a sharp eye for the foibles of his fellow Cariocas. In such fiction as his short story ˮA Segunda Vida" ("The Second Life") and the novel *Quincas Borba* (translated into English as *Philoso-*

pher or Dog?), Machado de Assis inverted the relationship that Menezes claimed to exist between reincarnation—a core Spiritist belief—and insanity. Whereas for Menezes a knowledge of past lives was part of the disobsession therapy that could cure mental illness, for Machado de Assis belief in reincarnation was a step on the road to insanity. In his newspaper columns, Machado de Assis occasionally lampooned Spiritism, and he adroitly caught Spiritists at their most embarrassing moments (U. Machado 1983).

Although Menezes was a member of the same elite group of medical leaders and intellectuals as Nina Rodrigues and Machado de Assis, they did not accept his attempt to bring scientific legitimacy to what they saw as popular religion and magic. The intellectuals and the medical profession as a whole viewed Menezes and his fellow Spiritists as slightly wacky betrayers of the establishment rather than as earnest reformers deserving a fair hearing. In September 1886, one month after Menezes announced his conversion to Spiritism, Machado de Assis alluded to Menezes sarcastically, commenting that "one cannot serve two lords; either it must be Baepend or Allan Kardec" (1956: 36). Baepend was the president of the Senate and a conservative politician from Pernambuco, Menezes' home state, so Machado de Assis portrays Menezes as less a reformist leader than a conservator of traditions.

The elite's hostility toward Spiritism was not limited to witty newspaper columns. A federal decree in 1904, concerning sanitary regulations, provided the grounds for a series of prosecutions against the president of the FEB, the FEB itself, and a well-known homeopathic medium (FEB 1907). Similarly, in 1917 the outspoken Spiritist intellectual Eurípedes Barsanulfo, from Sacramento, Minas Gerais, was accused of practicing medicine illegally.[12] Likewise, the Spiritist Redeemer Center (Centro Redentor) of Rio de Janeiro, which had developed an independent form of "scientific" Spiritism and ran a clinic for disobsession treatment, faced prosecution in 1914 and again in the 1920s and 1930s (Spínola and Barros 1915; Maggie 1988: 194ff.).

Spiritists based their defense primarily on the religious freedom argument, but they also brought to bear testimony regarding the scientific validity of their practices, and some cases, such as those against the FEB in 1904, ended in acquittal. Still, the external pressure from the state and the medical profession had its effect, and Spiritists carefully articulated their practices as both scientifically valid and religious in character (therefore falling under the constitutional provision for freedom of religion). Perhaps this is the most fundamental of the mediations in *Insanity*

Through a New Prism; certainly the three sections of Menezes' text (on materialism, Catholicism, and the Spiritist synthesis) are constructed around this science/religion mediation.[13] Like Kardec, who built a philosophy across the gap between science and religion, Menezes constructed his bridge in the form of a therapy that combined exorcism and neurology.

Menezes' bridging of exorcism and neurology was also parallel to the mediation that the new dynamic psychiatrists were achieving at the same time. Like Freud's psychoanalytic method, which borrowed from the Catholic confessional even as it used a biomedical idiom, Menezes' disobsession therapy borrowed from Catholic exorcism but instead used the spirit idiom. Like Freud, Menezes challenged the accepted dogmas of both the Catholic church and biomedicine. Yet, instead of mapping out an unconscious, Menezes mapped out a spirit world—one that was as real to most Brazilians as the world of repressions, automatisms, and psychic energies was to the psychological reformers of Europe.

Menezes' disobsession therapy was similar to the new dynamic psychiatries in a second way: the triad of spirit of light/client/errant spirit is in many ways similar to that of superego/ego/id. The mutual translatability of the idioms of Spiritist therapy and psychoanalysis is a point that social scientists such as Bastide (1967) and Garrison (1977) have already made. One can apply their analysis to a case, discussed by Menezes in *Insanity Through a New Prism* ([1897] 1939: 142–43), in which a medical student feels guilty about the death of his father—so much so that he no longer studies medicine and must fight off suicidal impulses. In this case, the disobsessor ("clarifying medium"), who is guided by the spirit of light, represents the role of Spiritist morality (the equivalent of the superego), whereas the errant spirit represents the guilt that the medical student feels over his father's death. The disobsession session, then, articulates the internal conflict within the medical student by creating a drama between the disobsessor/spirit of light and the errant spirit.[14] As a result of the disobsession treatment, the boy was able to overcome his suicidal impulses and return to his medical studies. The fact that he was a medical student is important: Menezes chooses a case that shows his new Spiritist therapy supporting the orthodox medical profession, not working against it.

In addition to the parallel between the spirit of light, victim, and errant spirit on one side and the superego, patient, and unconscious conflict on the other side, the passive figure of the medium plays a role similar to that of the silence of the analyst: both are empty stages on which the drama of unconscious conflict plays itself out. The comparison of medium and analyst shows how similar the structure of disobsession is to psychoanalysis, even as it replaces European drives with Brazilian spirits: Brazilian Freud.

In summary, one sees in this comparison yet another example of Menezes' role as a medium—not in the literal sense of someone who bridges the spirit world and the human world, but in a metaphorical sense of one who bridges diverse ideologies. *Insanity Through a New Prism* bridges divisions not only within the Spiritist movement and among the spirit-mediumship religions, but also between the Spiritist movement and the official ideologies of the Catholic church and the medical profession. To restrict the comparative context of Menezes' text to the field of spirit-mediumship religions would miss the way in which he is also confronting the elite and Eurocentric ideologies of Roman Catholicism and neurological psychiatry with a therapy that is deeply rooted in the spirit world of Brazilian popular culture.

CHAPTER FIVE

POLTERGEISTS AND BRICOLEURS
Spiritism and the Parasciences

The Spiritist intellectuals of contemporary Brazil continue to read Kardec's and Menezes' works, but they read them in a different context and give them a different meaning. Kardec, for example, was writing in the world of Mesmerism, positivism, utopian socialism, Swedenborgianism, and Spiritualism, whereas the Spiritists of contemporary Brazil read the "codifier" in a context that includes Umbanda, Candomblé, Catholic parapsychology, Northern Hemisphere parapsychology, biomedicine, and a multitude of psychotherapies. As a result, Kardecist doctrine has become just one element of Spiritist scientific thought, which synthesizes that doctrine with various ideas borrowed from the other traditions. Perhaps the most important of these traditions is Northern Hemisphere parapsychology, the heterodox science that studies extrasensory perception, psychokinesis, and other paranormal phenomena. A variety of schools of parapsychology exist in the Northern Hemisphere, and in a process that one might term "scientific bricolage"[1] these schools reappear in Brazil as markers of different social categories: namely, the Catholic church, the medical profession, and the Spiritist movement.

This proposition becomes clear when one examines the thought of the Spiritist Hernani Guimarães Andrade. A retired engineer, Andrade is a native of the interior state of Minas Gerais who has lived in São Paulo since the 1920s. An elderly man, he enjoys visits from foreigners and will sit for hours telling anecdotes and jokes that would charm any but the most virulently anti-Spiritist Jesuit. He works with his secretary, Suzuko Hashizume, every day in his tiny Brazilian Institute of Psychobiophysical Research (IBPP), where he maintains a rigorous schedule of writing and research. In addition to writing—frequently under pseudonyms—for Spiritist newspapers, he also engages in psychical research of cases of reincarnation and poltergeistery.

"Poltergeist" is the German word for a "noisy spirit" that wreaks havoc on the domestic tranquillity of the household. It throws and breaks valuable objects, brings in sticks and stones from the street, and causes fires, puddles, and other unwanted natural processes to appear inside the house. A kind of carnivalizing spirit, the poltergeist takes miscellaneous objects that are in their place, whether in the house or on the street, in culture or in nature, and disorganizes them.[2] Although one may try to trace Andrade's ideas to Kardec's discussion of poltergeists in *The Book of the Mediums*, this Spiritist intellectual's theory and research come to life only when situated in the context of the contemporary ideological arena in Brazil. My method of analysis, therefore, begins with the interpretation suggested by Bastide and his followers, who view Spiritist-intellectual production as an elite ideology within the field of spirit-mediumship religions. After examining how the text under consideration distinguishes Spiritism from Umbanda and Candomblé, I then show how consideration of other positions in the ideological arena allows for a more detailed understanding of the meanings of the text.

Andrade's *"Poltergeist" of Suzano* (1982) is an unassuming monograph published by his institute.[3] Printed on ordinary white paper and bound with staples, the physical appearance of the monograph is that of a scientific research report; at first glance, it does not even appear to have a connection with the Spiritist movement. When one opens the cover and surveys the monograph, the text appears to be a routine case study of a poltergeist attack, similar to the many case studies in the parapsychological or psychical research literature of Western Europe and the United States. The ninety-four-page case history is even more detailed and more fully researched than most of its Northern Hemisphere siblings: flipping through its pages, one finds a detailed floor plan of the house with a numbered key for each "paranormal event"; a narrative of the case with transcriptions of interviews and photographs of the burned objects; a summary of the events that occurred (falling stones followed by fires); other relevant facts (Catholic, Protestant, and Spiritist "exorcisms"); and then the analysis, hypotheses, and conclusions. Except for the bibliographic references to Allan Kardec and André Luiz, the study would not appear to have any connection with Spiritism.

Nevertheless, Andrade's final interpretation of the poltergeist of Suzano is a Spiritist interpretation. In his conclusion to the study, Andrade argues that the factor which effectively controlled and blocked the poltergeist was the Spiritist "exorcism." His use of the term "exorcism" instead of "disobsession" suggests that his implied reader is a non-Spiritist intellectual, such as a Brazilian doctor, a North American parapsychologist, or a social scientist. He then argues that because the disobsession ritual was the factor which effectively ended the poltergeist, the reader should examine seriously the Spiritist hypothesis. He opens this discussion with a remark on Allan Kardec by the French psychical researcher Charles Richet, who admired Kardec's "intellectual energy" but was critical of his "exaggerated credulity" (Andrade 1982: 88, citing Richet 1923: 33). Warning that "exaggerated skepticism . . . has been more prejudicial to science" than exaggerated credulity, Andrade then examines Kardec's discussion of poltergeists in *The Book of the Mediums* ([1859] 1944e: ch. 5, #90). Kardec concludes that the cause of the poltergeist is "discarnate agents," which are generally mischievous rather than malevolent (Andrade 1982: 89).

At this point, Andrade comments on Kardec's ideas in a way that reinterprets the doctrine, a step which epitomizes the role that the intellectuals are able to play in the Spiritist movement. Although the nonintellectuals of the Spiritist movement tend to view Kardec's doctrine as sacred and immutable, many intellectuals treat him as a great thinker of another century who was wrong on many points. As a result, within the Spiritist movement, the intellectuals can play a progressive role—in the sense of making the doctrine more adaptable and flexible in a changing world. Andrade's comment on Kardec is as follows:

> Allan Kardec recognizes that things are not always so simple, a fact that we verified personally in dealing with innumerable cases of household infestations by aggressive poltergeists. In the major-

ity of the events of this type, we always encountered the same indices: conflicts among the dwellers of the house and people connected with "works of the *terreiro*" [an Afro-Brazilian temple; see Glossary]; objects used in this category of "works"; [and] threats or implications on the part of individuals affiliated with those organizations of black magic. The codifier gathered these difficult cases under the heading of *obsession* and *haunted places*. (1982: 90)

These observations lead Andrade into a discussion of black magic: "We were surprised by the coincidence, in a significant number of cases, of evidence suggesting maleficent action induced at a distance by '*macumbeiros*' (a type of black magician), whom one can find in 'Quimbanda *terreiros*' in Brazil" (1982: 91). Andrade concludes that such cases are increasing in Brazil: "The number of persons affected by this type of 'paranormal aggression' is growing at a frightening rate." Moreover, he says, this new type of crime is "still not officially recognized" and, as a result, is "not foreseen in the laws" (1982: 93).

Andrade's discussion of black magic as a criminal activity is reminiscent of the medical profession's attitude toward all forms of spirit mediumship—Spiritist included—during the 1930s.[4] In the medical texts of this period, "espiritismo" was an umbrella term that lumped Spiritism (which they called "Kardecism") together with other spirit-mediumship religions such as Umbanda and the Candomblés. During this period, Spiritists stressed the scientific nature of their creed in order to distinguish Spiritism from the Afro-Brazilian religions. When Spiritist intellectuals such as Andrade study the Afro-Brazilian religions as scientists, they further differentiate Spiritism from these religions and instead associate Spiritists with doctors, lawyers, social scientists, and other elites.

Knowledge of the stratified domain of the spirit-mediumship religions enriches a reading of The "*Poltergeist*" of Suzano in another way: one can examine how the internal dynamic between the Spiritist intellectuals and the evangelists plays itself out in the text. As noted above, Spiritist evangelists tend to read *The Gospel According to Spiritism* and sometimes *The Book of the Spirits*, but they almost never read *The Book of the Mediums*, which is widely considered to be Kardec's most scientific and difficult book. When Andrade cites and discusses this book, he is therefore being consistent with the intellectuals' effort to get the Spiritist movement as a whole to take a greater interest in *The Book of the Mediums*.

The intellectuals also try to get the rest of the Spiritist movement to pay more attention to parapsychology, which many Spiritists have written off as an anti-Spiritist discipline. One can see this process at work in a paper Andrade gave at the First Brazilian Symposium on Spiritism, Medicine, and Parapsychology, held in São Paulo in October 1986. Titled "The Three Faces of Parapsychology" (probably in reference to the famous "three faces of Eve" case of multiple personality), the paper reworks an article of the same name that he had published in the *Folha Espírita*, seven years before, under the pseudonym Lawrence Blacksmith.[5] Andrade writes under many pseudonyms for the *Folha Espírita*, a Spiritist newspaper of wide circulation in which the Paulista Spiritist intellectuals address other Spiritists and laypeople; he explained to me that he uses these pseudonyms to protect himself against popularity. The different names therefore distinguish between his popular and elite readerships.

Andrade's conference paper and the related article were more or less identical—with one significant difference. "Blacksmith" adopted a more explicitly pro-Spiritist position, whereas Andrade made the following comment regarding the three faces of parapsychology: "I am neither Janio nor Fernando Henrique, not even Eduardo Supplicy." This was a reference to the two main candidates of the 1985 mayoral race in São Paulo politics (Jânio Quadros and Fernando Henrique Cardoso), whom Andrade was implicitly calling the "superpowers" of São Paulo politics (like the U.S. and Soviet faces of parapsychology), in contrast to the underdog Supplicy, who was a minor candidate just as Brazil is a minor actor on the world stage.[6] Because Andrade's position is more explicit in the article, I will use the article as the basis for outlining his ideas on the role of Spiritist parapsychology.

According to Andrade, the three faces of parapsychology are the "Soviet face," a materialist school that has given the new name "psychotronics" to parapsychology; the "Western face," which refers to the parapsychology and psychical research of Europe and the United States; and the "Brazilian Spiritist face." In regard to the first, Andrade notes that the materialist ideology of the Soviet Union impedes the free investigation of paranormal phenomena. As for the second face, Andrade writes: "We could compare Western parapsychology to a coin with its usual two sides: heads and tails. One of these sides corresponds to the parapsychology that presents itself officially, showing a scientific and positivistic orientation. The other is a more internal aspect, which awaits an incommensurable body of evidence that supports a position which is still considered metaphysical, that of the survival of the personality after death" (Andrade/Blacksmith 1979b: 5).

The third face of parapsychology mediates between the opposing materialist and metaphysical schools; it is neither materialist nor metaphysical, and (implicitly) neither Soviet nor North American: "Brazilian Spiritist [parapsychology] expands the concept of matter, admitting its extension beyond those three strict dimensions of Kardec—out of which the paranormal properties of living beings occur" (Andrade/Blacksmith 1979c: 4–5). Andrade then discusses his theory of a "biological organizing model" (MOB), which he says the spirit of André Luiz had already predicted. By showing that André Luiz also discusses a "quintessential matter" with quantum physical properties equivalent to those of the MOB, Andrade shows how his MOB is in accordance with Spiritist doctrine. Although the MOB is not exactly identical to the perispirit, it expresses and legitimates in more scientific language the idea of the perispirit (more or less what in English is called the "astral body"), one of the key elements of Spiritist doctrine.[7]

The pair of terms MOB/perispirit (like the pair of names Andrade/Blacksmith) therefore repeats his heads/tails formula for Western parapsychology: the term "MOB" is more suitable for dialogue with skeptical outsiders, such as orthodox Northern Hemisphere parapsychologists or Brazilian doctors, whereas the term "perispirit" is more common among Brazilian Spiritists. Note, however, that within the house of Brazilian Spiritism he is Lawrence Blacksmith (a foreign name), whereas on the street of scientific discourse he is Hernani Guimarães Andrade. One cannot reduce this situation to a case of double discourse; it is more complicated than that. Andrade represents the external discourse of official science within the Spiritist movement, just as he represents Spiritist discourse to an external scientific world: a medium of discourses.

The translatability of these names and terms corresponds to Andrade's view that parapsychology translates into, or at least provides evidence in support of, Spiritist doctrine. Andrade therefore chastises those Spiritists who reject parapsychology as anti-Spiritist: "Before going any further, we wish to alert those Spiritists still influenced by the ridiculous campaign alluded to above that parapsychology never was nor ever will be the adversary of Spiritism. Very much to the contrary. The two complement each other" (Andrade/Blacksmith 1979c: 4). The "ridiculous campaign" to which Andrade refers is Brazilian Catholic parapsychology. For Andrade this is "pseudo-parapsychology," what many orthodox scientists would probably consider an oxymoron generated by this complex process of heterodox heterodoxies: "There has been a proliferation of pseudo-parapsychologists with unnecessary and nonscientific objectives. Among these adventurers, some religious and intolerant fanatics have managed to disseminate confusion in the breasts of the lay masses, improperly using the name of parapsychology as a support for their absurd attacks on Spiritism" (Andrade/Blacksmith 1979c: 4). Andrade speaks to the evangelical, nonintellectual Spiritists and warns them about their simplistic tendency to dismiss parapsychology. In the process, he is drawn into one of his rare moments of polemic, in which he attempts to free Brazilian Spiritism of its anti-intellectual tendencies, which he blames on Catholic intellectuals.

To summarize, Andrade's interpretation of the poltergeist of Suzano and his discussion of the three faces of parapsychology bring out divisions among intellectual Spiritists, evangelical Spiritists, and followers of Afro-Brazilian religions. However, in the process of interpreting these class and status divisions within the field of spirit-mediumship religion, one encounters other significant groups: namely, the medical profession, Catholic intellectuals, and Northern Hemisphere parapsychologists. Thus, the elite/popular dialogue within the religious system of spirit mediumship leads into a series of dialogues between Spiritist intellectuals and other elites. A fuller interpretation of The "Poltergeist" of Suzano requires us to situate that text in this broader context.

Catholic Variations

It is interesting that "fanatic," the term which Andrade used to describe Catholic parapsychologists, is also the word which Padre Oscar González Quevedo, S.J., used to describe Andrade when I brought up his name during a visit to Quevedo's school in August 1983. Quevedo is a Spanish Jesuit who ran the Latin American Center of Parapsychology (CLAP) of the Anchieta College in São Paulo, both of which have been closed since my first visit there. A generation younger than Andrade, Quevedo is also much more of a polemicist; he clearly states his own position and seems to enjoy a good debate. His influence is considerable: this Jesuit priest has trained many of the Catholic parapsychologists of Latin America, and his parapsychology courses for Catholic priests and laypeople have drawn large audiences across Brazil.

Quevedo's interpretation of parapsychology differs strikingly from that of his Spiritist "colleague." To begin, Quevedo provides a different classification of the various schools of Northern Hemisphere parapsychology. In his book *What Is Parapsychology?* Quevedo argues that Northern Hemisphere parapsychology can be divided into three schools: the "materialist school" of the Soviet bloc countries; the "spiritualist school" of the United States; and the "eclectic school" of Europe, which brings together the first two approaches.[8] This is not so different from Andrade's viewpoint, but Quevedo adds to this threefold scheme a fourth approach: the "theoretical school" of Catholic parapsychology. This last school is derived from the eclectic school but differs from it by deducing certain theoretical implications from the research findings. Among these implications is the existence of a category of phenomena that are neither extranormal (Soviet, "materialist") nor paranormal (U.S., "spiritualist") but that instead are "supernormal." These phenomena belong to the domain of the theologian, and they include biblical prophecy, raising the dead, the cure of lepers, the phenomena at Lourdes, and speaking in multiple languages (which is associated with Catholic saints [Quevedo 1974: 100–103]). Because these miracles require direct intervention from the otherworld, they lie outside the domain of parapsychology; however, the same does not hold for demonic possession, spirit communication, or reincarnation, which the theoretical school of parapsychology classifies as extranormal or paranormal phenomena. In short, in Quevedo's scheme the phenomena which legitimize Spiritist doctrine are merely extranormal or paranormal, whereas those which legitimize Catholic theology are truly supernatural.

Quevedo therefore situates his parapsychology in a mediating position between science and Catholic doctrine, a position that is parallel to the mediation between science and Spiritist doctrine accomplished by Andrade's parapsychology. Yet, although both of these parapsychologies serve as mediating discourses between science and "religion," and in this sense are structurally equivalent, they are diametrically opposed in content. This point becomes clear when one considers Quevedo's interpretation of the poltergeist. For Quevedo and his followers in the Catholic church, poltergeists are products of "telergy," a physical energy and "a type of electricity that, however, does not obey the common physical laws which govern electricity" (Quevedo 1974: 44). The Jesuit intellectual also makes clear that telergy bears no relationship to the Spiritist concept of the perispirit: "We may also do away with the false presupposition of the 'perispirit.' The perispirit is inadmissible. It is only ectoplasm or body energy and never 'matter in the spirit,' 'semi-material spirit,' or 'semispiritual' matter, which implies a logical contradiction in terms" (Quevedo 1968: vol. 2, p. 358). For Quevedo and his followers, such as the Jesuit Edvino Friderichs, telergy is a physical energy that is directed by the unconscious.

This theory of telergy is closely linked to the Jesuit parapsychologists' treatment strategy for poltergeists: namely, psychotherapy, as opposed to exorcism or the Spiritists' disobsession. Regarding one poltergeist case, Friderichs writes:

> Before my visit, they had already called in Umbandists, then Spiritists, and finally a Catholic priest, who blessed the house, prayed with the landlords of the house, performed exorcisms, and prayed a mass on the spot, all without any result.
>
> It is in such cases that one should call a specialist. When some-one suffers from poor eyesight, one goes to the optometrist . . . and so on. In the same way, we are dealing here with a subject that demands a specialist, and the right man is the parapsychologist. (1979: 181)

For the Jesuits, the parapsychologist plays the role of clinical psychologist. The Catholic intellectual's psychotherapy substitutes for the disobsession of the Spiritist, the exorcism of the Umbandist, the psychiatric treatment of the medical profession, and even the exorcism of traditional Catholicism (on Friderich's treatment, see Hess 1991b, 1991c).

The Jesuit priest John Fitzpatrick had these ideas in mind when the family victimized by the Suzano poltergeist called on him to exorcise their house. In his book *The Power of Faith*, Fitzpatrick writes:

> A haunted house, for example, is not caused by strange occult forces but, normally, by a member of the family who lives in the house and who is generally a boy or girl undergoing puberty. At this age, the imagination is at its highest point of development. It is very fertile and uncontrolled, extremely lively and creative, and capable of producing uncommon phenomena.
>
> Haunting, therefore, can be understood as the result of a body of energy created by the person. It appears to be under the sub-conscious control of whoever is causing it, and it can be brought forth to interfere with persons and situations in the most varied of ways. Usually it is a symptom of a moderate form of mental disturbance such as extreme jealousy, hatred, resentment, or dissatisfaction with some person or situation. (1983: 19)

Before he arrived, Fitzpatrick notes, the afflicted family sought help from a variety of other sources, including the police, a *macumbeiro* (probably an Umbanda or Candomblé priest or priestess), Protestant pastors, and Spiritists (1983: 19). According to Fitzpatrick's account, the family turned to him out of desperation. The family believed that a woman in the neighborhood had called on a *macumbeiro* to perform black magic against them and that this is what had caused the poltergeist. This "native" interpretation (one that the Spiritist reading defends in more scientific language) constructs the poltergeist in terms of a set of personalistic and hierarchical relationships. In other words, from the family's point of view, the poltergeist is a product of a personal relationship between the father of the family and a neighbor. This relationship is mediated by two sets of hierarchies: the neighbor goes to a local *macumbeiro*, who in turn calls on his evil spirits to help do the work of sorcery; in return, the father appeals to a religious figure (a priest, the Protestant pastors, another *macumbeiro*, or a Spiritist medium), who in turn asks for help from a more powerful otherworldly being (either God or the spirits of light).

In contrast to the family's interpretation, that of Quevedo, Friderichs, Fitzpatrick, and other Jesuits—which derives from European and North American parapsychology—situates the individual, who is called the "poltergeist agent," as the central figure and encompassing value. Instead of encompassing the poltergeist in a series of personal and hierarchical relations (neighbor/*macumbeiro*/evil spirit versus father/priest, medium, etc./God, spirits), the cause is reduced to the fourteen-year-old girl's "telergy," which reflects her unconscious hostility. Thus, the solution is not exorcism or disobsession, which would institute hierarchical and personalistic values, but instead a session of psychotherapy, which focuses on the girl as an individual and on her psychological motivations. The Catholic interpretation, then, represents the values that DaMatta (1978) and Dumont (1980) associate with individualism and the modern West (for a more detailed discussion, see Hess 1989c).

Thus, Fitzpatrick, following this "modern" interpretation, believed that the fourteen-year-old girl harbored a profound resentment of her father (apparently with good reason; Andrade [1982: 17] notes that he beat her). The Jesuit states that several years earlier the father had left the family to live with another woman in the neighborhood and that he had returned about two years before Fitzpatrick's visit; his return corresponded with the beginning of the poltergeist activity. According to his report, Fitzpatrick then recommended that the family send the girl to visit relatives for two weeks in order to see whether the poltergeist attack would subside. The priest reports that he returned after two weeks and encountered the girl, who had returned the day before. During her absence, there were no fires; as soon as she returned, they began again. Fitzpatrick concludes: "With this in mind, I took Irene for an interview in which I tried to get her to accept her father consciously, forgive him for what he had done, and end the resentment. As far as I was able to ascertain, this was the end of the incidents, as incredible as it seems" (1983: 23).

Andrade, like a fiery poltergeist, burns a hole in Fitzpatrick's account. According to Andrade's research, the daughter was away for only four days, from May 23 to May 27, 1970 (1982: 71). He reasons that Fitzpatrick visited the house on May 22 or 23; if so, two weeks after this date would be well into June, but the phenomena stopped on May 28. Andrade concludes that Fitzpatrick's counseling session occurred well after the phenomena had stopped (p. 71). The Spiritist intellectual does not consider the possibility that Fitzpatrick simply made a mistake and wrote "two weeks" (fourteen days) instead of "four days"; instead, Andrade argues that the most likely cause of the poltergeist's extinction was the Spiritist disobsession meeting (pp. 73ff.). His report, however, does not specify the date of that meeting; it states only that he interviewed the Spiritists on May 30, or two days after the phenomena stopped (p. 73). One is therefore left not knowing when the Fitzpatrick counseling session actually took place or when the Spiritist disobsession meeting occurred.

It is not necessary to resolve these questions here. Indeed, the open-endedness of these questions is an almost certain guarantee that the poltergeist of Suzano will return to haunt the dialogue between Catholic and Spiritist parapsychologists. Nor is this dialogue likely to end in the near future, for the underlying values that structure this dialogue and that the dialogue reproduces are in fundamental conflict over the very nature of the world. The Spiritist viewpoint reflects, in a more intellectualized language, the family's own diagnosis of the symptoms: the cause of the poltergeist was black magic initiated by the father's lover. In contrast, the Catholic viewpoint corresponds more closely to the interpretation that one would find among Northern Hemisphere parapsychologists as well as among Brazilian social scientists, psychologists, and doctors, the official discourse which is heavily influenced by that of their colleagues in the United States and Europe. In this respect, it is interesting to note that two of the Jesuit parapsychologists discussed above (Quevedo and Fitzpatrick) are not Brazilians. In contrast to the interpretation of the

Spiritist intellectuals, theirs is a markedly "foreign" reading of the meaning and dynamics of the poltergeist.

In short, in this context the Spiritist reading links up with "Brazilianness" and popular ideology, and the psychodynamic/psychoenergetic reading is connected to "foreignness" and elite ideology. Yet, Catholics and Spiritists alike can legitimately call themselves parapsychologists, because both positions are represented within the parapsychology of Europe and North America. What is whole in the Northern Hemisphere comes apart in the Southern Hemisphere.

A Northern Interlude

Parapsychology, or psychical research, is a general name that embraces a variety of schools and traditions, including, we have seen, the Soviet school of psychotronics as well as the various European and North American schools. For the moment, this discussion will leave aside the Soviet school and will concentrate instead on a key division within European and North American parapsychology.

Although skeptics may cordon off the entire field of parapsychology as "pseudoscience," those within the field see important divisions of skepticism and belief within European and North American parapsychology. The previous name for the field, psychical research, also entailed a somewhat different perspective and what has sometimes been likened to a different "research paradigm" in Thomas Kuhn's sense (1970): the first generations of researchers inspected psychic phenomena with the hope of answering the question of whether or not the personality survives death.[9] In the United States during the 1930s, Joseph Banks Rhine of Duke University brought about a major reorientation of psychical research, arguing that researchers could not take seriously the hypothesis of survival until the limits of extrasensory perception and psychokinesis were better understood.[10] This shift of research interest was accompanied by a shift of research methods; Rhine moved psi research out of the parlor and into the psychology laboratory. He also used the term "parapsychology" to refer to his new approach, but since his time the word has become an umbrella term that includes other traditions, such as the older paradigms of psychical research.

Although Rhine showed little interest in poltergeist cases, the opposing opinions of Rhineans and many psychical researchers on the "survival question" are similar to the opposing Catholic and Spiritist interpretations of the poltergeist. A majority of European and North American parapsychologists today adopt the perspective that poltergeist activity, when not explainable by normal causes (e.g., electrical failure, pranks, animals, hoaxes, dissociated behavior, etc.), is caused by the "recurrent spontaneous psychokinesis" (RSPK) generated by a living human agent or agents. Theories of the mechanism of RSPK vary from the psychoanalytic type, in which the poltergeist outbreak is an alternative expression of repressed emotions (e.g., Fodor 1948), to the physiological type, in which the poltergeist outbreak is an alternative expression of central nervous system disorders such as epilepsy (e.g., Roll 1977). Against this interpretation, a smaller number of parapsychologists/psychical researchers continue to support the theory that at least some poltergeist outbreaks are caused by "discarnate" human spirits (e.g., Stevenson 1972).

Thus, divisions within West European and North American parapsychology appear in Brazil as divisions between Catholic and Spiritist parapsychology. Fitzpatrick's idea—to look for an agent and employ psychotherapeutic counseling—follows a model that Brazilian Catholic parapsychologists have adopted from post-Rhinean Northern Hemisphere parapsychologists. In contrast, Andrade's spiritic interpretation of the Suzano poltergeist finds some support among a minority of Northern Hemisphere parapsychologists who still embrace the old psychical research framework. Andrade cites these parapsychologists in the section of his case study titled "The Participation of the Epicenter," in which he criticizes agent-oriented theories of the poltergeist (1982: 80–85). In fact, Andrade reinterprets the term "agent" from the human to the spirit world, and he replaces what Northern Hemisphere parapsychologists call the "agent" with the term "epicenter":

> Rhine's experiments managed to demonstrate the reality of paranormal functions and phenomena. However, they also served to support the positivist and materialist interpretation of these facts. In this way, poltergeist phenomena were also generically placed in the category of purely psychokinetic events. In accord with a *materialist* interpretation, they would be the *only* and *exclusive* result of the paranormal faculties of the *epicenter*. (1982: 80)

Andrade does not deny that a living person can furnish energy to the poltergeist, but for him this is not a sufficient explanation. He argues instead that four conditions are necessary for this type of poltergeist to occur: (1) the existence of a sorcerer (*feiticeiro*); (2) the existence of one or more discarnate agent(s); (3) magical practices capable of activating the discarnate agent(s); and (4) the presence of an "epicenter," or living agent, at the site of the poltergeist (1982: 94). For Andrade, the "epicenter" is a necessary, but not sufficient, condition; he encompasses the post-Rhinean and Catholic interpretation of the poltergeist in this framework of relationships among the sorcerer, the spiritic agent, and the epicenter.

Andrade, then, is himself making a kind of poltergeist attack on what he terms "materialistic" and "positivistic" theories of the poltergeist, and as a result *The "Poltergeist" of Suzano* presents a dilemma of values for Northern Hemisphere parapsychology. On the one hand, it is a carefully researched, empirical study, rather than an expository or programmatic statement; therefore, it is representative of a genre of parapsychological writing that Northern Hemisphere parapsychologists value highly. On the other hand, this Spiritist case study arrives at theoretical conclusions opposed to the orthodox, individualistic, and agent-centered interpretation favored in the Northern Hemisphere.

The solution to this dilemma appears in a review of *The "Poltergeist" of Suzano* in the *Journal of the Society for Psychical Research*.[11] The reviewer, Carlos Alvarado, is a Puerto Rican educated in the United States in post-Rhinean parapsychology and, more recently, in the history of science, but he is also an expert on the older literature of psychical research. In conversations with me, he has described his role as one of introducing "other perspectives" into contemporary parapsychology, especially perspectives drawn from the literature in Spanish and Portuguese. His Puerto Rican background places him in an ideal position as a cultural mediator. He sees his review of *The "Poltergeist" of Suzano* as part of an effort to open up new (or revive old) theoretical perspectives within parapsychology. Although his review succeeds in this regard, it also raises questions that reflect the values of the North American parapsychologists for whom he is writing. For example, while Alvarado praises the thoroughness of the Suzano poltergeist study and consequently invokes the value of empirical research—"it is the most systematic and detailed report on record of fire poltergeist phenomena" (1984: 395)—he also questions Andrade's spiritic interpretation by arguing that "alternative explanations could be considered in more detail" and by explicitly mentioning the impact of the Spiritist disobsession on the group's psychodynamics (pp. 394–95). Just as the translation of Northern Hemisphere parapsychology into the Brazilian Spiritist context involved a cultural reinterpretation of that parapsychology, here one sees a hint of the reverse process as the Brazilian variant is translated back into the domain of Northern Hemisphere parapsychology.

More Catholic Variations

Returning now to Brazil, the division between the Spiritist and psychotherapeutic interpretations of the poltergeist also has a parallel within the Catholic church. Fitzpatrick notes that the father of the afflicted family wanted him to bless the house; but he refused, arguing that "according to my understanding of the nature of the problem, I did not think that a blessing would have resolved the case" (1983: 21).

The attitudes of the priest and the family represent a division of values within the church—not just between the elite and the masses, but between two elites. On one side, Quevedo observes the following (in a passage that reminds one of Kardec's description of possession, cited at the end of Chapter 3): "All of the cases in history—biblical or postbiblical, even the most celebrated, such as the possessed [sic] of Loudun, the 'possessed' Cafre, the Pausini brothers, the Cemetery of Saint Medardo, the 'possessed' of Ilfurt, the young Cassina Amata, etc.—are easily explained scientifically and parapsychologically, and it is absurd and illogical to employ the demonological interpretation" (Quevedo 1974: 116). In contrast, the Franciscan intellectual (currently bishop of Bahia) Boaventura Kloppenburg, who is just as critical of Spiritism as Quevedo, has a very different view of spirit mediumship and demoniacal involvement. In his book *Spiritism in Brazil: Orientation for Catholics,* Kloppenburg warns Brazilian Catholics of the many alternative explanations for poltergeists and concludes: "If a given case is not . . . mixed up with naughty little girls, ornery boys, interested shysters, rats, or gusts of wind; if the reports have not been made by mythomaniacs or paranoid types; if individual hallucinations and mental contagions have been eliminated as a possibility—and still the haunting continues—then one can ask a priest to do an exorcism according to the rule, because diabolical infestation would then be a possibility" (1960: 271). This comment sets the stage for the next chapter in Kloppenburg's book, "The Processes of the Demon in Spiritism." In that chapter, the Franciscan intellectual argues that spirit mediumship may be "the occasion," even if it is not "the cause," of otherworldly intervention, and because this may mean the intervention of the devil, Spiritism is a very dangerous practice (p. 289).

Quevedo's strongly skeptical stance with respect to demonic possession and intervention has led to conflicts with the Church hierarchy. His Latin American Center of Parapsychology was closed in 1984, and, like the liberation theologist Leonardo Boff (Kloppenburg's rebellious protégé), albeit for different reasons, Quevedo was also prohibited from speaking in public. In an interview with me on April 2, 1986, Kloppenburg explained that Quevedo was under prohibition because he "did not stay within the bounds of science"—in other words, because he used parapsychology erroneously to explain demoniacal intervention.[12] In this case, the personalistic and hierarchical interpretation has not only encompassed the individualistic one, it has repressed it.

The Case of the Anomalous Doctor

In August 1985, I traveled to Florianópolis to interview Dr. Osmard Andrade Faria, who has written an important textbook of parapsychology (1981) as well as a more popular book, *What Is Parapsychology?* (1984), for the "What Is It?" series of the publisher Brasiliense. Faria's position on parapsychology is anomalous:[13] as a medical man with a long-standing research interest in hypnosis, he finds himself drawn neither to the Catholic nor to the Spiritist interpretation of parapsychology. Instead, he sees himself as a materialist, although he admits that he is drawn to some of the ideas of Zen Buddhism.

Faria's neutrality with respect to Catholic and Spiritist parapsychology can be seen in his textbook of parapsychology, where the Suzano poltergeist makes its appearance among summaries of other poltergeist cases. Faria draws his data from Andrade's research, but he follows Fitzpatrick's interpretation and makes no mention of Andrade's spiritic theory (Faria 1981: 175). He then ends the section with a quote from Andrade; "For reasons of ethics and prudence, we believe that for the time being it is more reasonable to withhold judgment with respect to solving the problem of the cause of the Suzano poltergeist" (p. 175). In *The "Poltergeist" of Suzano*, which was published the next year, Andrade provides his solution.

Faria respects Andrade for his research and knowledge rather than for his Spiritist philosophy, and he describes himself, in contrast to Andrade, as only a kind of journalist rather than a parapsychology researcher. Indeed, before he became a doctor, Faria was a journalist who thought of himself as a kind of debunker; and his first book, *Hypnosis and Lethargy* (1959), was a critique of the Catholic therapist Irmão Vitrício (Paixão 1981). He described himself in my interview with him:

> To be honest, I can't be called a researcher like Hernani Guimarães Andrade. I'm not exactly what Hernani is. I'm more of a journalist—a doctor—more of a scientific journalist than a man dedicated to laboratory work. I don't do laboratory parapsychology. I did hypnosis. I did a lot of surgery by hypnosis. I taught it a lot and practiced it a lot.
>
> Given the situation in Florianópolis where I live, it's very difficult to do laboratory parapsychology. So I did the opposite. I hunted down information. Everyone seems to know what parapsychology is, but I didn't. Everyone knows, don't they? The Spiritist knows, the Catholic knows, the man in the street knows. Everyone knows. My mother-in-law knows, my maid knows. I was the only guy who didn't know what parapsychology was. The result: twenty years of research and a "journalistic work."

What Faria set out to do in his parapsychology textbook was to provide an introduction to the field that scrupulously avoids siding with either the Catholic or the Spiritist interpretation, both of which he opposes to his own "scientific" vision of parapsychology:

> Spiritists do everything to prove that parapsychology is a spiritual phenomenon, so they start with preconceived notions and foregone conclusions. If someone is a Spiritist, he's going to show that the phenomena all prove Spiritism. The Catholic does just the opposite. He's going to show that it's all part of the Catholic religion. I started from a different point of view. I didn't have any preconceived ideas. But I knew that the phenomena were not [part of] Spiritism, religion, magic, superstition, or belief but, instead, that they are scientific phenomena.

Faria is disheartened by parapsychology in Brazil. After attending several parapsychology conferences in Rio and São Paulo, he resolved never to go to another one because, in his words, "I didn't know whether I was attending a scientific congress or a Spiritist session." He notes that even some Spiritists were disappointed by the way Spiritism had taken over the parapsychology conferences, and one Spiritist said to him that "he himself didn't like the distortion that occurred in these conferences."

Despite these negative comments, Faria's relations with Spiritist intellectuals are slightly more friendly than those with Catholic parapsychologists. This was not always so. In the first edition of his widely read and translated textbook *Manual of Medical and Dental Hypnosis* (1979), he argued that phenomena of spirit mediumship were fundamentally hypnotic, and he made other assertions that caused an uproar in the Spiritist press (Casella 1961/62; Faria 1961/62; Imbassahy 1961, 1962a–d). Since then, however, tempers have cooled, and Faria says that Spiritists have told him they would even use his new textbook on parapsychology as an empirical (albeit not a theoretical) textbook in their college in Curitiba. He also became friends with the late Carlos Imbassahy and says that Hernani Guimarães Andrade is "today very much my friend." Still, Faria distinguishes his personal friendship with Andrade from Andrade's beliefs as a Spiritist. "Hernani is an extraordinary thinker," he told me. "It's just a shame that he's a Spiritist. Tell Hernani this: 'The only thing wrong with you is that you're a Spiritist,' " he said, laughing. Then he went on: "But he isn't one of those orthodox Spiritists, that fanatic, dogmatic, type."

As for Padre Quevedo, Faria's previous experience with Irmão Vitrício seems to have influenced his present opinion:

> Quevedo was here in Florianópolis. . . . He seemed to me to be much more of a stage performer than a scientist. He even performed tricks—easily demonstrated—and it's a good thing no one saw that they were stage tricks, prestidigitation. But anyone who knows a little about the subject would be able to tell that they were just . . . a trick [performed] in order to get the public to believe in the phenomena. This demoralizes me a lot.
>
> Did he really do this? [I had asked.] He didn't explain at the end of the talk that they were just tricks?
>
> No sirree. He really did it, seriously.

If Faria is opposed to Catholic as well as to Spiritist interpretations of parapsychology, that does not mean his own version is completely neutral. As a medical man, he has a certain allegiance to his own profession, even if its attitude toward parapsychology is lukewarm at best. When I asked what his profession thinks of parapsychology, he answered: "They're against it because they're afraid of a bad interpretation. Outside Brazil, there's a great deal of university study of parapsychology. In North America, for example, there are a lot of universities that study parapsychology, such as Duke and UCLA. . . . But in Brazil there's no place for it in the universities. Because if they had a parapsychology course in a university here, they would *certainly* have to contract a Spiritist or a priest to give the course." Despite the unwillingness of the universities to offer parapsychology courses, Faria said that most doctors who had read his book "agreed with it and liked it." He also said that many engineers had liked it. Spiritists, however, thought he was a crypto-Catholic, and vice versa.

Like Andrade and Quevedo, Faria portrays himself as speaking from a neutral position, and his authority is anchored not only in this neutrality but also in links to orthodox medicine, science, and Northern Hemisphere parapsychology. Faria's brand of parapsychology does not fit into either the Catholic or the Spiritist school, and unlike many post-Rhinean parapsychologists in Europe and North America, Faria is a materialist. He sees the world through the lens of a background in physiology, medicine, and medical hypnosis. Given this background, he tends to look for physical explanations of paranormal phenomena, and he therefore tilts more toward Soviet parapsychology ("psychotronics") than toward the parapsychology of the North American Joseph Banks Rhine, who believed that his research on extrasensory perception and psychokinesis supported mind-body dualism. This anomalous position means that Faria finds himself agreeing and disagreeing at different points with Catholics as well as with Spiritists. Like Quevedo, for example, Faria believes that a physical energy generated by the agent causes poltergeists; but, unlike Quevedo, Faria also believes that all paranormal phenomena, including precognition, must have some physical explanation. Faria therefore believes that the Spiritists' concept of the perispirit was a positive step toward a physical explanation of parapsychological phenomena; yet, for him it was just a step, and he regards the most exciting advances to be those of the Soviets on "bioplasmic fields" (Faria 1981: 295, 312).

Thus, in this process of bricolage, a school of Northern Hemisphere parapsychology which has so far been missing in Brazil—namely, Soviet psychotronics—appears in Brazil in the figure of a medical doctor and hypnosis expert. A division in time in the Northern Hemisphere (psychical research/post-Rhinean parapsychology) appears in Brazil as a division within the religious system (Catholicism/Spiritism), just as a division in space (Soviet/Western) appears as a division within the ideological arena (medical/religious).

A *Polterabend* Ending

Andrade's critical comments on "materialism" and "positivism" in *The "Poltergeist" of Suzano* take on new meaning when contrasted with the thought of Faria and the Catholic and Northern Hemisphere parapsychologists. By comparing the ideas of Andrade with those of rival elites, Spiritist science appears to be a defense of Brazilian or popular thought against the ideas of foreigners and domestic elites. In other words, one arrives at a conclusion diametrically opposed to the assumptions at the starting point of this chapter, which drew on a Bastidean framework: Spiritist science as an elite, white, middle-class ideology in conflict with the popular, mulatto, working-class ideology represented by Umbanda and the Afro-Brazilian religions. But my intent here is not to make a poltergeist attack on the house of Brazilian social science and then replace it with an alternative social science (an antisyncretic and puritanical move). Rather, my intent is to Brazilianize Brazilian social science by syncretizing the two interpretations of Spiritist scientific thought: "Spiritism as elite ideology" and "Spiritism as popular ideology." Toward that end, let us turn to a context in which *The "Poltergeist" of Suzano* makes another appearance—and in which its meaning is inverted.

From June 5 to 9, 1985, a joint conference met in Brasília: the Fourth Brazilian Congress of Parapsychology; the First National Meeting of Researchers in the Fields of Parapsychology, Psychotronics, and Psychobiophysics; and the Third Congress of Natural Medicine. Less an academic conference than a gathering of Brazil's occult and New Age tribes, the business of this meeting took place not only in the two large lecture halls but also in smaller rooms where "minicourses" were offered in astrology, chiropractic, acupuncture, applied psychotronics, past-lives therapy, and iridology. Stalls and expositions featured Spiritist and occult books, psychically inspired paintings, pyramids, and various perfumes and herbs. In addition, there were tours to such sites as the Umbanda-occultist community in the Valley of the Dawn; Cristalina, a center for crystals and precious stones; the mineral water park in Brasília; and other sights of the Brazilian capital, the up-and-coming center of Brazilian esotericism.

The Mexican novelist Carlos Fuentes once said that the plight of being a writer in Latin America lies in the fact that its history continually outdoes its literature. A case in point is the symbolic transformation of Brasília, a city known for its promise of utopian modernism which the realities of Brazilian society ultimately subverted. The anthropologist

James Holston (1989) has investigated the many ways in which Brasília has become Brazilianized, particularly how class and status distinctions have been reinscribed on the urban landscape; the 1985 gathering of parapsychologists, ufologists, and occultists revealed yet another dimension to this process. In the brief two or three decades since the city was built, the local population has imbued this planned, rationalized city with occult meanings, rereading its modernist architecture with esoteric numerology and finding parallels between its edifices and Egypt's pyramids. As the "Egyptologist" Iara Kern explained during the opening group of speeches, the setting of the conference was auspicious because Brasília is both the city of Juscelino Kubitschek (the charismatic, modern, Kennedyesque president who built it) and Akhenaton, the Egyptian city of magic. Brasília residents at the conference went on to quote a NASA specialist who says that the central plateau of Brazil would be one of the most secure locations on the planet in the event of a nuclear war. This city of steel and concrete has become, in their words, the "city of the third millennium." Thus, the Lusitanian tradition of Sebastianism—after the king who disappeared on a crusade to Africa but who one day would return to save Portugal—has been reborn on the central plateau of South America.

During the conference, this popular millenarianism commingled with the elite millenarianism surrounding the birth of the Brazilian New Republic. Thus, the opening session was the most carefully orchestrated, serving to identify the major groups at the meeting and to link them to the recent transition from two decades of military dictatorship to a civilian-ruled New Republic. The dignitaries at the conference predictably recognized their personal ties by sitting together at a large table which brought together the ufologists, the Brazilian Federation of Parapsychologists (a loosely Spiritist group), the Brazilian Association of Natural Medicine, the organizing committee (led by Octávio Ulysséa of the Spiritist college in Curitiba), and the New Republic leaders, represented by José Aparecida, governor of the Federal District of Brasília.

The conference took place shortly after the death of President-elect Tancredo Neves and the birth of the New Republic, and the major speakers flavored their speeches with millenarian rhetoric concerning the dawn of a new age of civilian rule and democratic hope. By examining these speeches in detail, one can begin to get at the double-edged quality—in the sense of being both elite and popular—of the "alternative thought," or counterculture, that the conference articulated. Governor Aparecida gave an opening speech that addressed the importance of natural medicine in the "Brazilian reality," and he noted that reforms were currently in process in the Ministry of Health, the Ministry of Welfare, and other departments of the federal government. Quoting Tancredo Neves, the governor hailed natural medicine as the medicine for the people, saying that it was "one more side of Brazil which must change."

After the governor's speech, the former general and current ufologist Alfredo Uchôa—on whom Márcio Souza may well have based the character General Pessoa in his novel *The Order of the Day: An Unidentified Flying Opus*—characterized the conference as a step in the formation of a community of alternative science, and he denounced official science as well as "materialist parapsychology." After Uchôa, the director of the Spiritist college in Curitiba, Octávio Ulysséa, called for educational reforms favorable to parapsychology. Ulysséa's speech, which stylistically recalled the political oratory of the great opposition-party protest speeches during the campaign for "diretas já!" (direct elections now!), called for educational reforms and "a new epistemology for the New Republic," and he argued that it was time for "psicobiofísica já!" (psychobiophysics now!). Several other of the opening speeches served to bring together the potentially contradictory groups of parapsychologists, ufologists, supporters of natural medicine, and so on. A shared opposition mediated potential contradictions: parapsychology and ufology are to orthodox science as natural medicine is to orthodox medicine as the New Republic is to the former military dictatorship.

The hope voiced by the speakers, and which the speech of Governor Aparecida fueled, was that a New Republic of science and medicine would emerge in the wake of the New Republic of the state. As if to prove that was not an idle dream, the program chair—Octávio Ulysséa—announced during the course of the conference that the Ministry of Welfare had accepted acupuncture, homeopathy, and naturopathy as alternative therapies. No one seemed to know exactly what this acceptance entailed, but the fact that some of the heterodoxies discussed during the conference could become "official therapies" revealed again the complex nature of the heterodox science and medicine of the conference, whose ambiguous position bridged both popular/alternative discourse and elite/official discourse.

Such ambiguity became evident in a remarkable episode during the opening session when a humble, self-educated herbal specialist made his appearance. Introduced not as a doctor or healer but as an intimate friend of the Spiritist medium Chico Xavier, Langerton Neves da Cunha spoke about "fitotherapy," which he confessed was a term he had never heard of before the natural medicine people explained to him that it was a fancy word for herbal remedies. Referring to himself as a poor *curandeiro* from the interior (a category which to him meant "folk healer" but, as the next chapter discusses, is illegal and which to many Spiritist intellectuals means "charlatan"), he announced that he had brought recipes for herbal cures as well as some medicine for gastritis and that he was willing to give it away. This caused a stampede to the podium, and the scientific revolutionaries at the table were forced to call for order. When order was restored, they praised the simplicity and goodwill of this man of the people: order and progress.

The appearance of this man of the people helped equate the heterodox thought of the conference with the people (*o povo*), but it also marked as scientific and elitist the heterodox science of the other conference speakers. Like the discourse of the New Republic of Brazil, that of the new republic of science represented itself as speaking for the people without necessarily letting the people speak for themselves. The discourse of the conference was therefore inherently a double discourse—both elite and popular. As such, it was a discourse of unity and inclusion; in fact, two key terms that emerged during the many speeches, talks, and lectures were "bioenergy" and the "integral man," both of which referred to a unity of spirit/mind/body parallel to the unity of spiritual and esoteric organizations at the conference. The "integral man" was a "man" aware of his "bioenergy," a term that symbolized the unity of "man" and of the occult tribes gathered at the conference. Everyone talked about bioenergy or energy; it was all things to all people, the mana of the discourse. One could feel it and photograph it, gain it or lose it, heal with it or hurt with it. Bioenergy was electromagnetic, psychokinetic, fluidic, vibrational, gravitational, auric, and more (depending on who spoke about it), but everyone agreed that it existed. It was both the mana and the doxa of the conference.[14]

Such a unifying symbol—a floating signifier, as Lévi-Strauss might say—was necessary, for the operative principle of this conference of the new republic of science was less the reformist principle of articulating a critical, alternative science—a principle that guides, for example, the parapsychology conferences of Western Europe and the United States—than it was the carnivalizing, Brazilian principle of letting all of the unwanted, marginalized groups speak. And speak they did, for nearly six days and nights: parapsychology of various stripes and shades, self-development through Oriental arts, mediumistic painting, Amazonian plants with paranormal effects, iridology, pyramid therapy (kefran therapy), acupuncture, yoga, alternative communities, Kirlian photography, ecology, past-lives therapy, meditation, paranormal music, interstellar biocommunication, astrological alchemy, radiesthesia, ufology, the power of the mind, interplanetary hierarchies, cosmobiology and, perhaps the most syncretic of all, the relationship between UFOs and *orixás*, the African deities of the Candomblés.

It was in this *polterabend* (charivari) of heterodoxies that we encounter, once again, *The "Poltergeist" of Suzano*. Ney Prieto Peres, a Paulista engineer who is close to Andrade and a member of the Spiritist Medical Association of São Paulo, presented the by-now-familiar case history in the sober, dry tone of a scientist reading a paper, in contrast to the informal and sometimes millenarian tone of many of the other talks. In heterodox scientific conferences in Brazil, apparently, one may present previously published materials; but, in fairness to Peres, I believe he chose this published piece of research in order to have something available to distribute to the audience, in order to set an example to the other groups at the conference, which he did not think were very scientific. In this context, the meaning of the Spiritist discourse was reversed from its meaning in the Catholic, North American/European, and medical-parapsychological contexts considered above. In the latter, the Spiritist case study represented a popular or "native" viewpoint to non-Spiritist elites: it defended the spiritic interpretation of poltergeists. In the context of the Brasília conference, the case study defended elite scientific values, such as empirical research and attention to methodology, against occult groups that were more interested in spiritual development, magical powers, and the dawning of the New Age than in scientific investigation. The reformist import of the Spiritist voice became even more evident in a talk by the Spiritists Ivo Ciro Caruso and Valter da Rosa Borges, "What Is and Is Not Parapsychology," which, like the lecture that Borges gave in São Paulo some months later, attempted to demarcate parapsychology from both Spiritism and religion.

Despite the Spiritists' call for a more scientific parapsychology, it is important to remember that their paradigmatic case study, *The "Poltergeist" of Suzano*, was written in the old tradition of psychical research rather than in the modern, experimental tradition that is de rigueur in cosmopolitan parapsychology. As General Uchôa clarified in his closing speech, modern science and laboratory parapsychology tell us "more and more about less and less." Regarding the laboratory parapsychologists of the cosmopolitan Parapsychological Association, he went on to say: "They're all so sophisticated, so full of science, so full of statistics, so full of quantitative, precise, mathematical facts. But with all of this, they sadly forget the value of qualitative facts [or facts of quality, *fatos de qualidade*]. . . . Well, these qualitative facts, unlike the statistical facts, don't exclude mother, Arí, Maurício. . . ." In place of a laboratory-based, post-Rhinean parapsychology, Uchôa advocated a return to the nineteenth-century tradition of psychical research (*metapsíquica*), a framework that does not forget these "facts of quality." In this formulation, laboratory parapsychology becomes doubly foreign: not only is it the product of a foreign culture, that of the North Americans and Europeans, but it turns people into facts—or insiders (*pessoas*) into outsiders (*indivíduos*)—and it remains anathema to the world of the home, with its family ties, emotional warmth, and quality facts.

To summarize, if one were to analyze Spiritist parapsychology only in the framework of the class and status divisions of the spirit-mediumship field, one would distort its meaning and fail to present an accurate depiction of its multiple meanings to Spiritists. Instead, by adopting the framework of a broader ideological arena—Jesuit and Northern Hemisphere parapsychologists, New Republic ideologues and New Age occultists, and so on—one sees the complex nature of Spiritist parapsychology, both as it appears in *The "Poltergeist" of Suzano* and as it appears in the 1985 Brasília conference, as a science of mediums and mediations. Spiritist parapsychology criticizes popular thought according to the standards and methods of elite science and, in doing so, represents an elite, modern voice within the field of spirit-mediumship religions and New Age movements; at the same time, however, this discipline translates popular thought into the language of science and consequently represents a popular, traditional voice within the field of orthodox science. In this sense, Spiritist science is both bricoleur and poltergeist: as bricoleur it reorganizes disparate elements from orthodox science as well as from popular tradition; as poltergeist it criticizes both orthodox science (as "positivistic" and "materialistic") and popular tradition (as "superstitious" and "occult").

CHAPTER SIX

SPIRIT SURGEONS AND WOUNDED LAWS
Spiritism and Medicine

An article that I cut out of the July 1985 issue of the *Folha Espírita* (Lex 1985) will serve as the starting point for this excursion into Spiritist-intellectual thought regarding medicine and alternative therapies. The method of this chapter is similar to that of the previous chapters. I begin with an interpretation that situates Spiritist medicine in terms of an elite/popular relationship within the Spiritist movement; then I consider other points of dialogue and comparison within the ideological arena: orthodox medicine, Catholic parapsychology, Northern Hemisphere parapsychology, law and political ideology, and other forms of heterodox medicine or alternative therapies.

The article, by Dr. Ary Lex, was part of the "Campaign of Clarification on Works of Healing" led by the Spiritist Medical Association of São Paulo (AMESP). In the column next to Lex's article, AMESP ran a general statement that explained the purpose of this campaign:

[O]nce again we are alerting our comrades, in the words of Bezerra de Menezes, in *Estudos Filosóficos* (first part), "to doubt, not in order to debunk, but to EXAMINE, OBSERVE, AND EXPERIMENT, as is the obligation of the man of science and the *man of good sense.*"

Works of healing occur in large numbers in the Spiritist Centers, and they need to be studied and analyzed seriously, using the most rigorous criteria of good sense and scientific process, without mysticism and idolatry, without fanaticism and disinformation.[1]

From the perspective of the intellectuals, the rank and file of their movement have an overly credulous attitude toward Spiritist healing, and this could endanger not just their clients but the Spiritist movement itself. Nowhere is this danger more evident than in the case of "mediumistic surgery" (*cirurgia mediúnica*, often called "psychic surgery" in English) or "surgical mediumship" (*mediunidade cirúrgica*). In order to educate the Spiritists who believe in or practice mediumistic surgery, Dr. Lex lays out the facts from the perspective of the Spiritist intellectuals.

Lex has been involved in the Spiritist movement of São Paulo for more than forty years; during this time, he has been an exponent of empirical research and scientific approaches within the movement. However, as he stated in a lecture late in 1985, and as he emphasized again to me when I spoke with him, during these four decades he has watched Spiritism become "less and less a science and more and more a mystical religion— *lamentably!*" He described his frustrations as a scientifically oriented Spiritist who has tried to do research in Spiritist centers:

For sixteen years, the Spiritist Medical Association [AMESP] tried to study scientifically the phenomena [of Spiritism], especially spiritual therapeutics or Spiritist healing. And the Spiritist Medical Association, despite having tried and having been criticized by many people in the medical profession for not having done any research, has never managed to do scientific research, especially in the area of healing, because the mediums, Spiritist centers, circles, and the Spiritist public in general usually consider research and scientific controls to be threats to the medium or the group. The simple fact of analyzing, raising a few doubts, suggesting methods of control—the simple fact of doubting a communication becomes extremely antipathetic. . . .[2]

As a surgeon and an elder statesman of the Spiritist movement, Lex exhorts Spiritist mediums and evangelical Spiritists to practice science as he understands it. And his understanding of science is backed by impressive credentials: Lex was a professor at the Surgery Clinic of the University of São Paulo's prestigious Medical Faculty, and in 1985 he was the executive director of the Central Institute of the Hospital das Clínicas of the same faculty. As for his Spiritist credentials, he is a former president of the AMESP and a board member of various Spiritist organizations in São Paulo. This Spiritist doctor, then, speaks as a leader in the medical profession and in the Spiritist movement.

"The subject is provocative," Lex begins his article on mediumistic surgery. "One always encounters reports by laypeople concerning folkloric cases that have not been studied scientifically and that instead are surrounded by much fanaticism and easy credulity" (1985: 6). In contrast to polemically "contra" or credulously "pro" accounts, Lex presents his article as an expository and neutral account of the various pitfalls of belief and skepticism in the study of mediumistic surgery. He notes that when he observed Arigó, the famous Brazilian medium-surgeon of the 1960s, he discovered that, contrary to popular reports, the medium did not stick a knife into the patient's eye but between the eyelid and the eye. Lex urges Spiritists to be more skeptical, to observe with greater care, to use orthodox diagnostic procedures and meticulous follow-up methods, and to be aware that many miraculous cures may be the result of suggestion.

Lex proceeds to outline two basic types of mediumistic surgery. In the first type, the mediums and spirits work exclusively on the perispirit (the spiritual body) and do not cut open the body of the patient. Generally they operate by giving the patients *passes;* in some cases, though, mediums do pantomime-like operations on the perispirit using invisible instruments and scalpels. Like the other doctors of the AMESP, Lex prefers *passes* to these invisible operations, but most AMESP doctors are not opposed to the invisible operations because they do not endanger patients and may even help them. In general, however, AMESP doctors are strongly opposed to the second type of mediumistic surgery, the physical-intervention type, which can endanger the patient because it involves breaking the skin.

Lex has the distinction of being one of the few Spiritists who have carefully observed Arigó, the most famous of the Brazilian surgical mediums of the second type. In his article and also in a conversation I had with him, Lex noted that he observed Arigó on many occasions as he extracted lipomas (tumors of fatty tissues) and performed hemostasis (stoppage of bleeding). He is critical of other claims, such as the widespread belief that Arigó's operations have never resulted in infection; because no one did any follow-up studies, Lex argues, it is impossible to verify any such claims. Nevertheless, Lex notes that in the cases of surgery that he himself observed, the healer did not use anesthesia and yet the patients did not feel pain. Lex ends his discussion of Arigó by noting: "The speed and dexterity in a layperson practicing medicine [and] the absence of adequate instruments or anesthesia lead us to admit that his 'operations' went beyond the normal capacities of a surgeon. Were these supernormal powers or [cases of] mediumship? Certain details that we observed speak in favor of the second hypothesis (1985: 6). Lex thus concludes that Arigó was indeed a true medium (one who was in fact receiving a spirit who could perform such operations); however, he warns Spiritists about jumping to the same conclusion in regard to other healers, particularly Arigó's emulators, whom Lex dismisses as "ambitious charlatans."

Whatever the standing of Arigó's surgery as a medical fact, as social facts Lex's opinions are clear. They raise the interpretive problem of explaining why a surgical medium from Minas Gerais who worked in the 1950s and early 1960s—two or three decades before the article was published—would be such a "tema apaixonante" (provocative subject) for Spiritists in São Paulo during the mid-1980s, and why the AMESP would find it necessary to engage in a "Campaign of Clarification on Works of Healing" at that time. What is the meaning of Arigó for Spiritists and other actors in the world of spiritual healing in Brazil? A clue surfaces when Lex comments on how Padre Quevedo violently contested his observations in a recent article: "but the contestations do not have the power of taking a phenomenon that has been repeatedly proved and making it disappear" (1985: 6). Once again, the internal dynamic between the elite and popular levels of the Spiritist movement appears to be linked to a Catholic/Spiritist conflict.

An Out-of-Court Trial

To understand the linkage between these two dynamics, one must journey back in time to a courtroom in Congonhas do Campo, Minas Gerais, in 1956. On trial is José Pedro de Freitas, known more commonly as

Arigó, "the surgeon with the rusty knife." He is accused of *curandeirismo*, of carving up innocent victims with unsterilized utensils such as a rusty kitchen knife. The pilgrims flock to Congonhas to view this "miracle worker," just as they have always come to Congonhas to see the monuments cut by Aleijadinho, the famous handicapped artist who carved the statues of Christ and the twelve biblical prophets that make Congonhas a capital of tourism and pilgrimage. The state authorities, however, do not find it interesting or desirable to compare the work of this twentieth-century bartender and public functionary to that of the disabled sculptor.[3] To them, Arigó is not a saint but a *curandeiro*, a word that is sometimes translated as a "faith healer" but that, in this context, is better translated as "charlatan."

Arigó was known as a devout Catholic, a family man, and a humble bartender, but he was also involved in local politics and is said to have discovered his powers as a healing medium in 1950, when he allegedly operated on his friend Senator Lúcio Bittencourt and cured him of lung cancer. Arigó soon discovered that he was receiving the spirit of Dr. Fritz, a German physician who died during World War I and who had decided to return to the terrestrial plane to finish his work through Arigó.[4] The humble bartender soon became a well-known healer whose claims to fame included writing out complicated prescriptions and performing minor surgical operations without anesthesia or antiseptics. Gradually his fame spread, and with it came condemnation from the Catholic church and the medical profession—as well as increasing involvement with the Spiritist movement.

In the Spiritist versions of the Arigó story, the Catholic church and the Minas Gerais medical profession prodded the state to action, and in 1956 the courts convicted him of violating the *curandeirismo* law.[5] However, President Juscelino Kubitschek, a surgeon by profession and fellow Mineiro by origin, pardoned Arigó in 1958 (the medium is said to have cured one of the president's daughters of kidney stones). After Kubitschek left office in 1960, investigations resurfaced as Arigó attracted increasing international attention. This included a visit from two North Americans, Dr. Andrija Puharich and Henry Belk, both of whom were interested in parapsychology, although they were by no means members of the inner circle of the international Parapsychological Association. Puharich let Arigó remove a lipoma in his arm, and the operation attracted coverage in the mass media, which may in turn have speeded up the impending second trial. In November 1964, Arigó was again found guilty of *curandeirismo*, and in March 1965 Puharich wrote a letter to the appeals court judge asking him to consider the case "with compassion and justice" (Fuller 1974: 176). In response to this letter, the widespread public outcry, and the recommendation of the appeals court judge, the Federal Supreme Court canceled the sentence in November 1965 and ordered Arigó released from prison (Fuller 1974: 183).

In May 1968, a team of North American physicians arrived to investigate Arigó and to document claims of clairvoyant diagnosis. Media reports, however, resulted in a public outcry that the North Americans were going to take the healer back with them to the United States, and the project ended prematurely amid charges of imperialism: *o curandeiro é nosso* (the healer is ours). The North Americans met with a group of Brazilian doctors led by Ary Lex, and plans were made for the Brazilians to form a team and continue the investigations that had been set up. There were even plans to build a hospital in Congonhas where scientists could study Arigó's operations, but the famous medium died in a car accident on January 11, 1971.

The desire of the medical profession (beyond those few Brazilian doctors who agreed with Lex) and the Catholic church to efface Arigó from the public memory appears to have been fulfilled not by the *curandeirismo* trials, which (like the auto-da-fé for Kardec nearly a hundred years earlier) served only to give him publicity and martyrdom, but instead by the medium's premature death. In Congonhas today, there is neither monument nor museum erected in the medium's memory, and when I spoke with his widow in January 1985, she claimed that all documents relating to her husband had been destroyed in a flood. Arigó carved patients rather than statues, and the family recommended that I visit the latter. If Congonhas has returned to the business of serving the memory of the sculptor Aleijadinho, it has likewise devoted itself to the business of forgetting this other carver.

Still, Arigó continues to live in the broader public memory of Brazilian national culture by means of numerous Spiritist publications on his mediumship and through a corresponding criticism from Catholic parapsychologists such as Padre Quevedo. Although Arigó was convicted long ago in the courts of the state, he continues to be tried in this out-of-court contest of books and pamphlets. This out-of-court trial provides a key to understanding the meaning of Spiritist medicine in the following decades.

One may begin with the doctors whom the Spiritist intellectual J. Herculano Pires, in his book *Arigó: Life, Mediumship, and Martyrdom*, calls to the stand as witnesses on behalf of Arigó. These include Oswaldo Lidger Conrado, a cardiologist; José Hortêncio de Medeiros Sobrinho, a radiologist and cancer specialist; Sérgio Valle, an ophthalmologist; and Ary Lex, a surgeon. Pires introduces Lex as "Professor Dr. Ary Lex, author of the well-known compendium *Biologia Educacional [Educational Biology]*, . . . a professor (*assistente*) of surgical medicine with the Faculty of Medicine of the University of São Paulo, a current member and ex-president of the Surgery Section of the Paulista Association of Medicine, a member of the Academy of Medicine of São Paulo and of the medical team of the Hospital das Clínicas" (1973: 172). Within Brazil, these are very prestigious titles, equivalent to working at Peter Bent Brigham Hospital and Harvard Medical School in the United States. More important, Pires introduces Lex as a doctor; he is presumed to speak as a doctor and as a leader of the medical profession. As a professor of surgery, Lex should be a leading authority on the topic and in a good position to evaluate Arigó's spirit surgery. His favorable testimony is therefore important evidence in the court of public opinion.

Let us consider how the "prosecuting attorney" in this court of public opinion, Padre Quevedo, cross-examines the witness. Quevedo first argues that, according to Arigó's testimony during the second trial in 1963, the medium stopped operating in 1957 and only preached after that time (1978: 263). It is not clear whether Quevedo interprets this to mean that all of the operations supposedly witnessed after this date did not take place, or that they were simply tricks, or that the medium was lying during his second trial. In any case, Quevedo dismisses all the medical testimony as the product of a group of Spiritist-inspired doctors, which he terms the "Arigó trust." In regard to Lex, the Jesuit parapsychologist writes: "The Spiritist doctor was carried away by his enthusiasm, which caused him to abandon his specialty when he gave the following opinion: 'The simple fact of Arigó's having realized this [surgical] intervention brought me face to face with a paranormal operation' " (1978: 273). One might wonder how a surgeon discussing surgery could have strayed from his specialty, but Quevedo clarifies his comment: "Any parapsychologist halfway familiar with his specialty knows that this antique technique is very simple and is neither paranormal nor of merit" (1978: 273). Thus, Quevedo carves up the witness by making him out to be a Spiritist and part of a Spiritist conspiracy, and he further disqualifies Dr. Lex by arguing that he is outside his specialty.

The objections that Quevedo raises regarding the first group of witnesses, however, cannot so easily be brought to bear on the next witness the Spiritists present: the North American Andrija Puharich. It is not so easy to dismiss a North American (or, as Puharich is, a foreign-born resident of the United States) as just another member of the "Arigó trust." Likewise, Spiritists present Puharich as a parapsychologist as well as a physician. For example, Pires introduces Puharich as "the North American doctor and parapsychologist" who is quoted as saying that "parapsychology in the United States and Europe is insufficient to explain the case" (1973: 37–38). Let us see how the Spiritist Nazareno Tourinho presents Puharich (and his colleague William Belk) in a series of articles written for the *Folha do Norte* of Belém, in which he criticizes another series of articles by Dr. Jofre Moreira Lima, who described Arigó as a psychopath:

> It so happens (and certainly Dr. Lima does not know this) that among the people susceptible to "suggestion" by Arigó, one finds an esteemed North American scientist, Dr. Henry Puharich, doctor, president of the Intelectron Corporation of New York, consultant to NASA, and specialist in medical electronics.
>
> This scientist, accompanied by Mr. William Belk, president of a parapsychological research society, brought from his country electronic apparati to test Arigó. Upon meeting the medium, [Puharich] asked him to examine his eyes. Dr. Fritz, incorporated in the medium, said that [Puharich] had no problem with his eyes, but that if he wanted, [Fritz] would take out a lipoma that North American doctors had thought prudent not to remove because the extraction might affect a nerve. Then Dr. Fritz, after receiving permission, took out the lipoma in less than a minute with a pocketknife, without causing any pain!
>
> In an interview granted to the magazine *Edição Extra* on September 7, 1963, Dr. Puharich said, "Arigó is a challenge to international science." (Tourinho and Imbassahy c. 1967: 42)

Such is the testimony that the North American parapsychologist and doctor gives. Given the high prestige that North American science has in Brazil, it is not clear which is more impressive—that Puharich is a North American or that he is a scientist—but, for many Brazilians, both characteristics suggest neutrality and contribute to the authority of the testimony.

Quevedo argues that, upon seeing a film of the Puharich operation, it was clear that the "operation"—and he puts the word in quotation marks—was a trick. He also puts the word "scientist" in quotation marks: "The North American 'scientist' on whom Arigó allegedly operated (to whom Arigó himself alluded in the trial) is Andrija Puharich. It so happens that he is a Spiritist, known as such, and is the author of the books *The Sacred Mushroom, Beyond Telepathy*, and *Uri: A Journal of the Mystery of Uri Geller*—full of Spiritist theories and flying saucers and extraterrestrials; absolutely antiscientific, aprioristic, and plainly fantastic" (1978: 269). Quevedo then argues that even Puharich has refuted some of the Spiritist versions of the supposed operation. In a later passage, the Jesuit professor-parapsychologist concludes: "In the first place, though, Puharich is neither a professor nor a parapsychology researcher in any university in the world" (1978: 280).

Who, then, would have been a better witness? Quevedo argues that the only acceptable witnesses are parapsychologists at the university level, a criterion that implies the following:

> Of the parapsychologists (at the university level) in Brazil, Dr. Cesário Morey Hossri—professor of parapsychology in the College of Philosophy, Sciences, and Letters of Santos—has made manifest in his classes, on television, [and] in the newspapers, his clear position against Arigó and his trust. As director-president of the Latin American Center of Parapsychology of the Anchieta College of São Paulo, I can testify that none of the researchers or professors of our Center (professors in various faculties) supports, approves, endorses, or finds any parapsychological or miraculous phenomena in Arigó. And there are no other parapsychologists (at the university level) anywhere in Brazil. (1978: 278)

Quevedo then calls to the stand his chief witness for the prosecution, whom he introduces and quotes: "The parapsychologist and physician Cesário Morey Hossri, after citing the parapsychological qualities that can sometimes occur in a *curandeiro*, adds, 'We think that Arigó does not have any such attributes. He is simply an instrument of economic or political forces or elements that have as their only objective, through the fraud or the farce that they practice, a pecuniary advantage and gain in all realms of life' " (1978: 281).

Quevedo takes this testimony from a series of articles Hossri wrote with the psychiatrist Rui Melo for the *Folha de São Paulo* (Melo and Hossri 1962). Regarding those articles, the Spiritist J. Herculano Pires writes: "The spokespersons of Campinas, professors Melo and Hossri, limited themselves to the rash premise of diagnosing Arigó as a paranoid, confusing things with hurried psychiatric interpretations that were made in a heavy-handed manner and with the original sin of a preconceived conclusion" (c. 1973: 126).[6] Furthermore, the Spiritist Moacyr Jorge argues that Hossri has changed his opinion since 1962 and that he "no longer attacks [Arigó] with the vehemence of two years ago" (c. 1964: 213).

The court of public opinion goes on and on, but this sample is enough to give a sense of the nature of the dialogue between Catholic and Spiritist intellectuals, one that has a polemical tone reminiscent of the dialogue between skeptics and parapsychologists in the United States. We are left, then, with an out-of-court trial in which the prosecution and the defense have disqualified all the witnesses. I would not presume to resolve this Catholic/Spiritist/medical aporia by playing the role of judge—if for no other reason than the fact that in the Brazilian reality the figure of the judge is far from sacred. Judges are frequently judged, as Moacyr Jorge makes clear in a comparison of Arigó's two judges:

> The judge of 1958 was a sort of stable mule for the penal code. Only the penal code existed for him. He saw only the letter of the law. He did not discern anything else. He was tied to the letter of the code, to the items and paragraphs. . . .
>
> Judge Dr. Márcio Aristeu Monteiro de Barros is not the judge of 1958. He has a different mentality. He does not know pressures of any kind, be they political or religious. He has even declared this recently. He is a modern judge. (c. 1964: 159–60)

Note that in this formulation sticking to the letter of the law is seen not as a symbol of neutrality but, instead, as an indication of a judge's bias; conversely, the ability to bend the law—*dar um jeitinho*—represents an absence of pressure. Of course, this is a Spiritist testifying, and one could probably elicit the opposite statement from a Catholic parapsychologist.

To summarize, the trial of Arigó today has little to do with the legal trials of 1956 and 1964. Today Arigó remains on trial in the court of public opinion, long after he has died and gone on to Nosso Lar. What survives him is the ongoing dialogue of the ideological arena: the Spiritist (and some medical) "attorneys" for the defense continue to call up witnesses against the Catholic (and some medical) "attorneys" for the prosecution, who in turn call up other witnesses, and each attempts to disqualify the other. Why do intelligent Catholic and Spiritist intellectuals continue to spend so much time debating the abilities of a popular healer who died nearly a generation ago? One is inclined to write it all off to religious (or medical? scientific? rhetorical?) fanaticism. But more is at stake than writing and rewriting history. As the sections that follow will demonstrate, writing past history is integrally tied up with the struggle to write present history, and this is a struggle that deeply concerns Ary Lex and his AMESP colleagues.

Pernambuco Permutations

Although Arigó died in 1971, "Dr. Fritz" continued to operate in Brazil. The spirit doctor returned to carry out his terrestrial mission through a series of mediums, all of whom are said to have died prematurely in freakish accidents, a belief that feeds the legend of Dr. Fritz.[7] Among these mediums was Edson Queiroz, a gynecologist from Pernambuco who in the 1980s received the spirit of Dr. Fritz. Unlike Arigó, Queiroz used surgical scalpels and other medical instruments, but he operated without using anesthesia; the assertion that his patients did not feel pain or experience infections was the basis of his claim to have paranormal powers. Although the Spiritist federation in his home state renounced any ties with him, Queiroz still had widespread support at the grass-roots level of the Spiritist movement, and the heat he took from the medical profession and the Spiritist federations seemed only to increase his popular support. He made constant trips to the South, where he attracted huge lines of patients who waited for hours and sometimes days to be treated in the Spiritist centers that hosted him.

Queiroz's colleagues within the medical profession were less enthusiastic about his performances than the laypeople who awaited his psychic healing; however, the Queiroz case is different from that of other surgical mediums, since this medium was also a licensed member of the medical fraternity. Still, this did not prevent the Pernambuco Regional Council of Medicine from voting to revoke his license to practice medicine, reportedly because he did not charge for his services when working as Dr. Fritz. Later, the National Council of Medicine voted to overturn that decision and to return the case to the regional level, because they could find no positive evidence that Queiroz had harmed any of his patients; but, after all this (in July 1988), the Pernambuco Regional Council of Medicine again voted to revoke his license.[8]

Ironically, the most vociferous critics of Queiroz are neither the orthodox medical profession nor Catholic parapsychologists but the Spiritists of the AMESP. As Lex underscored in his article (1985), the AMESP tolerates and accepts mediumistic surgery of the noninvasive type, but it is extremely cautious about the kind of mediumistic surgery that involves physical intervention. In regard to Edson Queiroz, the AMESP doctors would prefer that he stopped practicing his mediumistic surgery. They believe that suggestion explains any analgesic effects that Queiroz obtains, and they think that his failure to use sterile procedures jeopardizes the health of his patients.

The AMESP's criticism has drawn replies from other Spiritists, who blame the AMESP for playing a role in Queiroz's condemnation by the Pernambuco medical establishment:

> Note that a Spiritist group made up of doctors and located in São Paulo has collaborated a great deal in this condemnation. No, the entity in question did absolutely no research on the medium. Beyond a report having no scientific value but sufficient to reinforce the prejudice and ill will of the [Pernambuco] Council, this group played a deplorable and unforgettable role.
>
> The doctor appealed, according to his rights. He continues, in the meantime, to practice his profession. The dispute promises further developments in the future.
>
> They want to take away his title of doctor. Maybe they will succeed. It remains to be seen whether they will manage to take away his mediumship.
>
> The entity calls itself the AMESP. . . .
>
> Repeating Kardec, who repeated the critics, we say, "Ah! How stupid smart people can be." (Garcia 1983: 30; see also Tourinho 1983)

This criticism of the AMESP comes from a Spiritist group from the ABC, the working-class cities on the perimeter of São Paulo and one of the strongholds of support for the Workers' Party (further evidence in favor of the interpretation that the controversy over Queiroz within the Spiritist movement resonates with class and status divisions). Despite this resistance and strong criticism from within the movement, AMESP members and other Spiritist intellectuals have remained strongly opposed to Queiroz. Evidently the stakes are very high indeed, if the intellectuals are willing to side publicly against one of their own members and to risk a divisive conflict within the Spiritist movement.

The AMESP campaign and Lex's 1985 article become more understandable in light of the Queiroz affair. Although Lex does not mention

Queiroz directly, his expository account concerning Arigó carries with it an implicit polemic against the Pernambuco gynecologist-medium. Lex, by showing that in the case of Arigó he accepts the possibility that mediumistic surgery of the physical type may involve genuine mediumship, makes his skepticism regarding Querioz more plausible. Lex shows that in the case of Arigó, he—a leader of the AMESP, the representative of routinized Spiritist medicine—is capable of recognizing the powers of a charismatic surgical medium. Thus, he appears to be motivated by purely scientific values. Undoubtedly he and other AMESP leaders see themselves from this perspective; however, it is also true that mediumistic surgery represents a threat, for it interferes with their campaign to win acceptance of Spiritist therapies within the orthodox medical and psychology professions. AMESP Spiritists have their own agenda of alternative therapies; and mediumistic surgery is not only not part of this agenda, it is its very nemesis.

The AMESP's Alternatives

Lex's article appeared only a few months after the First International Congress on Alternative Therapies, which was held in São Paulo in February 1985 and which was cosponsored by the AMESP, whose members joined with other leading Paulista Spiritists in order to articulate their ideas on Spiritist and other alternative therapies. Their vision of alternative therapy of a Spiritist orientation contrasted sharply with the type of mediumistic surgery practiced by Queiroz; their vision of Spiritist medicine reveals more interest in alternative psychiatry and psychotherapy, and they view Spiritist therapies as complementing rather than replacing the treatments of orthodox medicine.

The AMESP doctors and most other Spiritist intellectuals regard the use of *passes* in the treatment of spirit obsession as a much more important therapy than mediumistic surgery. They believe that a large number of mentally ill patients in psychiatric hospitals are victims of spirit obsession, and although there are differences of opinion among the AMESP doctors, some have said that as many as 90 percent of such patients are victims of spirit obsession. It is true that Spiritist doctors with a background in psychology or psychiatry tend to use a lower figure, and the Theosophist/Spiritist/psychiatrist Alberto Lyra has argued that even in cases where standard psychiatric treatment was unsuccessful and Spiritist treatment (*passes* and disobsession) was successful, one could still not conclude that the illness had a spiritic origin (Lyra 1984: 75). Nevertheless, the question of whether psychiatric illness has a psychogenic or spiritic etiology does not preoccupy Spiritist doctors, for they believe that in practice the two processes overlap. In other words, mental illness can expose the patients to spirit obsession, and spirit obsession can lead to mental illness. As a result, patients must be treated both at a psychological-physical level and at a spiritual level, as Dr. Maria Júlia Peres of the AMESP explained at a lecture given during the First International Congress of Alternative Therapies: "I wish to make clear that spiritual treatment does not exclude medical treatment. It should be complementary to medical and psychiatric treatment, not a substitute" (my transcription; for abstract, see M. J. Peres 1985).

Spiritual problems are further complicated because they call for therapies both for the obsessing spirit (disobsession) and for the patient (Franco 1982). Such therapies include biomedicine and psychotherapy, alternative psychotherapies (e.g., past-lives therapy), and "fluidotherapy" (*passes*); but AMESP Spiritists stress that disobsession, psychotherapy, and the *passe* can only alleviate symptoms. In fact, there is a danger that people with spiritual ailments can become dependent on *passes*, as Dr. Peres goes on to explain:

> Fluidotherapy, or the *passe*, consists of an individual or mediumistic transfusion or donation of energy. It should be applied only when necessary in order for the person to avoid dependency. There are people who go to Spiritist centers just to receive *passes*, and they can become dependent on the *passe*, going from one center to another just to receive *passes*. In contrast, our work methodology proposes . . . that the *passe* be used as one of the phases [of Spiritist treatment] inasmuch as it is necessary.

Spiritists such as Dr. Peres emphasize that patients must study and practice Spiritist doctrine and Christian morality in order to eliminate the root cause of their spiritual ailments. In one Spiritist psychiatric hospital that I visited, for example, the administration puts a copy of one of Kardec's books in each patient's room, and another Spiritist hospital encourages patients to form study groups and attend Spiritist sessions where they learn more about Spiritist doctrine. The more rapidly patients understand and enact the Christian moral principles of Kardec's doctrine, the more rapidly they convalesce. The study of doctrine may in turn lead patients to develop their own mediumship; however, this is optional, and the key to alleviating spirit obsession remains an inner spiritual metamorphosis.

The therapies for obsession proposed by AMESP doctors, therefore, encode the moral principles of Spiritist doctrine. This differs strikingly from mediumistic surgery and other forms of popular healing within the Spiritist movement. In mediumistic surgery, patients may walk away with no inner moral change; this therapy may leave them in the same moral and spiritual condition (and with the same susceptibilities to illness) that they had before. Thus, Spiritist intellectuals, far from negating the moral side of Spiritist doctrine, integrate it into their therapies, whereas evangelical Spiritists may use mediumistic surgery to attract laypeople, then force them to listen to long hours of evangelization where they pay with their time and ears for their "free" Spiritist treatment.

Despite these strong beliefs about what constitutes appropriate spiritual healing, at the First International Conference on Alternative Therapies, the Paulista Spiritists adopted an ecumenical attitude and welcomed a diversity of perspectives, including many presentations that were compatible with a broadly Spiritist perspective on alternative medicine. Many non-Spiritist therapies and therapists were still welcomed because their beliefs and practices coincided with aspects of Spiritist doctrine and therapy. For example, the "meridians" of acupuncture, the "vital energy" of homeopathy,[9] and the "chakras" of yoga all were acceptable because they were consistent with the Spiritists' understanding of the perispirit. The AMESP Spiritists also warmly received papers by North American parapsychologists (Dean 1985; Rauscher 1985) and a Brazilian doctor (Sobral 1984, 1985), all of whom presented quantitative studies of ostensible healing effects on biological systems ranging from bacteria to human beings. While the healers in these studies were not necessarily Spiritists, the latter could point to these studies as support for their claims regarding the energy transfer of the *passe*. The Spiritist conference organizers also welcomed the California past-life therapists, who endorsed reincarnation and claimed that their patients were sometimes victims of a possessing (what Spiritists would call "obsessing") entity. These therapies, which have become popular among some Hollywood movie stars, are consistent with the Spiritist principles of reincarnation and spirit obsession, and it is therefore not surprising that the Spiritists affiliated with the AMESP have pioneered the introduction of past-lives therapies and therapists into Brazil.

Most of the therapies discussed at this conference were therefore consistent with basic Spiritist ideas regarding spiritual energy, a spiritual body, energy transfer, reincarnation, and spirit obsession. In addition to selecting from among alternative therapies, the conference sponsors—among whom AMESP Spiritists played a prominent role—also selected from among Spiritist therapies. The AMESP's notion of alternative therapies was thus "doubly alternative": first, it helped present alternatives to orthodox medicine; second, it presented alternatives to the popular medicine of the Spiritist movement itself.

Mediumistic surgery was just one of several therapies with which the AMESP doctors found themselves in disagreement. In the interest of fairness and freedom of expression, they allowed the advocates of alternatives to their alternative therapies to have their say at the conference, but they also scheduled these presentations at the end of the conference, after many people had gone home, in a kind of grab-bag session. These therapies are interesting because they highlight other communities with which the AMESP Spiritists are in dialogue, among them the Catholic church, the Afro-Brazilian religions, and the popular side of the Spiritist movement itself.

Outstanding among the alternative psychotherapies developed according to principles of the Catholic church is the work of Frei Albino Aresi, who presented a paper on "parapsychological cures." Aresi defined parapsychology in a way that excluded basic Spiritist principles such as reincarnation, the perispirit, and spirit communication and obsession. Aresi had himself sponsored two congresses on parapsychology and medicine, in which participants examined the relationship between his version of parapsychology and therpeutic and legal medicine; these conferences also introduced his spiritual therapy (called "noosofrology") to a wider medical audience (Aresi 1975, 1976, 1979, 1984). At the First International Conference on Alternative Therapies, Aresi was less interested in introducing his therapy than in showing how parapsychology negated fundamental Spiritist principles.

Equally or perhaps even more controversial to the Paulista Spiritists is the "psychotrance therapy" of Dr. Eliezer Mendes, a Bahian psychiatrist who at the time of the conference maintained a clinic in São Paulo. One aspect of Mendes's extremely complex therapy entails using "sensitives," persons who act out or personify the illness of the mentally disturbed patients and, in the process, relieve the patients of their symptoms.[10] On the surface, Mendes's therapy represents an upgrading of Spiritist disobsession concepts into a less heterodox psychotherapeutic language. The terms "sensitive" and "energies" replace "medium" and "obsessing entities," and it has therefore been easier for Mendes to present his work at conferences of psychiatrists, hypnotists, and psychologists.

However, there are certain crucial differences that make psychotrance therapy unacceptable to AMESP doctors. The model for Mendes's therapy is the medium-conducted exorcism of Umbanda and Afro-Brazilian religions rather than the disobsession of the Spiritists, and some sensitives who work for Mendes are also members of those religions. Mendes has therefore succeeded in translating Umbanda and Afro-Brazilian exorcism into a scientific or medical language, a process that rivals the Spiritist intellectuals' upgrading of their own work as alternative therapies. In turn, Spiritists are very uncomfortable with this rival alternative therapy, and one Spiritist intellectual even told me that he believes Mendes practices black magic by keeping his sensitives spiritually "subjugated."

At the session of alternatives to alternative therapies, two therapies indigenous to the Spiritist movement were also in evidence: chromotherapy and mediumistic surgery. The former involves both clairvoyant diagnosis of illness via the colors of the patient's aura and spirit healing via the application of color-coded *passes*, sometimes with electric lights (Armond 1978). Although some AMESP Spiritists have shown an interest in chromotherapy, others question its scientific validity, especially some of its claims regarding the chromotherapeutic treatment of conventional diseases such as kidney stones, pneumonia, and tumors (e.g., Nunes 1981: 71).

Finally, this grab bag session included a paper on mediumistic surgery. Queiroz himself did not appear at the conference; instead, a North American journalist and supporter of Queiroz presented a paper on Queiroz's mediumistic surgery. Privately, the AMESP doctors told me that they thought the North American journalist "knows nothing about parapsychology or medicine," and in turn the journalist told me about how his proposal to talk on Queiroz's behalf had been mysteriously "misplaced" until an influential Paulista Spiritist intervened and "gave the *jeitinho*" for him. Queiroz himself appeared only in a private home near the conference site, where he gave demonstrations to conference guests. The Paulista Spiritists stayed away from the private demonstration, and the controversial surgical medium attracted mainly guest speakers from other countries, some of whom volunteered themselves as patients for one of his minor treatment procedures, which involved sticking needles into their bodies in acupuncture-like operations.[11]

Placing Spiritist popular therapies in a session together with competing, non-Spiritist therapies suggests that both have, from the perspective of the AMESP and Paulista Spiritists who organized the conference, an "outsider" or anomalous status. This ordering of alternative therapies provides one more indication of how Spiritist intellectuals play a complex role of mediating between the Spiritist movement and other social groups outside it. On the one hand, the intellectuals (e.g., Ary Lex) inject orthodox medicine and science into the Spiritist movement by challenging popular therapies indigenous to the Spiritist movement (e.g., mediumistic surgery). On the other hand, they represent Spiritist therapies such as *passes* and disobsession as scientifically valid to the medical profession and other alternative therapists. By emphasizing the importance of the moral change in the patient as a crucial part of the healing process, the medical discourse of the intellectuals combines both the science of the Spiritist intellectuals with the morality of the Spiritist evangelists: it brings together these two strands of Spiritist thought for the purpose of representation to the outside. Thus, like other elites with respect to their groups and movements, the AMESP intellectuals serve as mediums for the entire Spiritist movement—representing the voice of orthodox medicine and science to the Spiritist movement and representing Spiritist thought to outside groups.

Finally, the Spiritist intellectuals seem to be attempting to impose some order on the broad field of rival and complementary alternative therapies. Thus, some therapies (e.g., Mendes's psychotrance therapy) represent to them the undesirable influence of Afro-Brazilian religions and black magic, whereas others (e.g., California past-lives therapies) are more welcome. With respect to this latter category, the First Conference on Alternative Therapies provided an opportunity for Spiritists to engage in productive dialogue with other exponents of alternative medicine who do not necessarily accept all aspects of Spiritist doctrine. By sharing with these groups a scientific and therapeutic discourse, Spiritists were able to sidestep potential divergences and to expose these potential rivals to Spiritist doctrine.

Legal Operations

Still, there remains the mystery of why the AMESP leaders and other Spiritist intellectuals have such a negative attitude toward mediumistic surgery of the physical-intervention type. True, it may not combine Spiritist doctrine and alternative medicine as ideally as other Spiritist therapies; but, still, why are the intellectuals so set against it, particularly when they seem open-minded enough about other, non-Spiritist alternative therapies? The reason, I will argue here, is that they see mediumistic surgery of the physical-intervention type as a potential *curandeirismo*, and this would work against their effort to divorce their own therapies from any association with *curandeirismo* and even to reform the *curandeirismo* law.

To understand the difference between *curandeirismo* and the alternative therapies supported by the AMESP, one might begin with the division between mind (or spirit) and body. Although both the popular and elite Spiritist therapies are based on the importance of the perispirit and its mediating role in the healing process, the two types of therapy differ according to where they locate the illness. The therapies that the AMESP supports operate more at a verbal or spiritual level: disobsession, past-life therapies, *passes*, doctrinal study, neurolinguistic programming, and so on. Mediumistic surgery, in contrast, entails an invasive procedure and claims that it can heal *bodily* ailments; thus, it might be easily confused with *curandeirismo*. Although Queiroz cannot be prosecuted for *curandeirismo* so long as he retains his medical license, the law has been applied to Arigó and other surgical mediums and today may still be applied to Spiritist mediums.

Regarding the *curandeirismo* law, a former district attorney of the state of São Paulo, Djalma Barreto, writes that only Peru and Argentina share with Brazil this "true legislative curiosity" (1972: 37–38). The law provides a kind of catchall category for the prosecution of popular healers who might not otherwise be punishable under the other articles in the penal code, such as stellionate (unspecified types of fraud), the illegal practice of medicine, and charlatanism. *Curandeirismo* is therefore defined broadly:

1. Habitually prescribing, administering, or applying any substance;
2. Using gestures, words, or any other means;
3. Making diagnoses.
   Penalty: detention from six months to two years. (Delmanto 1981: 293)[12]

In addition to the *curandeirismo* law, a related series of federal public health regulations forbids the practice of religious therapy in the nation's psychiatric hospitals—for example: "Religious institutions of doctrinary sects and related associations are forbidden the practice, in psychiatric establishments, of their religion and any liturgical acts having therapeutic ends."[13] Although similar regulations would conceivably apply to Protestant services held in psychiatric hospitals, it is likely that their intent was to ban the Spiritist treatment of spirit obsession in the dozens of Spiritist-owned psychiatric hospitals.[14] Referring to legal regulations on Spiritist hospitals, the Spiritist psychiatrists Denizard Souza and Teresinha Fátima Deitos note: "In Brazil the law prohibits the exclusive use of Spiritist methods in any type of hospital or clinic. Newly created hospitals are encouraged not to use or advertise the word 'Spiritist,' and existing hospitals are encouraged to remove the word [from their names]" (1980: 192).

Yet, this impressive legal apparatus means only that spiritual healing is legally banned in Brazil, not actually banished. After a period of repression during the 1930s, religious healing has been on the increase and continues to be a "growth industry" today. Medical professionals bemoan an incompetent legal system and an overly mystical population; healers in turn decry an incompetent state medical service (INAMPS) and an overly materialistic science. Nevertheless, the *curandeirismo* law and its siblings are not an idle set of legislative scalpels. Now and then, the law does manage to cut into the social body and extract some practitioners of popular healing. Yet, what is of interest here is not how often this occurs—obviously only a small percentage of popular healers are arrested or brought to trial—but, rather, what the records tell us about how Spiritist intellectuals attempt to position their own therapies as alternatives within official medicine rather than as *curandeirismo*, a term that in this context is better translated as "quack" or "charlatan" than as "folk healer."

With the exception of Edson Queiroz, who was still a licensed physician in the late 1980s, surgical mediums clearly violate the *curandeirismo* law and related regulations. Still, Spiritists have also faced prosecution even for practicing the more innocuous *passe*, so the *curandeirismo* law throws into question the entire apparatus of Spiritist healing. Juridical opinion on the legality of the *passe* is divided; an examination of the cases in the *Revista dos Tribunais*, the journal that publishes precedent-setting cases, shows that juridical opinion sometimes understands the *passe* as being included under freedom of religion, like the priest's blessing:

> Thus, to prohibit the *passe* of the medium or the blessing of the padre is to disrespect the guaranteed freedom of religion. . . . As a medium of his center, the defendant disinterestedly attempted

to cure, or at least to alleviate, the "spiritual" maladies of his "brothers" with *passes* and blessings, and these means—which constitute religious expressions guaranteed by Article 141, section 7, of the Federal Constitution for religions "that are not contrary to the public order or *bons costumes*"—should be understood as innocuous by Justice, given that science itself recognizes and proclaims the benefits of suggestion and persuasion in the cure of maladies called "nervous." (*Revista dos Tribunais* 307, p. 565)

This district attorney's opinion, which the courts accepted, equates "spiritual" maladies with "nervous" disorders (i.e., psychiatric disorders), and argues that the *passe*, which treats spiritual/nervous disorders, is protected by the constitutional guarantee of freedom of religion.

Another court opinion, however, includes the healing of "psychical maladies" under the rubric of *curandeirismo:* "[One] characterizes *curandeirismo* as the treatment of physical or psychic maladies via *passes*, blessings, 'spiritual operations,' etc. by those who make themselves intermediaries for the beneficial action of forces from the beyond" (*Revista dos Tribunais* 433, p. 423, citing case no. 58.730, Batatais, June 6, 1966). ("Blessings" in this sense probably refers to the acts of faith-healing *benzadores* rather than to those of priests.) Still another opinion bases the legality of the *passe* on its intent: "The 'passe' of the Spiritists is a type of blessing with a spiritual nature; the 'passes' that are administered to the faithful have spiritual ends and not, properly speaking, healing ends. Therefore, one cannot speak of a crime in this instance" (*Revista dos Tribunais* 340, p. 275).

Together these interpretations form an ambiguous picture of the legality of the *passe*. If religions view some illnesses as spiritual illnesses—e.g., spirit obsession or diabolic possession—is the treatment of these spiritual illnesses (problems? syndromes?) related to "spiritual ends" or "healing ends"? The category of "spiritual problem" overlaps with that of "psychological problem," and both overlap with "physical illness" when the phenomenon of somatization is taken into account. The state is saddled with the impossible task of making black-and-white categories out of a gray reality, and as a result the jurisprudential discourse of the state itself becomes gray and muddled. One finds the Spiritist's *passe* and the faith healer's blessing interpreted alternatively as *curandeirismo* and as purely religious practice.[15]

The dubious legality of the *passe*-as-therapy as opposed to the *passe*-as-religious practice helps account for the dual way in which Spiritists talk about the *passe*. On the one hand, Spiritist intellectuals are trying to gain acceptance within orthodox medicine for the use of the *passe* as an alternative therapy. On the other hand, although the terminology of alternative medicine may help legitimate the *passe* in this context, the medicalization of the *passe* may make it illegal according to certain interpretations of the *curandeirismo* law. When legal prosecution threatens the *passe*, the strongest defense is the freedom-of-religion argument. Although Spiritists may invoke science, as did one of the court opinions, the stronger defense of the *passe* is that it falls under the constitutional guarantee of freedom of religion.

To argue that the *passe* is religious in nature, however, puts it in conflict with those federal health regulations which prohibit religious therapies in psychiatric hospitals. The only way to avoid being subject to such regulations is to argue that the *passe* is a "scientific" therapy—a "fluidotherapy"—and not a religious therapy; but that is what leads to a conflict with some interpretations of the *curandeirismo* law. Thus, Spiritists are caught in a legal double-bind, and this no doubt contributes to the "schizophrenic" language they use to describe their therapies—that is, a language that switches back and forth from scientific terminology and values to religious ones. For Spiritists, this is not a symptom of infirmities in their thought; rather, it reflects an unjust legal situation. Thus, what was meant to be a sound law that would extract pseudomedicine from the social body seems to suffer from internal contradictions: it is a wounded law. This leads Spiritists to make proposals to remedy the legal situation, proposals in which there is no room for mediumistic surgery.

Healing a Wounded Law

With the transition to the New Republic in early 1985, Spiritist intellectuals began pushing for changes in the penal code by forming commissions that presented Spiritist legislative proposals to the *Constituinte* (Constitutional Convention) of the New Republic. Among the leaders of this movement was Freitas Nobre, a federal deputy (equivalent to a U.S. congressman) and formerly a professor of law at the University of São Paulo.

In an interview on October 26, 1985, Deputy Nobre told me that

Spiritists do not wish to repeal the *curandeirismo* law in its entirety, and he outlined their proposal:

> We understand that with respect to healing, there is exploitation in certain times and places. However, when someone performs a work [of healing] without remuneration and attempts to help the sick, especially when this person has mediumistic abilities, penal justice simply cannot interpret this activity as one that violates the law. Violation of the law can exist only when there is exploitation or financial speculation. Spiritism itself does not allow for . . . the paid exercise of mediumship, so when the penal code is announced before the legislature, it will encounter a good part of the senators and deputies disposed to include the *passe* as a normal activity and to prevent the healing *passe* from being interpreted as a type of charlatanism, which it is not.

Nobre's discussion restricts legalized healing techniques to the *passe* itself. This seems to be a narrowly Spiritist program of legal reform; but when I asked him about this, he pointed out that his was an ecumenical position, since other religions also practice variants of the *passe*.[16] Clearly not included in this revision of the *curandeirismo* law would be mediumistic surgery, which involves physical intervention and poses a potential risk to the patient's health. By legalizing only that popular healing which would neither harm patients nor cost them money, Spiritists believe they would create a law that opens the field to a kind of spiritual healing which does not endanger the public.

Behind Spiritists' negative concept of presenting neither danger nor financial cost to the patient is the positive concept that these spiritual therapies are in fact efficacious, a belief that is grounded in Spiritist scientific thought. This is where Spiritist parapsychology returns to center stage; it legitimates Spiritist healing by anchoring its validity in the authority of science. However, there is a problem here, and once again the world of science enters the political arena. Spiritist parapsychology, like other parapsychologies, has a marginal and heterodox position in the world of science. Thus, the goal of winning state sanction for parapsychology education becomes crucial: such a change would elevate Spiritist parapsychology to the status of an official science and, in the process, would legitimate Spiritist claims for the efficacy of their healing practices. To date, three bills have appeared before the Federal Chamber of

Deputies in favor of parapsychology education in Brazilian medical schools, and these three bills have all borne a Spiritist imprint.[17] Although these bills may not represent a conscious attempt to legitimate Spiritist medicine via parapsychology, they are part of a general effort by diverse Spiritists to acquire the mantle of scientific orthodoxy for Spiritist parapsychology and alternative therapies.

Spiritist attempts to promote parapsychology programs in the nation's medical schools encountered predictable resistance from an associate of the Jesuit parapsychologist Pedro Oscar González Quevedo: "Already on three occasions Spiritists have proposed a law to make parapsychology obligatory in the faculties of medicine and psychology throughout Brazil. The Latin American Center of Parapsychology opposed these proposals and alerted the deputies to what could happen; for, without professors who have a scientific background, it would not be a true parapsychology, but only a covert Spiritism" (Cobêro 1983: 3). Quevedo makes his attitude about the relationship between parapsychology and medicine even clearer in his book *Curandeirismo: An Evil or a Good?* (1978), where he argues for more vigorous enforcement of the *curandeirismo* law. These views in turn make their way into the *Revista dos Tribunais* via Judge Sérgio Gischkow Pereira, who devotes the bulk of an article on *curandeirismo* to reviewing Quevedo's ideas (Pereira 1981: 216–82; see also Peixoto 1980).

Thus, Spiritists and Catholics again oppose each other, this time in the legislative-juridical field. Whereas Spiritists hope to heal the wounded *curandeirismo* law by cutting out those provisions which apply to the *passe*, Quevedo prefers to heal the law by injecting it with new repressive powers. Between these two opinions is a third, anomalous position, that of Djalma Barreto, the former Paulista district attorney and author of *Parapsychology, Curandeirismo, and the Law* (1972), a text that bears the outward signs of Catholicism: the publisher (Vozes); the citations of Boaventura Kloppenburg and Padre Quevedo; and the preface by Cesário Morey Hossri, the "clinical psychologist and sociologist" who was coauthor of the series of articles against Arigó and to whom Quevedo turned as his acceptable "neutral" witness. Nevertheless, Barreto avoids the Jesuit position and instead stresses the need to find a "formula for a Brazilian solution": "As soon as healers claim to be paranormally gifted, they should submit to tests formulated by a commission composed of doctors and parapsychologists that should verify the real existence of such gifts. If such a commission confirms such extraordinary faculties, the healers would then be permitted to exercise those proven faculties, even professionally, though always with a licensed physician" (1972: 117).

I asked Deputy Nobre what he thought about Barreto's proposal, and at first he seemed to like the idea, although his answer also reinterprets the proposal:

> In some countries such as England, there is already official authorization that enables mediums to exercise their works of healing even within hospitals. We understand that here [in Brazil] there is the possibility of an ethics committee in this regard, which would be able to judge the authenticity or lack thereof [of healers]. This commission would have to be based in the principal Spiritist entities, such as the state Spiritist federations or the Brazilian Spiritist Federation. There is also the possibility that some institutes of parapsychological research, some institutes of psychobiophysics, such as that of Dr. Hernani [Guimarães Andrade], might give their opinions on this issue, but it is difficult to come up with a precise plan that would allow an investigation to take place.

He went on to describe a legal investigation regarding the medium Chico Xavier's claim to receive the spirit of the author Humberto de Campos and the difficulty that the judge had in finding a suitable, neutral expert: "The judge found it impossible to locate someone who could undertake the investigatory work, and he could not even find someone to do the research who would be acceptable both to the judge and the involved parties. It is a complicated problem, but the day will arrive when it [legal recognition] will come about, both with respect to the authenticity of Spiritist works . . . and with respect to the program of works of mediumistic healing."

Nobre sounds a note of optimism here, but his suggestion that the members of this commission be drawn from Spiritist federations or institutes of psychobiophysics represents a strikingly different solution from that proposed by Barreto, who mentioned Quevedo's group at the (now defunct) Latin American Center of Parapsychology as a possible source of qualified parapsychologists. Nobre is undoubtedly aware that the question of who would be on such a commission will be extremely politicized, and as a result he seems to be concentrating his efforts on getting the *passe* recognized as a legal activity rather than on supporting Barreto's rather idealistic proposal.

Furthermore, when one looks at the Catholic side of the picture, there is a somewhat surprising reply from Quevedo: the Jesuit priest rejects Barreto's proposal and argues that, given the present level of knowledge in the field of parapsychology, it would be "charlantanism" to claim that one might harness for healing purposes the powers recognized by parapsychology—even under the supervision of doctors and parapsychologists—because such powers are spontaneous and uncontrollable (1978: 297–98, 357). Given these diverse opinions, it is unlikely that Barreto's vision will ever become a reality. As another Spiritist said to me, commissions such as those proposed by Barreto would lead to impasses among Catholic, Spiritist, and "materialist" parapsychologists: from *passe* to impasse.

Barreto bases his proposal on faith that the empirical fact, the world as a neutral court, would stave off any impasses between Catholics and Spiritists. "Parapsychologists," he writes, "be they Catholic or Spiritist, would not refuse to recognize paranormal gifts for purely religious motivations, if they were truly informed by scientific interests" (1972: 117). This viewpoint assumes the existence of an uncontested scientific discipline as well as loyalty to a profession which does not exist in Brazil, for in that country religious loyalties overdetermine the facts which parapsychologists recognize. It also assumes that scientific knowledge exists outside of society and can therefore be called upon to resolve political disputes. Barreto, therefore, does not recognize that scientific knowledge can be constructed in multiple ways according to different interests, particularly in politicized situations such as this one, where scientific truth is clearly conditioned by personal loyalties to Catholicism or Spiritism.

That is why the official sanctioning of a course of parapsychology studies in the nation's medical schools is so important to these groups: it would give one of the rival parapsychologies the legitimacy of official status. Through such a transformation, one of the parapsychologies would lose its adjective as Catholic or Spiritist and would become elevated to a kind of universality. This in turn would change the relationship among Catholics, Spiritists, and doctors in the domain of therapeutic orthodoxy: heterodox therapies could be transformed into orthodoxy if their legitimating heterodox science achieved orthodoxy.

Whatever the eventual outcome of these legislative proposals, Spiritists surveying their country in the ethereal glow of the dawn of the New Republic could envision the dawn of a New Age in Brazil. Everything seemed possible at this historical juncture. When I returned to Brazil in 1988, just three years after the First International Conference on Alternative Therapies, the mood was considerably gloomier. Still, Spiritists continued to hope for changes in the Constitution that would allow a more liberalized *curandeirismo* law, and the historical forces that control the destiny of the social body remain openly contested.

The operations of the Spiritist intellectuals, therefore, continue to take place on multiple planes. To the orthodox medical community, they present only the least controversial type of therapy: alternative therapies that involve no contact with the body—"psychotherapies" in the broadest sense of the term. Psychotherapy is already a zone within orthodox medicine where the lines between science and religion, art and politics are blurred; consequently, it is the area where Spiritists are likely to have the greatest credibility and success. With respect to the state, Spiritist intellectuals attempt to change those aspects of the *curandeirismo* law which they believe are unjust and out of touch with the Brazilian reality. Finally, with respect to the popular segments of the Spiritist movement, the intellectuals join with the orthodox medical community in an attempt to stop a therapy that threatens not only orthodox medicine but the Spiritist-intellectual reformist project. In the present study, likewise, I have grafted another perspective onto the social-scientific study of Brazilian religion, science, and medicine: the elite/popular disagreement within the Spiritist movement regarding the status of mediumistic surgery makes sense only in the broader context of the competing actors, ideologies, and therapies outside the Spiritist movement.

CHAPTER SEVEN

OBSESSIONS AND DISOBSESSIONS
Spiritism and the Social Sciences

This chapter moves from Spiritist views on parapsychology and medicine to Spiritist views on social science, which in Brazil means sociology, anthropology, and political science. Because I am writing here as a social scientist, adding this discourse to the picture involves a new level of reflexivity and complexity. This is to be welcomed instead of resisted, for one of my assumptions is that to classify Spiritist thought as "popular religion" or "occultism" is to seal it off as something fundamentally different from scientific thought (whether of the psychological, biomedical, or social-scientific variety). This in turn involves a distancing of the analyst's thought from that of the analyzed, an act which has its advantages when the analyst's legitimacy and authority are in doubt, but one which ultimately reifies the analyst as much as the analyzed. As a result of this reification, social scientists lose the opportunity not only to benefit from dialogue with the Other but also to inspect their own assumptions and categories of thought.

Thus, the empirical question of this book—the idea that understanding the scientific ideas of the Spiritist intellectuals means taking into account not only class and status differences within the field of spirit-mediumship religions but also the ideas of other groups in the ideological arena—necessarily leads to a broader methodological issue whose roots lie in a dialectical conception of anthropology as a critique of ethnocentrism and an inspection of one's own assumptions (Marcus and Fischer 1986). If one of the groups in the ideological arena is the social science profession, then the close inspection of Spiritist ideas may mean a rethinking of ideas in the social sciences—in this case, theories of Brazilian religious complexity.

Previous chapters have focused on one or another Spiritist scientific text which served as a starting point for an examination of the meaning and contexts of Spiritist scientific thought. This chapter begins with an older, polemical book—Deolindo Amorim's *Africanism and Spiritism* (1949)—and concludes with Pedro Mundim's essay "Spiritualist Therapies ('Nootherapies') and Psychopathologies" (1985). Amorim's text provides a Spiritist theory of Umbanda syncretism; implicit in the theory is a map of a portion of the Brazilian religious system.[1] Explication of this theory and map will require us to examine other points of view in the ideological arena, including the Catholic, medical, and social science theories and maps of the religious system.

A Spiritist Theory of Spirit-Mediumship Religions

Spiritist intellectuals worry that many Spiritist centers seem to wander from the orthodoxies of Kardecism and to intermesh, interpenetrate, or syncretize themselves with Umbanda. In addition, many Umbandists call themselves "Spiritists," especially when they talk with outsiders whose social status is higher than their own. I witnessed this on numerous occasions, and the sociologist Cândido Procópio Ferreira de Camargo also noted that this occurred when he interviewed Umbandists: "Enjoying higher social prestige than the Umbanda religion, the qualification 'Spiritist' is almost always employed by interviewees during the first contact; only later do they specify the Umbandist nature of their Spiritism" (1961: 14).

Spiritist intellectuals would bristle at such a statement and point out that Camargo confuses Spiritism with Umbanda by using the former term to include the latter. Umbandists, though, would agree with Camargo; consequently, at first glance, his terminology appears to take the Umbandist side of a Spiritist/Umbandist terminological feud. Spiritist intellectuals vehemently disagree with this inclusive use of the term "Spiritism"; for them, "Spiritists" refers only to the followers of Allan Kardec. The Spiritist Lippman Tesch de Oliver, for example, makes this point abundantly clear in his foreword to Amorim's *Africanism and Spiritism:*

> When we speak of Spiritism, the reader should know that we refer to Allan Kardec's scientific, philosophical, and moral codification—the only doctrine worthy of the title—which the master propounded in a series of notable works, published in France between 1857 and 1869, and not this conglomeration of witchcraft and fussy rituals, where one finds the fetishism of savages and the aberrations of bastardized mediumship; in short, the carnival of Umbanda. . . . (1949: 5–6)

All of this is a very familiar phenomenon to social scientists. If, as Michael Taussig (1987) has done for the Andean context, one can read the Spiritist view of Umbanda as a bourgeois fantasy that degrades Umbanda even as it empowers it with the imagery of wildness, one can also read the Umbandists' miming of Spiritism as a Veblenesque move to enhance their status and power by adopting the name, language, and customs of the higher-status group. The latter, the Spiritists, attempt to stop this process, or they adopt new cultural forms (in this case, science) in order to distinguish themselves further from the lower-status groups.

Again, we are back with the logic first described by Roger Bastide: the language of the Spiritist intellectual makes sense in terms of the class and status dynamics of Spiritism and Umbanda, for it provides a means for marking off a higher-status form of spirit mediumship from a lower-status form. Unlike the author of the foreword just cited, however, Deolindo Amorim does not simply push Umbanda back into "Africanism." Instead, the Spiritist intellectual actually proposes a new social theory of Umbanda in which he describes Umbanda not as a syncretism of the Afro-Brazilian religions and Spiritism, but as a syncretism of the Afro-Brazilian religions and Catholicism. He defends this theory by showing a series of parallels between Catholicism and Umbanda. For example, both religions share the use of altars, a belief in divinities and miracles, the use of "ritual," and so on (1949: 46, 73–74). He also argues that, in contrast to Umbanda and Catholicism, Spiritism is characterized by "an absence of rituals" and a "doctrinal base in natural laws" that "excludes miracles and the supernatural" (1949: 73–74). Although many Spiritists view the relationship of Umbanda, Catholicism, and Spiritism in terms of an evolutionary progression similar to the stages of Auguste Comte and Edward Burnett Tylor, Amorim is too sophisticated to adopt that sort of argument. His other works show him to be familiar with twentieth-century cultural anthropology, and in this study he restricts his argument to the similarities of form between Catholicism and Umbanda. Using this as his basis of evidence, he finds the link between Catholicism and Umbanda stronger than the one between Spiritism and Umbanda.

In short, unlike the introductory passage on Umbanda by Oliver, which merely rejects Umbanda by primitivizing it, Amorim presents a social theory of Umbanda that is anchored in his study of twentieth-century cultural anthropology. What is the meaning of this move? What is at stake in Amorim's definition of Umbanda as "Afro-Catholic" rather than "Afro-Spiritist"?

A Catholic Theory of Spirit-Mediumship Religions

Amorim lived through the years of the Getúlio Vargas dictatorship, when many Spiritist centers were closed, and this historical experience shaped the consciousness of his book *Africanism and Spiritism*. Beginning in the 1920s, the Catholic church grew much closer to the state, a big change from the early days of the Old Republic. In 1921, Sebastião Leme arrived in Rio as coadjutor, later to become cardinal and one of Vargas's closest confidants. Although Vargas was known for quickly shifting his political alliances, the partnership with Leme remained a key part of Vargas's political strategy throughout his regime. In return for cooperation with Vargas, Leme extracted concessions unparalleled in other Latin American countries (Bruneau 1974: 37). Among these were the decree of April 30, 1931, which called for religious education in public schools, and the changes of the 1934 Constitution, which contained articles allowing religious services for the armed forces, religious marriages with civil effects, and religious education in public schools (Moura 1978: 87–88). In addition, a 1934 law required Spiritists and Umbandists to register with the police—and in Rio this meant the police division that handled alcohol, drugs, illegal gambling, and prostitution (Brown 1986: 146). Likewise, the consolidated legal code of 1932 reconfirmed the older provisions of the 1890 penal codes that outlawed *curandeirismo* and *espiritismo* (D. Barreto 1972: 32). In short, while the Catholic church did not return completely to the position of official religion that it had held during the days of the empire, it made significant progress toward reinstating de jure recognition of its de facto status.

Amorim's book *Africanism and Spiritism,* appearing a few years after the end of the Vargas dictatorship, expressed Spiritists' concern to avoid confusion with (and repression alongside) Umbanda and the Afro-Brazilian religions. Catholic intellectuals, of course, paid little attention to the book and continued to identify Spiritism with Umbanda and Candomblé, and that is one reason why Spiritists are so quick to reject any identification of their movement as "popular religion." Even the census categories reinforced this perception; thus, the 1950 census data contained one category for all spirit-mediumship religions: from this perspective, even the categories of the census become permeated with ideological overtones. According to the 1950 census, the spirit-mediumship religions were growing even more rapidly than Pentecostalism and, for the Catholic church, they posed a far more radical doctrinal challenge.[2] In 1953, the National Council of Bishops declared Spiritism (the term included Umbanda in this case) the most dangerous doctrinal deviation in Brazil (Kloppenburg 1967: 771). The Catholic church followed with a substantial public-education campaign, of which the books by Álvaro Negromonte (1954) and Boaventura Kloppenburg (1957, 1960, 1961b) are perhaps the best known. This led to rebuttals by Carlos Imbassahy (1955), Mário Cavalcanti de Mello (c. 1958), and Deolindo Amorim (1955).[3] Although many of these debates centered on issues such as reincarnation, they also touched on the relationship among Spiritism, Catholicism, and the Afro-Brazilian religions.

In 1956, many of the leading Spiritists, including Amorim, issued a radio commentary that criticized Kloppenburg's use of the term "Spiritism" to include Umbanda. Nevertheless, Kloppenburg did not change his position, and in his pre–Vatican II study of Umbanda, he devoted an entire chapter to the defense of "the Spiritist character of Umbanda" (1961b: 61ff.). In that chapter, Kloppenburg rebutted the Spiritist radio commentary of 1956 and cited passages from Kardec himself to defend the idea that Spiritism includes "all spiritualists who admit the practice of the evocation of spirits," which implies not only Umbanda but other spirit-mediumship religions, such as Anglo-Saxon Spiritualism and Candomblé (1961b: 66). Thus, Kloppenburg articulated a Catholic perspective on the nature of Umbanda and, in contrast to Amorim, associated Umbanda with Spiritism and the Afro-Brazilian religions rather than with the Catholic church.

In the 1960s, two major political changes affected this general environment: the Brazilian military coup in 1964 and Vatican II. With the consequent development of liberation theology and the new rulings of Vatican II, leaders of the Catholic church rethought their policy toward popular religiosity in Brazil. Kloppenburg, who had been one of the most outspoken critics in the church's cold war against Spiritism and Umbanda, now issued a statement on "a new pastoral position with respect to Umbanda" (1972). However, it is important not to overestimate the change in his or the church's position. While the Franciscan scholar notes that Vatican II calls for an "appreciation of popular customs and traditions," and while he celebrates the African side of Umbanda as falling under "Africae Terrarum," he condemns both the "syncretism" of Umbanda with Spiritism and the Umbandists' acceptance of the doctrines of reincarnation and necromancy, both of which he argues are irreconcilable with Catholic church doctrine (Kloppenburg 1972: 61).

Such a statement amounts to a condemnation of spirit mediumship itself, and in this respect the revolution of Vatican II amounts to little more than a cosmetic change.[4] In an interview in February 1986, Kloppenburg told me that his position had not really changed over the years. He stated that he had waited for the dialogue called for by Vatican II to take place and, after spending ten years outside Brazil, he had returned only to find the same old Spiritist *propaganda* (a word that also means "advertising"); as a result, he was preparing a new edition of his 1960 book on Spiritism. Thus, even in his post–Vatican II writings, Kloppenburg continues to view Umbanda as a form of Spiritism. For Kloppenburg, Umbanda is a form of Spiritism that has African elements, and he adamantly defends the use of term "Spiritism" to refer both to "Kardecism" (what the present book calls "Spiritism") and to Umbanda.

As social theories, then, the positions of Amorim and Kloppenburg are diametrically opposed. Amorim argues that Umbanda is a syncretism of Afro-Brazilian religions and Catholicism, whereas Kloppenburg sees Umbanda as a form of Spiritism with African elements. Thus, both intellectuals deny the involvement of their own "religion" with Umbanda; instead, they view Umbanda as a syncretism of the other's "religion."

Some Medical Profession Theories of Spirit-Mediumship Religions

During the Vargas years, Spiritists also suffered attacks from the medical profession, particularly from the emerging mental health movement. The idea of public health had already garnered widespread public support earlier in the century from the work of Brazilian scientist Oswaldo Cruz, who used Pasteur's discoveries to combat yellow fever in Rio de Janeiro (Stepan 1976). In 1923, the birth of the Brazilian League of Mental Hygiene helped extend the idea of public health to include mental health, and in 1927 the Washington Luís government recognized this extension by creating the Service of Assistance to coordinate all public psychiatric institutions in Rio (J. F. Costa 1976: 25, 31). This was to have important implications for the spirit-mediumship religions.

The doctors of the League of Mental Hygiene were most preoccupied with antialcoholism campaigns, which received government support, but they also regarded *espiritismo* as a mental hygiene problem (J. F. Costa 1976: 46–49, 60ff.). Two doctors who were involved in the league, Murillo de Campos (Ribeiro and Campos 1931) and Antônio Xavier de Oliveira (1931), wrote extended tracts on Spiritism and other spirit-mediumship religions as a social problem. One doctor associated with the mental hygiene movement wrote that spirit mediumship was "one of the major factors in mental illness," and Oliveira claimed that 90 percent of the patients at the Division for Observation of Assistance to Psychopaths had gone to Spiritist centers.[5]

The medical studies, therefore, provided a mantle of scientific legitimacy for the repression of spirit-mediumship religions during the Vargas regime, sometimes quite baldly, as exemplified by a passage from a book by Leonídio Ribeiro and Murillo de Campos:

> The police authorities should [apprehend] . . . the so-called "mediums" in order to intern them in the Division for Observation of the National Hospital for the Mentally Ill. There it could be easily determined that the majority of these charlatans are themselves mentally ill, a great majority of whom would already be known by the doctors at the hospital. The other portion comprises clever and dangerous individuals, recidivists in this species of exploitation, who should be prosecuted and punished severely by the

judges, who unfortunately are still not sufficiently informed about the danger of these troubling elements in the life of the society. (1931: 144)[6]

In 1927, the chief of civil police published a report against "low Spiritism" (Maggie 1988: 27), and in the same year the Medical Society of Rio de Janeiro met to consider the problem of spirit-mediumship religions with respect to medicine (Ribeiro and Campos 1931: 179ff.). Leonídio Ribeiro, a specialist in forensic medicine, led the discussion and argued that the medical profession should take action against the numerous cases of illegal practice of medicine associated with Spiritist centers and other spirit-mediumship temples. The society created a commission to work for the enforcement of the anti-*curandeirismo* and anti-*espiritismo* laws, and the book by Ribeiro and Campos that followed in 1931 was a call to action aimed at judges and police officials.

According to Amorim, many Spiritist centers were closed during this period.[7] However, the state and the medical profession were not as successful with Kardecian and other "scientific" Spiritists as they were with the "low Spiritists" who had recourse to Afro-Brazilian magic. For example, new prosecutions against the non-Kardecian but "scientific" Spiritist Redeemer Center (Centro Redentor) in the 1930s were apparently unsuccessful (L. Ribeiro 1975; Maggie 1988: 194ff.; see also Sousa do Prado 1932: 297). Likewise, in 1933 the attorney general rebuffed a series of suggestions from the Brazilian Medical Association, which hoped to limit the rights of defense for Spiritists who were accused of the illegal practice of medicine (D. Barreto 1972: 48–49).

Several factors contributed to a long-term moderation of the medical profession's posture toward Spiritism during the years after World War II. First, beginning in 1926, Spiritists had started to build and staff psychiatric hospitals, which meant that some doctors were working in collaboration with Spiritist administrators and the occasional Spiritist doctor.[8] Likewise, the founding of the Society of Medicine and Spiritism of Rio de Janeiro helped counter the medical profession's perception that linked Spiritism to mental illness. The Brazilian Spiritist Federation, moreover, translated a group of European psychical research studies, and this allowed Spiritists to position their movement as a scientific endeavor allied more with the medical profession and the universities than with "low Spiritism."[9]

The development of psychoanalysis in Brazil, especially its use by anthropologists and sociologists, also contributed to the moderation in the medical profession's position. Although there was scattered interest in psychoanalysis prior to World War II, and although a short-lived psychoanalytic society was founded in 1927, Brazilian psychoanalysis is largely a phenomenon of the World War II years and later (Azevedo n.d.: 272; Galvão 1967: 46–64). Arthur Ramos's *The Brazilian Negro* (1940) was the first study to use psychoanalysis in the interpretation of Brazilian spirit-mediumship religions, and Roger Bastide ([1960] 1978: 21) credits him with breaking with the "racist" analysis of the early studies of Ramos's teacher, Raimundo Nina Rodrigues. Still, Ramos was a transition figure who continued to compare mediumistic trance to psychopathology, and it was Bastide and Melville Herskovits who would situate Brazilian spirit mediumship in its wider institutional context and criticize the interpretations of spirit mediumship as psychopathology. In defending the spirit-mediumship religions as nonpathological phenomena, the emerging social science profession situated itself between the medical profession and the spirit-mediumship religiosity of the lower classes, a position of mediation similar to that assumed by the Spiritist movement. As late as 1967, Bastide felt compelled to rebut the earlier medical profession's opinion: "We cannot consider the million or more Brazilian Kardecists to be mentally ill; we are sufficiently familiar with them to affirm the *normality* of the great majority" (1967: 7–8).

Given this background, one can reread Amorim's text in terms of its relationship with the emerging field of ethnology. From this perspective, in *Africanism and Spiritism* Amorim engages in a long dialogue with Arthur Ramos, whose work marks an important transition between studies by Nina Rodrigues, which were tainted by psychopathology and ethnocentrism, and those by Bastide and Herskovits, which adopted a sociocultural and relativist perspective. Although Amorim treats Ramos with the utmost respect, he does criticize the esteemed professor on one point: "Thus, what the eminent Professor Arthur Ramos labels 'Spiritist practices' in Afro-Catholic or Afro-Brazilian syncretism do not exist, for the reason that these Spiritist practices do not have characteristics that bear even the remotest similarity to rituals of African origin. . . . Spiritism is Spiritism, just as Africanism is Africanism: the subjects are quite distinct" ([1946] 1958: 27).

In his work *Spiritism and Criminology* ([1955] 1978), Amorim also took Ramos to task for his uncritical reliance on Freudian psychoanalysis. Amorim used anthropology to launch a cultural critique of psychoanalysis, arguing that Freud and Jung suffered from "the intellectual environment of the period," which was marked by "a positivist spirit with a strong propensity for the predominance of biology and physics in the concept of man" ([1955] 1978: 176–77). In place of Freud and Jung, Amorim preferred the neo-Freudian culturalists or even Adler, for whom "man is fundamentally a social, and not a sexual, creature" ([1955] 1978: 177).

Even if Ramos and the other psychiatrist-ethnologists whom Amorim criticized ignored his ideas, Amorim viewed himself as a participant in the social science reformation of the Brazilian medical discourse on spirit mediumship. His *Africanism and Spiritism* represented a Spiritist contribution to the ethnology of Brazilian religion, one that was allied with the new social sciences and sharply opposed to the older medical studies. However, even though social scientists have generally distinguished Spiritism from the Afro-Brazilian religions, not all of them have distinguished Spiritism from Umbanda. As the next section will show, the new social science discourse itself appears to speak in multiple voices.

Social Science Variations

One might think that social scientists would represent an outside voice or a neutral point of view on the issue of the relationship between Spiritism and other religions, but there is no "outside" to ideology, and social scientists are as actively involved in that tangled plexus of politics, science, medicine, and religion as the groups they study. This point becomes clear when one compares two social science texts on the issue of the "mediumistic continuum" between Spiritism and Umbanda.

In *Kardecism and Umbanda*—significantly not titled *Spiritism and Umbanda*—the Brazilian sociologist Cândido Procópio Ferreira de Camargo advances his theory of a "mediumistic continuum" between Spiritism, which he calls Kardecism, and Umbanda (1961: 13–15). Among the common elements of "Kardecism" and Umbanda that form the basis of the continuum, Camargo cites shared beliefs and practices such as mediumship, reincarnation, evolution, and karma (p. 83). He argues that the continuum is complex; in some cases, for example, the doctrine may tend toward Spiritism, whereas the ritual may tend toward Umbanda (p. 84). In addition, he cites groups that practice "in the same place, successively or simultaneously, Kardecist and Umbandist sessions" (p. 84). Likewise, individual actors may move on from Umbanda *terreiros* to Spiritist centers; but he also points out that one clearly Bahian (African-line) *terreiro* has attacked Spiritism and that, likewise, the leadership and elite of Spiritism "formally reject any similarity to Umbanda" (pp. 85–86). Camargo's overall view may be summarized as follows: "the extremes [of the continuum] repel each other, whereas the middle recognizes and accepts each other" (p. 85).

The anthropologist Maria Laura Cavalcanti disagrees with Camargo's theory of the mediumistic continuum. Her book *The Invisible World: Cosmology, Ritual System, and Notions of Person in Spiritism*—which uses the term "Spiritism" instead of "Kardecism," as does the title of the present book—argues that the point of departure for the social scientist should be "how the groups see themselves" (1983: 15, 139). When one assumes this methodological stance, one finds that Spiritists do not accept a continuum between themselves and Umbandists; thus, the mediumistic continuum makes no sense. Her argument, then, is rooted in the methodology of cultural anthropology and interpretive social science, as opposed to functionalist sociology and "explanatory" social science, which posits a continuum regardless of whether or not the people under study see themselves this way.

As already noted, Camargo acknowledges that Spiritist intellectuals and leaders reject any association with Umbanda, but he implies that the more popular levels of the Spiritist movement accept Umbanda more readily. Yet, Camargo also argues that even if the continuum is problematic at this level, which he calls the "subjective point of view," it still exists at the "objective" level:

> Objective forms and structures reveal in an even more evident way than the attitudes and opinions of the faithful the sociological reality of the "continuum." We refer to the modalities of organization of practice and the interpretations of doctrine that are intermediary, formed from combined elements drawn from Umbanda and Kardecism. One can affirm that there are innumerable combinatorial modalities in which one expresses the "continuum"— some more closely tied to Umbanda, and others closer to Kardecism, forming an axis between the extremes. (1961: 15)

When I spoke with Camargo shortly after Cavalcanti's book was published, he argued that her comments did not challenge his theory because, even if there is no continuum from the viewpoint of the groups involved, it still exists objectively.

The debate on the reality of the mediumistic continuum, therefore, appears to be rooted in methodological stances in the social sciences. Such an explanation of the debate, however, assumes that the social sciences operate in a vacuum; the framework of a broader ideological arena, in contrast, implies that things may well be more complicated. In fact, when one adopts the ideological arena as the point of departure, another continuum rapidly makes itself felt.

Camargo's emphasis on a continuum and his use of the term "Spiritism" are two areas in which he concurs with Umbandist thought. Furthermore, Camargo emphasizes the similar therapeutic functions of Umbanda exorcism and Spiritist disobsession (1961: 99–106), a perspective with which few Umbandists, but many Spiritists, would disagree. In contrast, Cavalcanti emphasizes a disjunction between Spiritism and Umbanda, and she uses the term "Spiritism" in a restrictive sense that excludes Umbandists. Furthermore, her reading of the disobsession ritual (1983: 127–31) emphasizes the ritual as an expression of the Western values of individualism and free will, a gloss similar to the one that Spiritists themselves give to the ritual and one that distinguishes the ritual from its sibling in Umbanda. The difference between Camargo and Cavalcanti, therefore, appears to repeat the division between Umbandists and Spiritists within the religious system. In other words, there appears to be a continuum that links a division in religious thought (Spiritist/Umbanda) to a division in social-scientific thought (Cavalcanti/Camargo).

Further inspection reveals that there may be yet another continuum at work: there are certain parallels in the thought of Camargo and Kloppenburg versus that of Cavalcanti and Amorim. Like Kloppenburg, Camargo uses the umbrella term "Spiritism" to include Kardecists as well as Umbandists, and like Amorim, Cavalcanti uses the term "Spiritism" to refer only to Kardecists. Kloppenburg and Camargo emphasize continuity between Spiritism and Umbanda, whereas Amorim and Cavalcanti emphasize disjunction. Furthermore, when one looks at the relations among the four writers, one finds, for example, that before his death in 1987, Camargo was a professor of ·sociology at the Pontifical Catholic University of São Paulo, and one also discovers that Kloppenburg wrote the preface for the Spanish-language edition—but not the Portuguese-language edition—of Camargo's book *Kardecism and Umbanda*.[10] In addition, the research for Camargo's book was funded by the Fédération Internationale des Instituts Catholiques de Recherches Sociales, which Camargo acknowledges in the Portuguese edition as the Fédération Internationale des Instituts de Recherches Sociales—that is, without the word "Catholic" (1961: ix). In the acknowledgments to her study, moreover, Cavalcanti cites Amorim, who was an important informant, and one of the two sites for her fieldwork was the Institute of Brazilian Spiritist Culture, of which Amorim was president at the time of her research (Cavalcanti 1983: 11, 16).

The discovery of a new continuum does not invalidate the ideas or results of any of the four researchers, but it does render problematic the division between researcher and researched. There appears to be a bit of leakage or, to use a metaphor borrowed from Spiritism, an obsession—albeit, in the realm of ideology, so therefore a "discursive obsession"—of social science thought by religious thought. This discursive obsession becomes even more evident in the case of Roger Bastide.

Disobsessing Bastide

Roger Bastide also criticized Camargo's theory of a mediumistic continuum:

> In a way, the idea of a continuum might seem to be correct, because one finds between Kardecism and Umbanda a whole series of transitions. However, in our opinion, the image is false, because this so-called continuum is composed of one true pole, Kardecism, and innumerable Umbanda tents that could not possibly make up an opposing pole. . . .
>
> We therefore have less a continuum than two concurrent groups, one well organized and the other a welter of sects. And this concurrence—as well as the Kardecian seduction, which plays itself out in certain Umbanda sects and might be responsible for Camargo's illusory continuum—can be definitely explained by the struggle between two classes, the middle and the proletarian, that is hidden in Brazil beneath the cover of religious ideologies. (1967: 11)

Instead of a continuum between Umbanda and Spiritism, then, Bastide sees a "concurrence," or coexistence, which is to say an opposition that is the expression of class conflict.

Bastide therefore offers a third point of view on the mediumistic continuum, one that is anchored in his fieldwork experience among the Candomblés of Bahia. This perspective informs his description of the

Spiritist disobsession ritual, which he sees as playing out the general psychological conflicts generated by the world of white, middle-class Brazilians:

> Hence the Oedipal complex, where all domestic conflicts are manifested, appears with an overwhelming monotony from one session to another, assuming the form of obsessing spirits. . . . All these interior dramas demonstrate that the puritanism of the lower-middle class is but a superficial veneer, a symbolic expression of a certain social status, the exterior manifestation of a class behavior, but one that has not yet destroyed the polygamous tendencies of the Muslim, the castrating tendencies of the mother, or the incestuous dreams of childhood. . . . We therefore find the mentality of the lower-middle class of Brazil attached to its puritanism as a defense, and all the more rigid as it is threatened by the sensual climate of the big tropical city or by the sexual liberty of the lower class, from which this lower-middle class is disengaging itself only with difficulty. (Bastide 1967: 15)

Our French informant (writing from Paris about a Brazil from which he was evidently still disengaging himself with difficulty) may be projecting his own puritanism onto Spiritists, but this should not sidetrack us from his sociological argument: Spiritism is for Bastide an expression of individual psychological conflicts that reflect a white, lower-middle-class mentality. His critique of Spiritist mediumship is further developed when he claims that Spiritist mediums experience only a "half-trance," which means that to some extent the medium controls the words of the spirits (1967: 14). He argues that in Spiritism the tremendous variety of spirits and the shallowness of the trance make the spirits into mere vehicles of individual psychological conflicts. Furthermore, the spirits of light counterbalance this expression of individual conflicts by articulating "the traditional Brazilian mentality, of the fraternal type, which places in the first rank the virtues of charity, and not justice" (1967: 14). As a result, Spiritism furnishes either spirits of light or errant spirits, and this reveals the complete structuring of the ego by the puritanical morality of the bourgeois mentality, on the one hand, and by repressed psychological conflicts on the other.

For Bastide, Spiritist mediumship and Spiritist disobsession meetings contrast sharply with the parallel practices in Umbanda, where the spirits are stereotyped characters drawn from popular mythology and, conse-

quently, are able to express the collective representations of an oppressed race and class rather than individual psychosexual conflicts. He
argues that, unlike Spiritist spirit guides, Umbandist spirits are stereo-
typical and compensatory, the first step to class consciousness based on
an independent ego that in turn can discipline the id for the interests of
the race and class. This in turn creates a revolutionary potential: "The
resentment [of Umbanda] is, on the contrary, the first expression of the
proletarian class, since it has not yet achieved a consciousness of its
strength in organized and militant syndicalism, and since it confusingly
forges its ideology behind the veil of religion. But this resentment is a
collective resentment, not the sum of a thousand individual resentments
[as it would be in Spiritism]" (1967: 16). In an effort to emphasize how
Umbanda is different from Spiritism, Bastide argues that the spirits of
the former are social rather than individual in nature, a feature which is
unlike Spiritist spirit guides but like Candomblé orixás.

Although Bastide uses the term "Spiritism" in the same way that
Camargo and Kloppenburg do (i.e., to include Umbanda, unlike the
usage of Cavalcanti and Amorim), he nonetheless emphasizes the differences between Spiritism and Umbanda and links Spiritism to Catholicism. He associates Spiritist disobsession with the "traditional Brazilian
mentality" of the Catholic church, in contrast to Umbanda and the Afro-
Brazilian religions, which are rooted in the collective experience of the
lower classes and people of color. He therefore adopts an interpretation
of Spiritism that is rooted in Afro-Brazilian perceptions of Spiritism: if
Camargo provides a Catholic (or even an Umbandist) reading of Spiritism and Umbanda, and if Cavalcanti provides a Spiritist reading,
Bastide provides an Afro-Brazilian reading.[11] Indeed, while he also believes, like the Afro-Brazilian priests, that Umbanda has (to use his word)
"betrayed" African religion with its acceptance of Spiritism and Amerin-
dian religion, he still sees in Umbanda the potential for a social consciousness rooted in the experience of people of color and the urban working
class—a consciousness which, like that of the Afro-Brazilian religions,
strictly opposes the "traditional Brazilian mentality" of Catholicism and
Spiritism. In short, Bastide attempts to put himself in the thongs of the
mulatto and African Brazilians at the bottom of the social pyramid, and
he locates a "continuum" not between Umbanda and Spiritism (the
Catholic reading) or between Umbanda and Catholicism (the Spiritist
reading), but between Spiritism and Catholicism (the Afro-Brazilian
reading). Bastide's role is that of a medium for the Afro-Brazilians,
whose voice no one hears in the realm of elite ideology.

Nor does his Afro-Brazilian reading stop with the religious system. Bastide also reads the social sciences in terms of similar class and race divisions. In the introduction to *The African Religions of Brazil,* the French scholar criticizes all previous studies of Afro-Brazilian religions—from Nina Rodrigues to Arthur Ramos and even Melville Herskovits—as "psychologism and ethnology" ([1960] 1978: 19–22). Later, he rejects these and other "international systems of explanation" as distortions of the Brazilian reality (1974: 113). In their place, he argues for the need to create an "Afro-Brazilian science" and to reject "what the black sociologist Guerreiro Ramos has so appropriately called 'consular sociology' " (1974: 113). This French intellectual's identification with an Afro-Brazilian perspective was so great that at the end of his introduction to *The African Religions of Brazil,* he wrote, "Africanus sum" ([1960] 1978: 28).

Bastide's reading of Umbanda as expressing the resentment of an oppressed race and class—an interpretation that subsequent research has rendered problematic (Brown 1986)—provides a good metaphor for the ambiguous status of his own Afro-Brazilian sociology. Bastide could not escape the irony that he—a white, cosmopolitan, French sociologist—was the prophet of this black, anticonsular, Afro-Brazilian science. His description of Umbanda might therefore be read as reflective of his attempt to identify his own sociology with Afro-Brazilian values. Thus, Bastide's formula for Umbanda applies to his own sociology; it was but the "first expression" of an Afro-Brazilian science, one that "confusingly forged" its ideology behind the veil of European sociology.

Transcultural Tranceformations

Although Bastide disagreed with Camargo on the issue of the mediumistic continuum, from another perspective they were writing less against each other than against the background of the medical literature that interpreted spirit mediumship as conducive to psychopathology (Bastide 1974: 112–13). By the early 1960s, at least some members of the medical profession had begun to accept the social scientists' argument (e.g., Martins and Bastos [1963], who discuss Camargo's work). Meanwhile, the emergence of transcultural psychiatry in the United States and Europe (Wittkower 1968) provided a new way for medical professionals to think about religious healers, and in 1968 the International Symposium on Transcultural

Psychiatry was held in Salvador da Bahia, the traditional locus of Afro-Brazilian religions. After this, the medical profession in Brazil increasingly began to concede that the spirit-mediumship religions could have therapeutic effects (Brody 1973; Pinho 1975; Leme-Lopes 1979; and Mariante 1975). In 1979, Ernesto La Porta, a psychoanalyst and clinical psychiatrist at the Federal University of Rio de Janeiro, wrote the following about Umbanda and the Afro-Brazilian religions:

> From the state of being a patient, one becomes a novice; and with time the faithful belong to the cult and, when initiated, are capable of receiving divinities, and thus reach the third stage, that of "therapist." They do not use this designation; it is simply what happens, as these are the people who will become veterans and adepts in the exercise of "passes" and capable of effecting acts and gestures that "drive out" the evil spirits, the "obsessors" . . . (1979: 103)

One need only recall the statement of Ribeiro and Campos (1931) to see how radically medical opinion has shifted. Yet, the change within the medical profession during the 1960s and 1970s, like the change within the Catholic church after Vatican II, should not be overemphasized. Even after the advent of transcultural psychiatry (what one might call a medical Vatican II), many doctors and psychiatrists continued to look at spirit mediumship through the prism of psychopathology; moreover, careful examination of the texts of transcultural psychiatry reveals how they preserve rather than subvert long-standing hierarchies. For example, the psychiatrist Clóvis Martins views the practices of spirit-mediumship religions as psychotherapeutic but nevertheless "primitive": "Poverty, malnutrition, illiteracy, and disease align themselves with *primitive processes of interpretation of the world* to facilitate the proliferation of magico-religious rituals, notoriously useful in the absorption of the impact of mental disequilibrium, either in the individual or the group" (1969: 52).

In an earlier paper, Martins and a colleague argued that although Spiritism and other spirit-mediumship religions "permit a restoration of equilibrium in the short run," they are no substitute for orthodox psychiatric treatment or psychotherapies because they work through suggestion (Martins and Bastos 1963:52). In other words, transcultural psychiatry preserves the same hierarchy as the older medical discourse, which labeled spirit mediumship as psychopathology: both transcultural psychiatry and the older medical discourse align biomedicine with the real and the scientific in opposition to spirit-mediumship religions, whose spirit idiom they associate with the imaginary and the primitive. The difference is that transcultural psychiatry now recognizes the benefits of spirit mediumship, rather than viewing it as a recipe for mental illness.

Transcultural psychiatry, then, preserves the hierarchy of orthodox medical therapies over ethno- or religious therapies. In so doing, Brazilian transcultural psychiatry also institutes the hierarchy of medical knowledge over anthropological knowledge. For these doctors and psychiatrists, the anthropological principle of cultural relativism does not imply the critical self-inspection of medical knowledge; it implies only that other, "nonscientific" therapies may have some limited efficacy. This perspective allows medical doctors to collaborate with religious healers or "ethno-therapists," particularly in conditions where the rival healers have tremendous popular support; however, such collaboration occurs on the terms of orthodox medicine. In other words, the process of self-reflection and introspection vis-à-vis one's own categories of understanding and one's assumptions about the nature of reality—so important for a humanistic mode of anthropology—is forgotten in this interpretation of transcultural psychiatry, for which such anthropology becomes as supplementary as the religious therapies themselves.[12]

From this perspective, anthropology is useful for an understanding of how spirit mediums might be primitive versions of doctors; that is to say, anthropology can help translate the spirit-mediumship discourse into the idiom of Western psychiatry and biomedicine. This line of transcultural psychiatry therefore relegates anthropology to the status of a supplementary science, just as it relegates religious therapies to the status of supplementary ethno-therapies rather than complementary alternative therapies. In contrast, the emergence of the category of alternative therapies, especially alternative psychotherapies, renders problematic the division that Brazilian psychiatrists such as Martins and Bastos have maintained between primitive, religious therapies and modern, scientific therapies. For Spiritists, especially Spiritist intellectuals, if the price they must pay to have their practices recognized as therapeutic involves accepting the label "primitive," the price is too high. They want recognition of their therapies as alternative, scientific therapies within the world of orthodox medicine, not as hyphenated, "ethno-" therapies.

These unsatisfactory implications of transcultural psychiatry have driven one Spiritist intellectual back to anthropology as a new source of cultural critique—this time at a higher level of dialectic. Just as Deolindo Amorim drew on cultural anthropology in order to undermine the

Freudian psychoanalysis of Arthur Ramos, so Pedro Mundim, a professor of psychiatry at the Federal University of Mato Grosso, draws on
contemporary anthropology to think critically about orthodox Brazilian
medicine. In a lecture given at the Spiritist Medical Association of São
Paulo on August 3, 1985, Mundim first returned to the critique of the
older psychiatric discourse of mediumship as psychopathology. Much as
Amorim had done nearly four decades earlier, Mundim criticized the
work of Arthur Ramos: "In other words, Ramos is locating mediumistic
phenomena in the realm of psychiatric nosology, especially hysteria, epilepsy, and [so on]. . . . This is what we call the 'psychiatrization' of mediumistic phenomena, for it implies a reductionist tendency in the psychiatric viewpoint" (my transcription). Mundim noted that this viewpoint is
still heard among members of the medical profession, but he also noted
that it was changing. He went on to link these changes to the political
abertura, or "opening," and the birth of the New Republic as well as to the
beneficial influence of sociology and anthropology:

> We understand that we are living in an opportune time—very
> opportune—and in medicine itself there is an opening regarding
> the study of these [alternative] therapeutic practices, and not only
> in medicine but also in the area of anthropology and sociology. We
> might even say that we have found a greater enthusiasm for these
> practices on the part of anthropologists and sociologists, especially
> anthropologists and sociologists connected to medical anthropol-
> ogy. (My transcription)

Thus, medical anthropology and sociology are, for Mundim, allies in
this process of provoking an "opening" for alternative therapies in official medical discourse. In a paper that Mundim wrote and presented at a
conference held the previous month, the Spiritist psychiatrist takes this
statement one more step. Citing the work of Jacques Lacan, the article
"The Effectiveness of Symbols" by Lévi-Strauss (1963), and a commentary by Sérvulo A. Figueira (1978) on Lévi-Strauss's and Peter Berger's
ideas of the symbolic, Mundim called into question the hierarchy between orthodox psychotherapies (especially psychoanalysis) and religious therapies:

> Do "scientific" and religious psychotherapies have in common the
> same symbolic efficacy? Does symbolic efficacy provide the foun-
> dation for the "therapicity" of psychotherapeutic practices that

are apparently disparate, but essentially similar? Do not "scientific" psychotherapies imply an "irrational" component, or belief, which is in some way similar to religious psychotherapies? Can one therefore subsume "scientific" and religious psychotherapies under the generic designation of "symbolic therapies"? And does not the psychotherapist, in the final analysis, have the same social function as the religious agent of healing? (1985: 18)

Mundim therefore uses an anthropology and sociology of the "symbolic" in order to neutralize the hierarchy between what he terms "scientific" and "religious" therapies; he accomplishes this neutralization by replacing both terms with a new umbrella term: "symbolic therapies."[13]

Mundim then carries through his deconstruction of "religious" and "scientific" therapies with an alternative hierarchy that finds a new scientific basis for what were called "religious" therapies. In completing his inversion of these two types of therapy, Mundim retreats from the anthropologist's discourse of the symbolic to that of the psychiatrist, physicist, and parapsychologist. More specifically, he argues that the so-called imaginary world of the spirit "possesses a space and time of its own, with 'complementary properties' to that of the space-time of 'reality' " (1985: 38), and he grounds the reality of world of the spirit in the authority of speculation by quantum physicists and of research by parapsychologists. Anthropological discourse allows Mundim to relativize all psychotherapies as "symbolic therapies"; once he draws this conclusion, however, he no longer seems to need anthropology, which can only relativize the two types of therapy rather than establish an alternative hierarchy, a move that requires the new physics and parapsychology.

As an anthropologist listening to Mundim's lectures, reading his paper, or talking with him, I want to encourage him to stop his argument at the point after he relativizes therapies with the notion of the "symbolic" but before he jettisons anthropological discourse and reformulates a new hierarchy by switching to quantum physics and parapsychology. Mundim's discourse may seem "anthropological" to Spiritists, but to this anthropologist his use of anthropology is as problematic as that of the transcultural psychiatrists: both use anthropology not to relativize their own discourse by comparison with other therapies and worldviews, but instead to render the Other's discourse in some sense "less scientific" than their own, which in turn is held to represent the most modern vision of scientific knowledge. My own preference is to see both discourses as being grounded in untestable assumptions about the nature of the world, one materialist and the other dualist. Of course, one might ask in turn whether *this* argument suggests that the anthropologist's relativizing viewpoint is better than the others. If so, is it no different from the viewpoints of transcultural psychiatry or Spiritist parapsychiatry in this regard?

Paradoxical Sciences

Mundim's anthropological analysis of psychiatry appears at first to have little relationship to Amorim's anthropological análysis of Umbanda. However, the two share an underlying structure that employs anthropology to invert an established hierarchy of the modern over the primitive. Amorim drew on anthropological sources to take one division between the modern (represented by the Catholic church) and the primitive (Spiritism and Umbanda) and to invert it, making Spiritism the modern and Catholicism/Umbanda the primitive in the sense that the latter share rituals, altars, belief in miracles, and so on. Likewise, Mundim drew on other anthropological sources to take another division between the modern (represented by official psychiatry) and the primitive (Spiritist therapy and other so-called religious therapies) and to invert it, making Spiritist parapsychiatry the modern in contrast to official psychiatry and other so-called scientific therapies. Anthropology therefore plays a special role in the dialogue between Spiritists and their Others, a dialogue that is in part a debate over how the cultural space they share should be divided up into a hierarchy of modern over primitive.[14] Spiritists turn anthropology back on ethnocentric statements by doctors to show that the sword of cultural relativism cuts both ways.

Thus, it should not surprise the reader that on one of my visits to the Faculdade Bezerra de Menezes in Curitiba, Director Octávio Ulysséa took me to a house that he said would eventually become their college's "Para-Anthropology Center." A sort of school within a school, the Para-Anthropology Center is the latest and most ambitious of the movement's attempts to attain the ideal that runs like an Ariadne's thread through the history of the Spiritist movement, from Amorim's Faculty of Psychic Studies to Menezes' and Cirne's school for mediums to Kardec's vision of a Spiritist Port-Royal and the Pestalozzi Institute of the young Rivail. Spiritists plan to use the Para-Anthropology Center to study popular religions such as Umbanda, the Afro-Brazilian religions, popular Catholicism, perhaps evangelical Protestantism, as well as popular beliefs regarding magic and the supernatural, but it is also envisioned as a place where a dialogue between Spiritists and their Others can take place. Instead of being just one more group on the list of popular religions, Spiritists see themselves as scientists who study these manifestations of popular culture, but with a difference: their stated goal is to reach out to and initiate a dialogue with the popular side of Brazilian religion.

During another visit to the campus, I attended a meeting and listened as Ulysséa discussed his plans for the Para-Anthropology Center with leaders from the local Umbanda federation who, owing to their previous experience with Spiritists, were skeptical of the proposal. Only later did I find out that Ulysséa had chosen me to give the college's first class on para-anthropology. The original choice, a local Spiritist who was trained in the social sciences, was unable to accept the honor; like the young Kardec in Switzerland, this crisis was the occasion for my first teaching experience.

Diana Brown (1986: 12) notes how Umbandists continually proselytized her and how she eventually had a trance experience; I also encountered good-natured proselytization, and although I did not go into trance or have any paranormal experience, I entered into the liminal zone in a way fitting to a study on science, religion, and ideology. Since my principal argument has been that one can understand Spiritist scientific thought only as a part of a larger ideological arena, it is perhaps defensible to conclude with a brief comment on how I personally became involved in this system of exchanges and differences.

Before accepting the teaching assignment, I asked Ulysséa what he had in mind, and he produced a course outline written by Hernani Guimarães Andrade which showed a Spiritist parapsychology combined with an evolutionary, Tylorian anthropology. The Spiritists realized that my own perspective on either discipline might be different from theirs; consequently, they guaranteed me complete academic freedom—free will and free speech are paramount Spiritist values—and told me that even the Catholic intellectual Albino Aresi had taught at their college. I accepted the offer (but refused payment, according to Spiritist principles and Fulbright rules), and—true to the Pestalozzian ideal of teaching students what the professor thinks they most need to know—I resolved simply to inform the students, as an anthropologist, about the ideas of the other cultures of "orthodox" anthropology and "orthodox" parapsychology. I taught what the culture of "orthodox" anthropology thought about magic and shamanism (assigning Frazer, Mauss, Evans-Pritchard, and Lévi-Strauss, among others) and what the culture of "orthodox" parapsychology thought about paranormal phenomena (summarizing basic experiments and research trends).[15]

As the anthropologist Jean-Paul Dumont (1978: 3) has argued, when an anthropologist begins to discuss his or her role in the other culture, the tendency is to lapse into the confessional mode of the travelogue. Adopting an I-hate-confessions-and-confessionals-yet-here-I-am tone that is reminiscent of *Tristes Tropiques,* Dumont sidesteps the problem by discussing how the Other perceived him, a tactic that I adopt here. Although Brazilians consider it "indelicate" to criticize someone they do not know well, I heard from one of the students what the general impression had been. When I emphasized the importance that the post-Rhinean school of North American and European parapsychology places on methodology and experimental design, they found me "positivist" and "parochial." The last adjective particularly interested me; they thought of the post-Rhinean tradition of parapsychology not as the cosmopolitan, international standard of this heterodox science but as a cultural aberration traceable mainly to the positivism of English-speaking countries. When I challenged the continuum that they posed between parapsychology and anthropology, and when I stated that many social anthropologists find irrelevant any kind of psychology—whether "para" or "ortho"—except as a cultural system worthy of study, they found me "narrow-minded."

In short, by presenting the orthodoxies of other disciplines, which may themselves be heterodoxies with respect to other disciplinary cultures (as in the case of "orthodox parapsychology"), I became heterodox in this one. We all liked one another and enjoyed some good dinners together, but this did not change their opinion that I was under the spell of a culture of materialism and positivism. In the terms of Spiritist thought, I was still a stage behind them in my own path of spiritual evolution. After the class ended, Ulysséa informed me diplomatically that my course had been a good introduction for the students and that perhaps now they would be prepared for a more advanced course that might be taught by Pedro Mundim.[16]

CONCLUSIONS

When people live in a country different from their own, the usual experience is that everything at first seems bewildering and foreign; then, with time and patience, it all becomes more familiar and commonsensical. But for this *norte americano* at least, the experience of living in Brazil was quite the opposite. At first Brazil appeared to be familiar: it is, after all, modern, urban, industrial, and Western, and even the visual landscape—peppered with Texaco stations, Levi's blue jeans, McDonald's "golden arches," Marlboro cigarettes, and Hollywood sit-coms on TV—seemed familiar. How different could it be? We are all, as Brazilians like to point out, *americanos,* and I found that my Brazilian friends were reading almost the same books, watching almost the same movies, and wearing almost the same kinds of clothes. But the surface similarities belie underlying differences, which gradually creep up on foreigners the more deeply immersed they become in the language and culture of Brazil. Time, friendship, love—in short, the fundamentals of everyday life—are all very different in the land "beside and below the equator," as the carnival song goes.

This is as true for the realm of ideology as it is for that of everyday life. At first, all the elements are familiar: the United States of North America (as they call us in the United States of Brazil) also has a Catholic church, a Spiritualist movement, a parapsychology community, a medical profession, a legal apparatus designed to stop the illegal practice of medicine, and even various forms of indigenous Afro-American religions and magical practices, such as rural-southern rootwork, New Orleans voodoo, and now the Afro-Cuban Santería of the large cities. The proportions may not be the same in the two countries, but the elements all seem, at first glance, to be familiar.

However, even if the elements were the same (and, on closer inspection, they are not), the relationships among them—their structure—is very different, and this is what makes Brazil seem increasingly foreign the longer one is there. Catholics and Spiritists tell doctors and scientists how to do medicine and physics; doctors, Catholics, and Spiritists advise legislators, judges, and politicians how to make, interpret, and enforce laws; and doctors inform Spiritists how to interpret "trance," while social scientists reinform doctors how to interpret "trance" and Spiritists tell social scientists how to improve their theories of Brazilian religion. In short, in Brazil there is a kind of leakage among discourses, a leakage that would be considered undesirable and even unusual in North America and Western Europe. In Parsonian terms, the relations among the various discourses are diffuse rather than specific. In Spiritist terms, the discourses obsess and disobsess one another.

The Brazilian case has several implications for the social studies of religion and popular science and medicine, one of which involves a question of methodology: in a society where discourses overlap and commingle with ease, an interdisciplinary method, such as the one adopted here, seems to be a better reflection of the social and cultural reality. More broadly, however, Brazil renders problematic those tidy frameworks which might define religion as a specific cultural system or as a demarcated field. Despite the methodological difference between apprehending (for example) religion as a system of meaning or as an ideology linked to power and social conflict, both approaches share an underlying assumption: they treat religion (or science, political ideology, etc.) as something that can be isolated and studied in some sense as an "individual." Thus, the Brazilian case encourages the social scientist to think more dialogically and to situate a given discourse within a broader ma-

trix of interpenetrating, overlapping, competing, syncretizing, and syn-
thesizing discourses. In other words, the study of ideology in Brazil
necessitates what Roberto DaMatta might call a "personalistic" social
theory of fields and cultural systems in place of an "individualistic" one.

As a result, the Brazilian case helps make questions possible that
might reorient the theoretical debate in the study of ideology or discourse away from the methodological dispute between a sociological
approach—i.e., the explanation of the "uses" of ideology, either in
terms of the needs it fulfills or the interests it serves—and a cultural
anthropological approach—the interpretation of ideological meaning
and the telling of the story from the point of view of the people who
practice it (Geertz 1973: 201ff.). The study of ideology in Brazil points
out that the problem may not be one of choosing between or synthesiz-
ing the different methodologies (after all, each has its truth) but, rather,
one having to do with the status of the object under study: that is, the
nature of "religion" or "science" or "medicine" as a system that can be
singled out and treated as a relatively discrete area of social inquiry.

Regarding religion, the Brazilian case adds another question to the
long tradition of anthropological skepticism. To a pair of more familiar
questions—Does totemism exist? Do dual organizations exist?—one
might also add, Does religion exist? It may be profitable to redefine
religion—to reorient the definition away from one that reifies religion
by constructing it around an essence such as Durkheim's sacred, Tylor's
spiritual beings, Lowie's supernatural, or Weber's questions of ultimate
meaning. An alternative to these approaches begins with the question of
religious syncretism or complexity and recognizes that all religion is
complex or syncretic, a truism that makes it possible to move on to the
idea that religious complexity or syncretism must be broadened to include a broader domain of ideology. As a strategy for interpretive social
science, it may make more sense, particularly in the context of modern
nation-states like Brazil, to assume that religion is best viewed as just one
position in the ideological arena, and to enter into dialogue with it by
showing how it is a lived discourse, to peek over its shoulder as it goes
about its everyday business of borrowing from, debating with, critiquing,
rejecting, and even admiring other discourses, including one's own. This
ongoing dialogue is what I have tried to portray in the preceding pages,
and to recognize this dialogue in one's methodology is, at least for the
Brazilian case, not only rewarding, but necessary.

To situate a religious, scientific, and philosophical movement like
Spiritism in terms of a broader "ideological arena" also means facing a

somewhat more complex issue than recognizing the dialogue among Spiritist intellectuals, Jesuit parapsychologists, New Republic ideologues, North American parapsychologists, the Brazilian medical profession, and so on. The ideological arena also includes, as I have discussed in Chapter 7, the place of social scientists in this ongoing dialogue. By viewing the social-scientific discourse as both the analyzed and the analyzing discourse—the observed observer, to borrow Stocking's phrase (1983)—one inevitably must grapple with that methodological problem and challenge which is sometimes identified as the "reflexivity" issue.

The word "reflexivity" is extremely slippery, but one of the key meanings of the term emerges from what Geertz has called "Mannheim's Paradox," a problem in the social theory of knowledge that he likens to Zeno's Paradox (1973: 194). In this sense, "reflexivity" means recognizing that any conclusions social scientists make about ideology/science must also apply to their own discourse. In recent years, this problem has become a topic of some concern both in the social studies of science (e.g., Woolgar 1982, 1988; Hess 1991a) and in anthropology, which has engaged in a series of critical rereadings of ethnographies as constrained by culture- and class-bound theoretical presuppositions and genre conventions (e.g., Boon 1985, 1987; Clifford and Marcus 1986: 24; Ruby 1982; cf. Watson 1987).

Recent experimental ethnography has attempted to address the reflexivity issue through a number of decolonizing textual and methodological strategies, and these discussions have influenced the construction of *Spirits and Scientists*. Marcus and Fischer (1986), for example, have emphasized the importance of adopting a global and historical perspective in order to explore relations between the world system and local communities and to develop a kind of reflexivity that examines the construction of the Other in the context of colonialism and neocolonialism. In the present book, by conceiving of the ideological arena for Spiritist discourse as one having international as well as historical dimensions, I have been able to examine a series of relationships between Spiritism in Brazil and various cosmopolitan Others, such as Catholicism, biomedicine, psychiatry, parapsychology, and even anthropology and sociology.

Another way in which one may write reflexively is via techniques that signal the constructed nature of one's cultural interpretation. An example of this kind of strategy has been the return to some of the conventions of the fieldwork account: the adoption of first-person narrative and the recording of dialogues with the informants. Because this genre may entail sacrificing the synthetic sweep and analytical depth of the holistic monograph, however, it has been used sparingly here (as at the end of Chapter 7), and the more moderate approach of making more room in the ethnography for the voices of Spiritist intellectuals (and their Others) has been adopted instead.

Some anthropologists have condemned the new experimental ethnography and have called for a return to an undisturbed, colonizing rhetoric of observer and observed, subject and object. However, the genie (or poltergeist) of reflexivity is out of the bottle, and notwithstanding the jeremiads of Marvin Harris and others, it is likely to remain on the loose. Some solutions are less radical than others (e.g., Latour 1988), and it seems clear at this point that "reflexivity" is complicated enough that it will be addressed in different ways and on different levels in the wide variety of new ethnographic experiments which are now emerging. The strategy adopted in *Spirits and Scientists* may add to this discussion in one rather specific way: instead of attempting to examine the dialogue between the social scientist and the community under study in the form of a conversation between individuals in the field, which is one solution that Clifford has considered (1983; cf. Rabinow 1986), I have chosen to interpret this dialogue as it is represented by two communities in the texts or public discourse (speeches and tape-recorded interviews) that they produce. My decision to examine the public and often published dialogue among social groups (including social scientists), rather than the informant/ethnographer dialogue, helps make it possible to focus the reflexivity problem on the relations among social scientists and Spiritists not as individuals but as members of discursive communities. In turn, moving to this level of analysis may put into question the individualist values implicit in some understandings of "dialogical ethnography" as restricted to the relationship between anthropologist and informant. The emphasis on public discourse also serves to relativize the positions of the social scientist and the Spiritist, for both communities can now be read on the same level through the lens of the ideological arena as producers of text/discourse.

Of course, this was a "choice" forced upon me to some extent by the nature of the groups under study: what intellectuals do (be they Jesuit, Spiritist, or social scientist) is write and lecture; therefore, their published texts and public speeches are the obvious place to examine the question of relations among discursive communities. This interpretive strategy may not be as obviously suited to the study of other communities as it is to that of Spiritist intellectuals. Nevertheless, all but the most remote tribal populations now face increasingly frequent contact with a global economy and its cosmopolitan culture, and with this they are becoming part of an ideological arena of dialogue and debate with their cosmopolitan Others, one that is frequently *mediated* by exchanges in publications, speeches, and the mass media. This process may be especially advanced among the articulate and cosmopolitan Spiritist intellectuals of southern Brazil, but Joralemon's essay (1990) about similar relations between Peruvian *curanderos* and North American New Agers suggests that it is occurring on a broader basis. If Spiritist intellectuals are not typical of the communities that anthropologists have traditionally studied, their cosmopolitan literacy certainly represents the future.

One may or may not wish to attach to this "cultural logic" the highly charged label of "postmodernism" (in Jameson's sense, 1984). It is now an anthropological cliché that the changing global political economy means that boundaries among cultures, discourses, and disciplines are increasingly transgressed, blurred, and, to use an older word, syncretized. It is no longer news that subdisciplines such as the anthropology of religion or the sociology of science look for their objects and find Others, or that the reality of the dialogue with the Other is forcing social scientists who study ideology to include their own discourse as part of the ideological arena they study. What the study of Spiritist intellectuals does accomplish is to point out some implications of the changes that everyone already recognizes: a world in which "informants" read social scientists' manuscripts (in English, no less) and respond with written comments (as one Spiritist intellectual has done for me); a world in which future Pedro Mundims will cite future Lacans and Lévi-Strausses as they redefine psychiatry in their own terms; and, more generally, a world in which local communities, popular religions, and social movements like Spiritism will increasingly articulate their own alternative vision of what cosmopolitan science and medicine—even anthropology—should be. No doubt, the Spiritist press will soon be publishing reviews of this book, and I may soon be responding to them . . .

A TYPOLOGY OF SPIRITIST
SCIENCE TEXTS

S pirits and Scientists maps out the ideological context of Spiritist science through a series of case studies of Spiritist doctrine and philosophy and Spiritist interpretations of parapsychology, medicine, and
the social sciences. It is also possible to think of these disciplines in
terms of a second system that crosscuts the first, the various "genres"
of writing represented in the different disciplines: (1) the empirical
genre, such as Andrade's 1982 monograph; (2) the expository genre,
such as Lex's 1985 article; and (3) the polemical genre, such as
Amorim's 1949 book, but especially the writings of Carlos Imbassahy.
These genres may overlap in each concrete instance, but they serve as a
useful set of ideal types that can make it easier to understand Spiritist
science writing. What follows is a summary of some of the major examples of each of these three genres, but first I discuss the idea of a
Spiritist "canon."

The Idea of a Spiritist Canon

The Spiritist and member of the AMESP (Spiritist Medical Association of São Paulo) Maria Júlia Peres (1985) has classified Spiritist books according to their importance—as "basic," "complementary," and "secondary" works. Although Spiritist intellectuals do not formally talk about a "canon," most of them would recognize certain books as the "classics" of Spiritist scientific and philosophical thought, and one can speak about a Spiritist "canon" in the same sense that one can speak of the works of Boas, Malinowski, Radcliffe-Brown, Mauss, and so on as constituting an anthropological "canon." What follows is my own impression of how the Spiritist canon was defined in the 1980s. The most important corpus of books, of course, is the doctrine of Allan Kardec (along with the writings of Jean-Baptiste Roustaing for Roustaingists and Pietro Ubaldi for Ubaldists). After the doctrinal works, for most Brazilian Spiritists the writings of Bezerra de Menezes, whose major books include *Philosophical Studies* (1977) and *Insanity Through a New Prism* ([1897] 1939), and those of the medium Francisco Cândido "Chico" Xavier, generally occupy the next most important place. Although other psychographic mediums, particularly Divaldo Franco (1982), are gaining increasing prominence, the work of Chico Xavier remains the most important of all the psychographic mediums in Brazil. Among the best known of the spirits who communicate through Xavier are the evangelical Emmanuel and the scientific André Luiz. Evangelical Spiritists read both Emmanuel and André Luiz in their sessions of doctrinal study, but they tend not to read the two most difficult and scientific of André Luiz's books, *Evolution in Two Worlds* (Xavier and Vieira 1958) and *Mechanisms of Mediumship* (Xavier and Vieira 1959), books that do, however, interest the intellectuals.

Finally, the Spiritist canon includes the texts of foreigners who were either Spiritists or psychical researchers and who held views acceptable to Spiritists. For example, works by Alexandre Aksakoff, Ernesto Bozzano, William Crawford, W. J. Crookes, Gabriel Delanne, Léon Denis, Camille Flammarion, and Oliver Lodge appear in many Spiritist bookstores. Spiritists translated many of these texts during the repressive years of the Vargas regime (1930–45) and shortly thereafter. During this period, life became increasingly difficult for Spiritists, and the government closed many Spiritist centers. By translating the European and North American psychical researchers, Spiritists could argue that their movement was scientific and philosophical, and not related to Umbanda or Candomblé. Likewise, by distinguishing their movement from these more popular spirit-mediumship religions, they hoped that they would avoid police persecution.

Although the opinion of psychical researchers was sharply divided between those who did and did not accept the phenomena of spirit mediumship as evidence of spirit communication, the Brazilian Spiritist Federation selectively translated those books which supported Spiritist doctrine. The Spiritist intellectual Hernani Guimarães Andrade told me that he believes this translation process had a double effect on the Spiritist intellectuals. The positive effect was that Spiritists had ammunition that they could use to defend themselves against detractors in the Catholic church and the medical profession; the negative effect was that many Spiritists adopted the attitude that all essential research had already been done, so there was no need to continue doing any more research. In other words, many Spiritists adopted the same attitude toward these texts as they had taken toward Kardec's works.

The Polemical Genre

Not all Spiritists were content with pointing their detractors to the translated texts; some penned polemical tracts against Catholic intellectuals and doctors. Like the translations of the European psychical researchers, these tracts are largely a product of the period beginning with the Vargas years (1930s) and ending in the 1960s. Pressure against Spiritists came from two major groups: the medical profession and the Catholic church. After the Vargas period, state repression eased up, but the Catholic church, led by intellectuals such as Boaventura Kloppenburg and Álvaro Negromonte, continued its war of words with the Spiritist movement. Perhaps the leading Spiritist polemicist of this period was Carlos Imbassahy. Against the Catholic intellectuals Kloppenburg and Negromonte, Imbassahy wrote *Evolution* (1955); he also answered the Jesuit parapsychologist Oscar González Quevedo's *The Hidden Side of the Mind* (1964) with *The Obscure Farce of the Mind* (1965). Other examples of these polemics include Imbassahy and Mello's *Reincarnation and Its Proofs* (c. 1945), Imbassahy's foreword in Mello's *How the Theologians Argue* (c. 1958), and Imbassahy's *On the Margins of Spiritism* (1950), which is a polemic against a variety of Protestant and Catholic critics. Against the medical profession, Imbassahy penned *Spiritism and Madness* (1949), *Phantasms, Fantasies, and Marionettes* (with Granja, 1950)—a response to the critical study by the well-known Dr. Antônio da Silva Mello (1949; see also Valle 1954)—as well as a critique of psychoanalysis (1969; cf. Gratton 1955), among other books and articles. See, too, Imbassahy's *Mediumship and the Law* (1943); his articles in the *Revista Internacional do Espiritismo* (1961, 1962a–d), on Dr. Osmard Andrade Faria's discussion of mediumship and hypnosis; and his *Enigmas of Parapsychology* (1967), which includes a polemic against the psychologist Cesário Morey Hossri, who had criticized Arigó.

Although Imbassahy was the most outstanding polemicist, other Spiritists wrote polemical tracts defending their doctrine and movement from outside criticism. The controversial work of the surgical medium Arigó led to books by the Spiritist journalists Jorge Rizzini (1963) and Nazareno Tourinho (with Imbassahy, c. 1967) as well as by the Spiritist intellectual J. Herculano Pires (1963, c. 1973). In addition, the books of Deolindo Amorim, which draw more on sociology and cultural anthropology than on psychical research, are sometimes polemical, although the tone of these books is usually more sedate and intellectual (e.g., Amorim 1955, which responds to Negromonte 1954; and Amorim [1955] 1978, which responds to psychiatrists such as Afrânio Peixoto, Arthur Ramos, and Nina Rodrigues using the neo-Freudian culturalists).

The Expository Genre

The expository texts have a didactic style and frequently read like textbooks. They do not appear to be polemical responses to critics; however, reading these texts with knowledge of their Others often reveals implicit polemicizing. The expository texts generally provide surveys of the field of parapsychology or psychic research, and they include frequent excursions into biology and physics. Although their model is the scientific textbook, in general the Spiritist expository texts do not simply reproduce the knowledge of other disciplines. They also reorder it, introduce new classificatory schemes, and encompass scientific research in a general Spiritist framework.

Hernani Guimarães Andrade's *Experimental Parapsychology* ([1967] 1984b) is a good example of this genre. This text outlines the parapsychology of Joseph Banks Rhine, a researcher at Duke University during the 1930s, but it also distinguishes this field from what Andrade sees as the encompassing discipline of psychical research, or *métapsychique*, which Spiritists view more favorably than parapsychology because it is less skeptical of spirit-mediumship phenomena, which Rhine viewed as having possible this-worldly explanations. Andrade's corpus also includes the three-volume magnum opus (1983, 1984a, 1986) that outlines his Spiritist science of psychobiophysics and places all Spiritist phenomena within a unified theory. More popular in approach is Andrade's essay "The Three Sides of Parapsychology" (Andrade/ Blacksmith 1979a–c). His work has earned a great deal of respect among Spiritists in the cities of São Paulo and Curitiba; it remains to be seen whether Spiritists in the rest of Brazil will eventually elevate his work to the status of Bezerra de Menezes or the European psychical researchers (see Marinho 1974).

Other expository texts of Spiritist scientific thought offer slightly different descriptions of parapsychology or the natural sciences. The Spiritist intellectual J. Herculano Pires (1964; n.d.) adopts an evolutionary approach to parapsychology, whereas the Spiritist engineer Carlos Alberto Tinôco (1982) discusses parapsychology with reference to modern biology and physics. The Spiritist psychiatrist Jorge Andrea focuses on biological processes (1984, 1982, 1980), and another Spiritist doctor, Waldo Vieira, known for having collaborated as a medium with Chico Xavier, compiled a massive annotated bibliography on "projectology" (1986), his term for the study of "astral projection" or "out-of-body experiences." Vieira's preference for the term "projection" over "out-of-body experience" expresses the Spiritist belief that such experiences are not purely subjective and that the perispirit and spirit actually leave the body. This contrasts with the belief of North American and European parapsychologists, who generally think that the experience is a variant on the "lucid dream." In all these texts, Spiritists present parapsychology, psychical research, and modern physics and biology in a nonpolemical manner, but they also reinterpret these disciplines in ways consistent with Spiritist doctrine. This tactic is similar to that of several Catholic parapsychologists, who present expositions of parapsychology in a non-controversial tone that in fact belies a substantial amount of reinterpretation according to Catholic church doctrine (e.g., Aresi 1978; Paixão and Silva 1974; Quevedo 1964, 1968, 1974, but *Curandeirismo* [1978] is more polemical).

Another group of expository texts provides descriptions of Spiritist disobsession and *passes* as alternative therapies. Probably the first Spiritist to institutionalize Menezes' ideas for the treatment of the mentally ill was Dr. Inácio Ferreira, who in the early 1940s founded a psychiatric clinic in

Uberaba, where he practiced disobsession as a psychiatric therapy. Yet Ferreira's books on the subject, such as *New Directions for Medicine* (1946; see also Ferreira c. 1940, 1963), lack the widespread acceptance and prestige that Menezes' work enjoys throughout the Spiritist movement. The *Boletim Médico-Espírita*, published by the AMESP, contains many expository accounts of Spiritist therapy, philosophy, and approaches to medicine. In addition, several Spiritist papers at the First International Conference on Alternative Therapies (1985), as well as the article by Ary Lex discussed in Chapter 6, fall into this category.

The Empirical Genre

The empirical texts constitute the smallest group; Spiritists in general have preferred to translate the research of North Americans and Europeans rather than do research for themselves. Although empirical research appears in all genres of Spiritist science writing, it is seldom the main focus of attention. This reflects both the Latin American cultural emphasis on deductive reasoning and the Spiritist movement's general tendency to value empirical research only as a way of confirming its doctrine. Likewise, in the medical field, Spiritists have produced relatively few empirical studies; again, they tend to rely on the research of North Americans and Europeans (e.g., Dean 1985; Rauscher 1985). Exceptions include the case studies of the Spiritist/Theosophist/psychiatrist Alberto Lyra (1984) and the hospital survey by the Spiritist psychiatrists Denizard Souza and Teresinha Fátima Deitos (1980; see also Souza 1983, 1985). Raul Sobral, a non-Spiritist doctor in Rio, has done empirical research on *passes* and healing (1984, 1985). There are also a few empirical studies of mediums (Fróes 1928; Ranieri n.d), and the Spiritist college at Curitiba has received government approval for a research proposal on the electrodynamic detection of plant infirmities.

An exception to the general lack of interest in empirical studies is the series of monographs written by Hernani Guimarães Andrade. These monographs follow the conventions of North American and European psychical research with respect to "spontaneous case research." Andrade's studies include an assessment of the validity of statements made by a medium's "drop-in communicator" (a spirit who is not part of the regular "control" spirits) as well as some investigations of reincarnation and poltergeist phenomena (Andrade 1980, 1982, 1988a, 1988b). Andrade concludes in favor of the spirit-communication hypothesis and in favor of the hypothesis of past-life memory. For Spiritists, Andrade's research offers empirical evidence in support of basic principles of Spiritist doctrine; his monographs, therefore, occupy a position of considerable importance in the general body of Spiritist science texts.

The Position of the Texts in the Ideological Arena

Whereas the polemical type of text generally has the non-Spiritist as its implied reader, the implied reader of the other genres can be either Spiritist or non-Spiritist. For example, intellectual as well as evangelical Spiritists read the works of Kardec, Xavier, Menezes, and the psychical researchers, but they will also give copies of these books, especially Kardec's *Book of the Spirits* or his *Gospel According to Spiritism*, to interested outsiders. English translations of some of Kardec's works are now available through the Spiritist Federation of the State of São Paulo, and Spiritists regard with interest the idea of "Kardecizing" their Spiritualist siblings to the north. In addition, numerous Spiritist books are available in Esperanto, reflecting the Spiritists' belief in the universal appeal of their doctrine (not unlike Latin in the history of the Catholic church) as well as the more general dilemma of a culture that speaks a marginal European language.

The other genres of Spiritist science writing have more specialized categories of implied readers. The textbook flavor of the expository genre makes it ideal for Spiritist study sessions or classes at the Spiritist college, and it also allows Spiritist intellectuals to address evangelical Spiritists or interested laypeople. With respect to laypeople, expository texts allow Spiritists to distinguish their movement from other movements that practice spirit mediumship, especially Umbanda, as scientific in nature; thus, laypeople sometimes refer to Spiritism as *espiritismo cientifico* (scientific Spiritism). At conferences, moreover, the expository mode is better suited than the polemical mode for addressing outsider intellectuals who are not necessarily hostile to Spiritism, such as occultists and sympathetic doctors or scientists.

The empirical texts are aimed more exclusively at elites, both within and outside the Spiritist movement. Some of Andrade's case studies, for example, have been reviewed in English, and colleagues make his texts available at Spiritist conferences in order to provide members of outside elites with examples of the scientific basis for Spiritist doctrinal tenets. Thus, as the threat of police repression subsides and as Catholic and medical polemics become more subdued, these Spiritist empirical texts may be replacing the Spiritist polemical texts as a mode of addressing outside elites.

Even the polemical texts—which Spiritists have written primarily for external elites such as Catholic intellectuals, legislators, medical professionals, and other groups skeptical of and/or hostile to Spiritism—may also have as their implied readers the large number of nominally Catholic laypeople who sometimes frequent Spiritist centers but who have misgivings due to Catholic-intellectual criticisms of spirit mediumship. In short, the implied readers of Spiritist texts vary both by genre and by context, and they may be either more or less "elite" or "popular." By having a variety of literary genres at its disposal, Spiritist scientific discourse is able to adapt flexibly to the discourse of different groups in the ideological arena.

A CHRONOLOGY OF THE DIVISIONS BETWEEN "SCIENTIFIC" AND "EVANGELICAL" SPIRITISTS IN THE EARLY HISTORY OF SPIRITISM IN RIO DE JANEIRO

The abbreviations for sources cited in this appendix are listed below. See Bibliography for full citations.

Abreu   *Adolpho Bezerra de Menezes* (1950)
Amorim   *Idéias e Reminiscências Espíritas* (c. 1980)
Aquarone   *Bezerra de Menezes* (1982)
Cirne 1   *Mensagem aos Meus Consócios na FEB* (1913/14)
Cirne 2   *Antichristo, Senhor do Mundo* (1935)
DA   L. Dos Anjos, "A Posição Zero," *Obreiros do Bem* (1979)
FEB 1   Federação Espírita Brasileira, *Memória Histórica do Espiritismo* (1904)
FEB 2   Federação Espírita Brasileira, *As Curas Espíritas perante a Lei* (1907)
FEB 3   Federação Espírita Brasileira, *Esboço Histórico da FEB* (1912)
Richard 1 P. Richard, article on the history of the FEB originally pub-

lished in *O Reformador,* September 15, 1901; cited in G.
Ribeiro, *Trabalhos do Grupo "Ismael" da FEB* (1941)

Richard 2 *Carta Aberta ao Presidente da FEB* (1914)

Wantuil   *Grandes Espíritas do Brasil* (1969)

August 2, 1873: The Society of Spiritist Studies–Confucian Group
(Sociedade de Estudos Espiríticos–Grupo Confúcio), was founded
in Rio de Janeiro (Wantuil: 118; Abreu: 25). According to their
statutes, they read only Allan Kardec, *The Book of the Spirits* and *The
Book of the Mediums* (Abreu: 28). Their spirit guide was named
"Confúcio" (Wantuil: 119), possibly the Chinese philosopher Confucius. This group lasted between two and a half (FEB 1: 58) and
three (Abreu: 26) years.

August 1874: The abolitionist and republican Antônio da Silva Neto was
elected president of the Confucian Group, which inaugurated a
new orientation that emphasized study sessions and called for
"the goal of a practical and theoretical school for Spiritist studies"
(Wantuil: 124–25).

January 1, 1875: The first Spiritist magazine in the capital, *Spiritist
Magazine—Monthly Publication of Psychological Studies (Revista
Espírita—Publicação Mensal de Estudos Psicológicos),* was founded
by Antônio da Silva Neto and his colleagues (Wantuil: 126); it
lasted only until its sixth issue (Wantuil: 129). The title provides
another indication of the "scientific" approach of Silva Neto and
his colleagues.

April 26, 1876: The God, Christ, and Charity Society of Spiritist Studies
(Sociedade de Estudos Espíritas Deus, Cristo, e Caridade) was
founded when a group of evangelical Spiritists left the Confucius
Group in order to read Allan Kardec, *The Gospel According to
Spiritism* (Abreu: 30; FEB 1: 58; cf. Wantuil: 147, who dates this
schism at March 23). This group also studied the works of Jean-
Baptiste Roustaing under the direction of Francisco Bittencourt
Sampaio (Wantuil: 389).

October 3, 1879: The God, Christ, and Charity Society of Spiritist Studies grew to include more than eight hundred members; then "dissidents" took over and transformed it into the God, Christ, and
Charity Academic Society (Sociedade Acadêmica Deus, Cristo, e
Caridade; Wantuil: 390). On this day, the Confucian Group dis-
persed (Wantuil: 131, 544).

According to Wantuil, the God, Christ, and Charity Academic

Society had a "purely scientific orientation" (p. 355), and I found that the first issue of their magazine—not published until 1881— also announced that the society has "the arduous mission to create an academy" and to study "Spiritist science" (*Revista da Sociedade Acadêmica Deus, Cristo, e Caridade,* January 1881: 1). However, in the second issue of this magazine, they called Jesus the "divine master" (April 1881: 1), and inside the back cover they recommended reading Jean-Baptiste Roustaing, so if Wantuil is right, concessions were evidently made to the Roustaingist elements. A group that was more clearly scientific, the St. Louis and Philosophical Spiritist Group (Grupo Espírita Filosófico e São Luiz), left the society, but little information on this group is available.

March 21, 1880: Dissatisfied with the scientific orientation of the God, Christ, and Charity Academic Society, the Roustaingists Francisco Bittencourt Sampaio, Antônio Luis Saião, and Frederico Júnior left to found the Spiritist Group of Fraternity (Grupo Espírita de Fraternidade; Wantuil: 147, 355; Abreu: 31; *Revista da Sociedade Acadêmica* . . . , June 1881: 173). The Spiritist Group of Fraternity held disobsession meetings and also studied Jean-Baptiste Roustaing (Wantuil: 356). According to Abreu (p. 31), the division between the "mystics" and the "scientists" began at this point.

June 6, 1880: Representatives of the Roustaingist Spiritist Group of Fraternity and the God, Christ, and Charity Academic Society met in order to discuss a possible reconciliation, but this did not work out (Wantuil: 147).

June 15, 1880: What would later be called the Grupo Ismael was founded under the spirit guide "Ismael" (Wantuil: 147). Eventually this group became part of the Brazilian Spiritist Federation (FEB), and its members included the Roustaingist Spiritist Group of Fraternity members Frederico Júnior and Francisco Bittencourt Sampaio (Wantuil: 356).

January 1881: The *Magazine of the God, Christ, and Charity Academic Society* (*Revista da Sociedade Acadêmica Deus, Cristo, e Caridade*) was first published.

August 28, 1881: The newspapers of Rio published a "police order that prohibit[ed] the God, Christ, and Charity Academic Society and all circles affiliated with it," but the emperor stopped the persecution (Wantuil: 483–85).

October 3, 1881: As an outcome of the First Spiritist Congress (September 6, 1881), the Spiritist Union Center of Brazil (Centro da União

Espírita do Brasil) was founded with the goal of uniting and orienting the diverse groups of Spiritists, perhaps in response to continued fears of police repression. Located in the God, Christ, and Charity Academic Society, its founders included Augusto Elias da Silva and the scientific Spiritist Afonso Angeli Torteroli (Wantuil: 191, 483, 544).

January 21, 1883: Augusto Elias da Silva launched *O Reformador* (Wantuil: 174), which later became the official magazine of the FEB.

January 2, 1884: The FEB was founded, led by Major Ewerton Quadros and Augusto Elias da Silva (Wantuil: 179, 232).

August 16, 1886: Adolfo Bezerra de Menezes announced his conversion to Spiritism in the Hall of the Old Guard, a large lecture hall that held more than fifteen hundred people and that was reported to be full on the occasion. In his speech, he "made a brilliant comparison between the Roman Catholic and Spiritist theologies, concluding that the latter and not the former was the apex of theodicy and Christian morality" (Wantuil: 232–33).

September 15, 1886: Antônio da Silva Neto, the former president of the Confucian Group who in 1874 had called for a school of Spiritist studies, gave a speech in the Hall of the Old Guard, evidently in reply to Adolfo Bezerra de Menezes, in which he warned "his future colleagues that Spiritism was in danger of becoming a religious sect, founding a church, and becoming swallowed up in dogmatic mysticism" (Wantuil: 134–35).

September 1886: The São Paulo Spiritist Francisco Júnior launched *Empirical Spiritualism* (*Espiritualismo Experimental*) in São Paulo, a magazine dedicated "especially to 'the Spiritist science' " (Wantuil: 189).

February 1889: The spirit of Allan Kardec transmitted a message (Aquarone: 76) through the medium Frederico Júnior (who later received the work of Jean-Baptiste Roustaing; Wantuil: 357) in the Spiritist Group of Fraternity (Wantuil: 396). Kardec's spirit asked for unity among the diverse factions, provided a method of disobsession, and asked, "And the school for mediums? Does it exist?" (FEB 3: 22–23).

1889: Adolfo Bezerra de Menezes was elected president of the FEB (Wantuil: 234).

April 21, 1889: Under Adolfo Bezerra de Menezes, the Spiritist Union Center of Brazil was reorganized as the Spiritist Center of Brazil (Centro Espírita do Brasil), and the effort to unite the diverse

Spiritist groups was renewed. The meetings of the Spiritist Center took place at first "inside the very house of Ismael"—in other words, within the FEB (Wantuil: 191, 236). According to Aquarone (p. 77), Menezes founded this center as a response to the request of the spirit of Allan Kardec to unite the Spiritists.

May 23, 1889: Adolfo Bezerra de Menezes inaugurated study sessions in the FEB for the discussion of Allan Kardec's *Book of the Spirits* (Aquarone: 85).

1890: Francisco Menezes Dias da Cruz, who had been vice-president of the FEB, was elected president (Wantuil: 291). In 1890 and 1891, Adolfo Bezerra de Menezes remained with the FEB as vice-president (Wantuil: 234). According to Aquarone (pp. 87ff.), he renounced the presidency in order to "dedicate himself more" to the Spiritist Center of Brazil and the goal of unification, but he was also "guided by a secret goal: to found a school for mediums." Elias da Silva, the founder of *O Reformador,* fought the idea of a school and it was not successful. Bezerra de Menezes then moved the Spiritist Center from the FEB to the Spiritist Fraternity Society (or "Spiritist Group of Fraternity"; Aquarone: 93).

The Roustaingists of the Spiritist Fraternity Society did not like Menezes' presence, and they abandoned that society for the FEB (Aquarone: 95; Wantuil: 308). "The leader of the dissidents was the medium Frederico Júnior, the same one who received the spirit of Allan Kardec and relayed the famous 'instructions' " (Aquarone: 96).

Under the presidency of Francisco de Menezes Dias da Cruz, the FEB began its program of Assistance to the Needy (Assistência aos Necessitados), where the homeopathic *receitista* mediums worked (Wantuil: 308). Pedro Richard later claimed that he had founded the program (Richard 2: 27).

October 1890: The new penal code of the Old Republic appeared (Wantuil: 547), and although the article prohibiting *espiritismo* was directed more against the Afro-Brazilian "low Spiritism," the general climate of political repression that surrounded the birth of the Old Republic made all Spiritists very anxious (Aquarone: 97–99).

1890 or 1891: The Spiritist Fraternity Society announced allegiance to the FEB (Wantuil: 185).

January 1893: Augusto Elias da Silva—founder of *O Reformador,* the official magazine of the FEB—was elected president of the Spiritist Union Center of Brazil (Wantuil: 191).

September 1893: According to Pedro Richard, there was a revolt within the FEB on September 6, 1893 (Richard 1: 23). According to Abreu (p. 57), the Spiritist Fraternity Society and the FEB fell into the hands of the scientific Spiritists in 1893. The Spiritist Fraternity Society changed its name to the Psychological Fraternity Society (Sociedade Psicológica Fraternidade; Abreu: 57; Wantuil: 398).

According to Aquarone (pp. 110–11, though he dates the event at mid-1894), the FEB reopened under a program of reconciliation among the "scientists" and the "mystics," led by Francisco Menezes Dias da Cruz, who remained president. He ended the study of *The Book of the Mediums, Genesis,* and "all the other works of Kardec" that had been instituted by Adolfo Bezerra de Menezes five years earlier. In place of these classes, he created Friday sessions in which there were "dry discussions of theses, without the intervention of religious sentiments." This corresponds to Abreu's statement that in 1893 "the FEB openly denied Kardecism—as far as it was concerned, Spiritism was a science" (p. 58).

April 4, 1894: The scientific Spiritist Afonso Angeli Torteroli, apparently now in charge of the Spiritist Union Center of Brazil, reorganized the center and renamed it the "Center of the Union for the Divulgence of Spiritism in Brazil" (Centro da União Espírita de Propaganda no Brasil); he also edited the *Spiritist Magazine of Brazil (Revista Espírita do Brasil;* Wantuil: 191–92, 236). Torteroli was the leader of "a group of dissidents . . . who were against the religious spirit of Spiritism" (Wantuil: 398).

January 1895: Júlio Cesar Leal was elected president of the FEB (Wantuil: 459). According to Abreu (p. 68), he was a "Kardecist" (for Abreu, this meant being a follower of the doctrines in all of Allan Kardec's books, including *The Gospel According to Spiritism),* while the official FEB magazine, *O Reformador,* remained in the hands of the "mystics" (in this case, the Roustaingists). Leal reestablished classes dedicated to the study of *The Book of the Spirits, Genesis,* and other works by Kardec (Aquarone: 113).

August 3, 1895: Adolfo Bezerra de Menezes was elected president of the FEB after Júlio Cesar Leal resigned (Aquarone: 113; Wantuil: 234) amid "serious financial problems" and "profound divergences among the Spiritist leaders" (Wantuil: 186). Menezes reoriented the FEB and "gave it the purely evangelical program of the former 'Spiritist Group of Fraternity'" (Wantuil: 398). Reading between the lines, one has to remember that the Spiritist Group of Fraternity held disobsession meetings and sessions devoted to the study of Jean-Baptiste Roustaing (Wantuil: 356). According to Dos Anjos (DA/April: 3), it was Menezes who "introduced, in the bylaws of 1895, an article that made obligatory the study of *The Four Gospels*," one of Roustaing's works. Menezes' disobsession therapy therefore seems to be part of the evangelical/Roustaingist program, but in his writings this medical doctor also portrayed disobsession in scientific terms as a kind of alternative psychiatry.

1896: Adolfo Bezerra de Menezes distanced himself from the Center of the Union for the Divulgence of Spiritism in Brazil (Wantuil: 460), which was now headed by the scientific Spiritist Afonso Angeli Torteroli (Wantuil: 191–92, 236). Menezes was "the first to raise his voice against the propositions of some of its directors, and the first to resign; only later did the facts confirm his assertions, thus resulting in the resignation of various others" (Wantuil: 192).

1897: Júlio César Leal, Augusto Elias da Silva, Ernesto dos Santos Silva, Pinheiro Guedes, and other Roustaingist/evangelical Spiritists resigned from the Center of the Union for the Divulgence of Spiritism in Brazil (Wantuil: 460).

April 11, 1900: Adolfo Bezerra de Menezes died (Wantuil: 237).

May 4, 1900: Leopoldo Cirne became president of the FEB (DA/April: 3).

1901: According to Dos Anjos, Leopoldo Cirne called a general assembly to consider new bylaws. Although Cirne was "a devoted student of [Jean-Baptiste] Roustaing," he wanted to omit the statute prescribing the study of Roustaing, the very statute that Adolfo Bezerra de Menezes had introduced in 1895 (DA/April: 3, 14).

1902: The Assistance to the Needy program was reestablished (Cirne 1: 46). Cirne's plan for a school for mediums received the support of the *receitistas* only when he included Jean-Baptiste Roustaing in the curriculum; the school functioned for only two years (DA/June–July: 15). Cirne saw the assistance program as a threat to his plans for a school for mediums (Cirne 2: 46).

March 10, 1904: Health regulations made healing legal only for licensed doctors (FEB 3: 35); prosecutions against FEB mediums began (Cirne 2: 256).

1904–1905: The FEB was prosecuted for the illegal practice of medicine (FEB 3: 36; FEB 2).

July 15, 1906: An article in *O Reformador* called for a hospital for the treatment of the obsessed (*O Reformador:* 225–27). The pages of *O Reformador* during this period show a strong interest in disobsession.

August 6, 1910: The plan for a FEB school for mediums was approved (Cirne 1: 34).

April 21, 1912: The new FEB school for mediums began to function (Cirne 1: 34).

February 15, 1913: An editorial in *O Reformador* declared Spiritism to be a religion (DA/June–July: 2).

1913–1914: Cirne supported a sanatorium for the obsessed and asked for changes in the Assistance to the Needy program, which he claimed had caused a financial crisis. Some mediums in the assistance program were against the school for mediums (Cirne 1: 43, 47–48, 51), and the mediums threatened to go on strike or transfer to another institution if Cirne were reelected. Many Spiritists left the FEB, and in 1914 it had only 60 percent of the members it had in 1913 (Cirne 2: 273).

February 10, 1914: In his *Open Letter to the President of the FEB,* Pedro Richard, who claimed that he had created and organized the program of Assistance to the Needy, criticized Leopoldo Cirne's criticism of the program. He further wrote that Cirne had never visited the Service of Cures, and he accused Cirne of having written against Jean-Baptiste Roustaing in his articles about "Animistic Evolution," which had been published in *O Reformador* during the administration of Adolfo Bezerra de Menezes. Richard also criticized the school for mediums and defended the study of Roustaing, and he said that the new mediums who perform cures in the Assistance to the Needy program could no longer "continue under a president who so severely and unjustly accused them" (Richard 2: 27).

1914: Aristides Spínola was elected president of the FEB; the vice-president was Pedro Richard. Immediately, the school for mediums closed (Cirne 2: 274).

1917: Aristides Spínola soon introduced a statute in favor of the study of Jean-Baptiste Roustaing, and the FEB approved that statute, which apparently remains in effect even today (DA/June–July: 14; DA/August–September: 2).

1918: A report called for the expansion of disobsession (Cirne 2: 281).

March 3, 1926: The National Spiritist Convention (Constituinte Espírita Nacional) resulted in the birth of the Spiritist League of Brazil

(Liga Espírita do Brasil), which was founded in order to protest the reforms of the regime of President Artur Bernardes and Federal Representative Plínio Salgado, who called for religious education in the public schools and the reestablishment of Catholicism as the official religion (Amorim: 49, 53; Cirne 2: 284). Despite the stated goal of defending the Spiritist movement as a whole against political reforms that were perceived to be anti-Spiritist, the Spiritist League appears to have been a locus for Spiritist intellectuals who were dissatisfied with the FEB. The Spiritist League published the *Spiritist Magazine of Brazil* (*Revista Espírita do Brasil*), which was the same name as Afonso Angeli Torteroli's publication of 1894, and it began a course on Spiritism (DA/August–September: 3–4). According to Spiritists whom I interviewed, the Spiritist League later became the Spiritist Federation of the State of Rio de Janeiro (Federação Espírita do Estado do Rio de Janeiro) in Niterói; it also supported the College of Psychic Studies (Faculdade de Estudos Psíquicos), which later became the Institute of Brazilian Spiritist Culture (Instituto de Cultura Espírita do Brasil; Amorim: 49, 163ff.).

May 1930: The Second Congress of the National Spiritist Convention adopted a resolution in favor of a school for mediums (*Revista Espírita do Brasil*, May 1930: 117).

July 1930: The article "Work Methods Suggested by the Spiritist League of Brazil" (*Revista Espírita do Brasil*, July 1930: 182) recommended the reading of Allan Kardec only (as opposed to Jean-Baptiste Roustaing) and called for a limitation on disobsession meetings and prescriptions.

TOWARD A COMPARATIVE STUDY OF SPIRITISM
Historical Development in Brazil and Puerto Rico

Although Brazil is the home of the world's largest Spiritist movement, followers of Allan Kardec reside in many lands, particularly other Latin American lands such as Argentina, Mexico (Finkler 1983; Loewe 1990; Macklin 1974), Puerto Rico (Koss 1976), and Venezuela, and among Hispanic groups in the United States (Harwood 1987; Garrison 1977). The field for comparative research, therefore, is wide open; this essay will suggest one possible direction for research oriented toward the comparative historical development of Spiritism as a social movement (also see Hess 1991d). Previous work on Brazil (Hess 1987b) resulted in a model of the dynamics of Spiritism's historical development. This essay will further develop that model by examining comparatively the historical development of Spiritism in Puerto Rico. It is hoped that this exercise will make the model useful not only for a general understanding of Spiritism, but for other heterodox social movements in Latin America.

Background

Puerto Rico provides a good counterpoint to Brazil. Although Puerto Rico has a relatively large Spiritist movement, the social and cultural context is in many ways very different. One obvious difference is size and political status: Brazil is a nation-state of continental proportions with a population exceeding 150 million people, whereas Puerto Rico has always had a colonial status and is a small island whose current population is about 3.5 million. In Brazil, one finds large Spiritist federations, Spiritist bookstores, a vibrant Spiritist press, famous and highly respected mediums, and clashing ideological tendencies within the movement—pure Kardecists versus Roustaingist and Ubaldist reformers or, more generally, "scientific" versus "evangelical" interpretations. In contrast, the relatively small size of the Spiritist movement in Puerto Rico has resulted in less internal differentiation, one federation for the island, no mediums of international stature, no remaining Spiritist bookstores, and a very small volume of published materials.

In addition to these "quantitative" differences, the social and political contexts of Brazilian and Puerto Rican Spiritism are markedly different. In Brazil, Spiritists have suffered persecution at three main points in their history. At the beginning of the New Republic (during the 1890s and the first decade of the twentieth century), the state and the medical profession attacked Spiritism and prosecuted some Spiritists. During the Getúlio Vargas years, particularly during the 1930s, a campaign by the medical profession combined with Vargas's strategic alliance with Cardinal Leme to close down many Spiritist centers. Finally, from the 1950s to the present, Catholic intellectuals, led by Jesuit parapsychologists, have attacked Spiritism not only as a doctrinal deviation but as a pseudoscience. The model of historical development for the Spiritist movement in Brazil can be summarized as follows: during periods of external repression and verbal attack, Spiritists have tended to develop a scientific discourse, to submerge factional disputes (a "centripetal" dynamic), and to close ranks behind the intellectuals; when external repression and verbal attacks were less fierce, the "centrifugal" dynamic of scientific/religious factional disputes has tended to become more evident (Hess 1987b).

To what extent is this pattern of historical development also evident in Puerto Rican Spiritism? Or, conversely, what insights does the history of Puerto Rican Spiritism provide for a more general, comparative understanding of the movement's historical development? In order to answer this question, an essay by the anthropologist Joan Koss (1976) and a book by the Spiritist Nestor Rodríguez Escudero (1979) on the history of Spiritism in Puerto Rico served to provide a sound starting point, and these were nicely supplemented with a book by the Spiritist Teresa Yáñez (1963) and two essays by the historian Carlos Alvarado (1979, 1980). In addition, during a trip to Puerto Rico in July 1989, I consulted primary sources at the Colección Puertorriqueña of the Universidad de Puerto Rico, and I visited the Casa de las Almas in San Juan and Círculo Lumen in Ponce. During this trip, I benefited from conversations and interviews with the following Spiritist leaders: Rafael Giraud, Jorge Quevedo, Luis Ramírez, and Nestor Rodríguez Escudero.

Spiritism in Puerto Rico

Koss (1976: 31) dates the arrival of Spiritism on the island at 1856, and by 1859 the Catholic church was attacking doctrinal deviations that included masonry, Protestantism, and Spiritism (Koss 1976: 31; Cruz Monclova 1952). The first Spiritist groups met privately in homes, where it was safer, and the first center was not founded until 1881 (Rodríguez Escudero 1979: 43). In 1888, the Law of Association liberalized the rules for the organization of societies, but nevertheless harassment by church and state continued in the 1890s (Rodríguez Escudero 1979: 44, 49).

With the U.S. occupation following the Spanish-American War in 1898, the First Amendment guarantees of freedom of speech, assembly, religion, and the press meant that Spiritists could openly espouse their philosophy. The documentary sources for the twentieth century show no evidence of police harassment or repression during the "American period," and Spiritists with whom I spoke had never heard of police repression or forced closing of Spiritist centers during this period. The only period in which one might find repression comparable to that of Brazil, then, is during Spanish rule. However, Spiritist journals from this period—e.g., *El Heraldo* (1880), *El Peregrino* (1884), *Luz y Progreso* (1885–86), *El Nivel* (1889), *El Estudio* (1892), *El Neofito* (1893), and *El Progreso* (1897)—were not available at the Colección Puertorriqueña, and Spiritists with whom I spoke did not know of any private collections. It is therefore difficult to assess the effect of state repression and attacks by the Catholic church on the internal development of the Spiritist movement during the nineteenth century.

There is documentary evidence of a "dialogue" between Spiritists and their detractors at the beginning of the twentieth century, and these documents allow some assessment of the impact of that dialogue on the relatively "scientific" or "religious" nature of Spiritist discourse. In general, attacks by the Catholic church were cast mainly in theological and philosophical terms, and Spiritists replied in kind. For example, in the reply by Francisco Vincenty, president of the Spiritist Federation of Puerto Rico, to attacks by the editor of the Catholic magazine *La Verdad,* the arguments revolve around theological issues, especially the importance of charity and internalized values in the role of salvation (Vincenty 1907). In other cases, such as letters in the Spiritist journal *El Buen Sentido* (e.g., 1908: 557–59), Spiritists were more concerned with the church's involvement in politics. Likewise, the debate between the Spiritist and political leader Rosendo Matienzo Cintrón and Padre Saturnino Janices involved philosophical, theological, and political discourse (Soler 1960: 634–40), and not scientific disputations over the claims of psychical research (cf. Bacón 1910).

As late as 1936, the Catholic intellectual Jesús López cast his critique of Spiritism in dogmatic or theological terms, but in 1948 a book by Jesús Martínez Barrena, C.M., combined theological and philosophical arguments with a critique of the psychical research upon which Spiritists based their empirical claims. This appears to be one of the very few cases in which Catholics attacked Spiritism in scientific terms; the polemical tracts of the Jesuit parapsychologists, which helped spur Spiritists in Brazil into developing their own scientific discourse, are absent in Puerto Rico. Indeed, I was able to locate only one parapsychology book published in Puerto Rico and written by a Catholic intellectual (Freixedo 1973); although he may not be very representative of Catholic intellectuals in Puerto Rico, he was very respectful of Spiritism.

In Puerto Rico, the scientific side of Spiritism developed either outside the context of external polemics and in contact with European and North American psychical research (e.g., Ponte Jiménez 1914) or in response to attacks from the medical profession. Although there may not have been a response to the book on hypnotism by Agapito Morales (1904), Spiritists were highly critical of a comment by a Dr. Goenaga, who at the turn of the century argued in the Catholic magazine *La Verdad* that the increase in reported cases of mental illness in Puerto Rico was a result of the growth of Spiritism, an argument that one also finds in Brazil, especially in the 1930s. In several articles published in the Spiritist magazine *Iris de Paz* (November 18, 1905: 1–8), Spiritists argued that the increased number of psychiatric patients was explained by the improvements in treatment subsequent to the U.S. occupation. In addition, they cited the authority of European psychical researchers, and one essayist concluded: "I do not hesitate to say that those who declare the phenomena of mediumship to be contrary to science do not know what they are talking about" (*Iris de Paz*, p. 2; see Suarez 1892 for a similar exchange in which a Spiritist uses psychical research to bolster a critique of a doctor's arguments).

One therefore finds the emergence of a scientific discourse in Puerto Rican Spiritism in a context similar to that of Spiritism in Brazil, but the Puerto Rican experience clarifies one aspect of the process in Brazil: scientific discourse, particularly the use of psychical research, emerges in these Puerto Rican dialogues in cases of critiques by doctors rather than those by Catholic intellectuals. In other words, the pattern appears to be that a scientific discourse emerges in response to external critiques which are phrased in a scientific idiom; and in Puerto Rico critiques couched in a scientific idiom were more evident among medical detractors than among Catholic intellectuals, who retained a theological idiom. Although the scientific discourse within Spiritism may emerge in contexts other than responses to external critique (as appears to be the case with Francisco Jiménez Ponte, and certainly this is true in Brazil, where the intellectuals formed a large enough group to develop their own publications and associations), the point here is that in the context of criticism from the outside, Spiritist scientific discourse tends to emerge more when the criticism is itself cast in scientific terms, as has been the case in Brazil much more than in Puerto Rico.

The other aspect of the Brazilian experience which may be relevant to understanding the historical development of Spiritism in Puerto Rico is that in periods of little or no external repression, factional disputes tend to be more openly expressed, and they tend to take place in terms of Spiritism as a scientific/philosophical, study-oriented enterprise versus a religious/evangelical, healing-oriented one. Kardec viewed Spiritism as philosophy with a scientific basis and moral implications, in which the morality was closely linked to the teachings of Jesus, but he stopped short of defining Spiritism as a religion. Furthermore, although he recognized the possibilities of healing via spirit mediums, he emphasized the use of mediumship for philosophical, moral, and scientific study. In Latin America, on the other hand, Spiritism has frequently been reinterpreted as a religion, just as the notion of healing mediumship has been given a much greater emphasis. For the intellectuals, this is a source of consternation, but the masses of Spiritists are unlikely to pay any attention to the "scientific" interpretations of the intellectuals unless they need the intellectuals for defense against state repression. Given the comparative absence of such repression in Puerto Rico, one would expect to see rather sharp divisions between relatively scientific intellectuals and the religious/healing-oriented masses.

Turning again to the history of Spiritism, in 1913 two key leaders—Rosendo Matienzo Cintrón and Hemeterio Bacón—died, and within three years the journal *Espírita* was lamenting the fact that "Spiritism appears to have entered into one of those periods of inactivity" (March 15, 1917: 1–2). In turn, it raised the cry that "the masses of Spiritists perhaps owed their indifference to a lack of preparation in the teachings of Allan Kardec." This was one early sign of how Puerto Rican Spiritism was quickly deviating from orthodox Kardecism and becoming, in a phrase that Rodríguez Escudero used in conversation with me, a "popular Spiritism": mediums who were nominally Kardecist but who did not study Kardec's works or practice his doctrine faithfully. Koss (1976: 35) argues that "Spiritism provided the legitimating element for folk religion," particularly that of the *jíbaros*, or peasants of the interior. This "popular Spiritism" includes the use of altars, prayers, and images of saints and Indians.

Instead of proselytizing this huge resource—Kardecizing the masses, so to speak—several of the intellectuals in Puerto Rico apparently moved in the opposite direction: they severed ties with the Spiritist movement and became Theosophists (Andino 1937: 51). One of the defectors even included Francisco Vincenty, the above-mentioned former president of the Spiritist Federation of Puerto Rico who had engaged in debate with the editor of the Catholic magazine *La Verdad*. The masthead of the *Heraldo Teosófico*, which began publishing in 1924, lists for that year eight "lodges" (a term that invokes comparisons with masonry, in which many of the first Spiritists were involved) and twelve in 1929, which gives some support to the view that Theosophy was healthy and growing during this decade.

During the 1930s, 1940s, and 1950s, the Spiritist intellectuals who remained in the movement engaged in several reform attempts, all of which seemed to be aimed at "cleansing" the movement of elements of popular religion and healing. For example, in a manifesto published in 1934, Spiritists associated with the Casa de las Almas in San Juan called for the need "to cleanse Spiritism of this great multitude of exploiters called *espiriteros* [Spiritoids]" (AEPR 1934: 11). They especially opposed those Spiritoids "who are dedicated to commerce and who exploit the ignorant" (p. 11), since charging for mediumistic services was expressly forbidden by the Kardecian doctrine.

A prominent reformer was Telesforo Andino, who attempted to win back the intellectuals by arguing that Spiritism and Theosophy were complementary (1937: 64), but who also viewed Spiritism as both a science and a religion. As Rodríguez Escudero points out (1979: 229), defining Spiritism as a religion was "easier for the masses to assimilate" than the other reform doctrine of the period: William Colón's scientific Spiritism, which held that "Spiritism is the antithesis of religion" (Colón and Sasport 1939: 14). Colón hoped to eliminate from Spiritism "the anthropomorphic God, prayers, candles, spiritually purifed water, spiritual *passes*, and images" (Rodríguez Escudero 1979: 229). Although in 1942 the Spiritist Federation of Puerto Rico condemned sorcerers, charlatans, and diviners, thus indicating some consistency with Colón's position, later that same year its leaders refused to let Colón speak before a general assembly (Rodríguez Escudero 1979: 99, 102), apparently because of his extreme antireligious stance.

In the end, neither the doctrine of Andino nor that of Colón became part of the Spiritist Federation's program or widely held among Spiritists of any type in Puerto Rico. In the federation's official magazine *Cosmos*, essays and editorials from the 1940s and 1950s continued to lament the "charlatans" who called themselves Spiritists; yet, popular Spiritism seemed to be healthy and even growing. A census held by the federation in 1959 claimed 100,000 Spiritists in 15,000 centers or groups throughout Puerto Rico (*El Mundo*, July 25, 1959, p. 4), but a vast majority of these were undoubtedly associated with a healing-oriented popular Spiritism, which, after the arrival of the Cubans in the wake of the Revolution, began to mix more with the Afro-American religion of Santería.

By the mid-1970s, the Spiritist Federation of Puerto Rico was so fragile that it fell apart when some Spiritists invited the Latin American Congress of Spiritists (CEPA) to hold its annual meeting in Puerto Rico. Lacking the energy and funds to host the congress, the Spiritist Federation declined the invitation; as a result, in 1976, a group of Spiritists formed a council that hosted the CEPA and later became the Confederation of Spiritists of Puerto Rico. As of my visit in 1989, the Spiritist Federation appears to exist only on paper, and the Confederation of Spiritists has replaced it as the federalizing body. Whether there was an ideological difference between the new confederation and the old federation is moot. Rafael Giraud, president of the Casa de las Almas, believes that the Confederation of Spiritists is more scientific and less tolerant of doctrinal deviations; but Jorge Quevedo, president of Círculo Lumen, sees the change more as a shift in leadership and organizational energy. In any case, both agree that the number of "scientific" Spiritists on the island is small, and that the vast majority of "Spiritists" are more concerned with popular healing, prayers, candles, altars, and a definition of Spiritism as a "religion."

Writing in the mid-1970s, Koss argued that Spiritism was "undergoing a florescence" (1976: 41), but Spiritists with whom I spoke some fifteen years later were less optimistic. Although Giraud, who spoke with the enthusiasm of youth, believed there was some movement toward "scientific Spiritism," Rodríguez Escudero, who spoke with the pessimism of an older generation, believed not only that orthodox or scientific Spiritism was in a state of "decadence," but also that "popular Spiritism" was declining, though not as rapidly as the former. Nor did he think that Catholicism was taking the place of either form of Spiritism; only Pentecostalism seemed to be growing rapidly, winning converts from Spiritism as well as Catholicism. Thus, the ultimate expression of the centrifugal tendency within Spiritism may not be a form of Spiritism at all, but Pentecostalism.

Conclusions

In general terms, the pattern of historical development outlined for the Brazilian case also applies in Puerto Rico. In response to attacks from the medical profession, Puerto Rican Spiritists replied with a scientific discourse and marshaled the results of psychical research. However, these attacks were so meager that it was not necessary for Puerto Rican Spiritists to develop a sustained scientific discourse. Nor was the movement large enough to foster an independent group of intellectuals with their own publications and organizations. Furthermore, the generally theological and philosophical nature of the "dialogue" with the Catholic church in Puerto Rico suggests a more general hypothesis that exchanges with the church will result in a recourse to and development of a scientific discourse only if the church uses science to delegitimize Spiritism, as is the case with Jesuit parapsychologists in Brazil but not with Catholic intellectuals in Puerto Rico.

As for internal divisions within the Spiritist movement, comparison of the Brazilian and Puerto Rican cases suggests that religious and healing-oriented variants of Spiritism tend to develop in the absence of state repression. However, the pattern of a divergence between an intellectual or scientific approach to Spiritism and a religious, healing approach differs in the two nations. In Brazil, the larger size of the Spiritist movement has led to an internal dynamic between those who follow an orthodox interpretation of Spiritism, as a philosophy with a scientific basis and moral consequences, and those who believe Spiritism is a science-religion. In Puerto Rico, this dispute can be seen in the divergence between the "scientific Spiritism" of William Colón and the interpretation of Spiritism as a religion-science by Telesforo Andino. In contrast to the situation in Brazil, in Puerto Rico this science/religion polarity has meant little for the development of the movement, probably because the number of Spiritists to whom such issues are accessible or important has been so small.

One can imagine multiplying Puerto Rico by a factor of fifty, creating a world in which "Colónistas" debate with "Andinistas" and in which the diverse wings of Spiritism align with regions and federations. One would then have something similar to the Spiritist movement in Brazil. These potential internal differences, however, have been overshadowed by what is a more meaningful division for Puerto Rican Spiritists, albeit one that expresses itself in terms of a rhetoric of religion and science: the "scientific Spiritists," who read and follow the teachings of Kardec, versus the "popular Spiritists," the so-called *espiriteros,* who have altars and who practice healing rather than study doctrine. The differences in Brazil between "evangelical" and "scientific" Spiritists seem in Puerto Rico to collapse into a single category of "scientific Spiritism." In turn, scientific Spiritism is defined in opposition to Puerto Rican "popular Spiritism," which may be compared with what is sometimes called Spiritist-line Umbanda in Brazil (Brown 1986), a point that one Puerto Rican Spiritist recognized in a short article written for *Cosmos* (Ceccarini 1952).

Thus, the relative lack of vitality of Puerto Rican Spiritism in comparison to Brazilian Spiritism may be explained in large part by the small size of Puerto Rico. It is also possible, though, that state repression and polemical attacks by the Catholic church and medical profession in Brazil may have had the paradoxical effect of invigorating the Brazilian Spiritist movement, and that the relative absence of persecution in Puerto Rico may have contributed to the relative anomie of Spiritism there. Certainly state repression gives the intellectuals much more power, for during these periods the Spiritist centers must close ranks behind the intellectuals and the federations, and the federations then have an opportunity to impose Kardecian orthodoxy. Enjoying a different political culture, the various centers of popular Spiritism in Puerto Rico have been free to go their own way and can pay less attention to questions of doctrinal purity.

In addition to these factors, the different pattern of the religious system in the two countries also warrants consideration. Nestor Rodríguez Escudero attributes what he views as the decline of Spiritism on the island to the growth of Pentecostalism, and Puerto Rico's colonial status has meant that it has been more open to U.S. Protestant missionary activity than most parts of Brazil, possibly even with the support of the U.S. government at different times. In Brazil, Pentecostalism is also growing rapidly, but it does not seem to have sapped the vitality of the Spiritist movement. This may be because Spiritism gains strength not only from converting former Umbandists but also from the peculiar relationship between Candomblé and national identity, the spirit idiom having become part of "Brazilianness." In Puerto Rico, the Afro-American religions do not have such an important role, and many regard them as a foreign import that came in with the Cubans who arrived after Castro came to power.

These speculations raise questions that might be answered by comparative analysis focusing on other countries—e.g., Argentina, where Afro-American religions are also relatively weak; Venezuela, where they are stronger in the coastal areas; and Mexico, where indigenous religions have played a more important role and where non-Kardecian forms of Spiritism have also emerged. Furthermore, a comparative study of the role of state repression and polemical attacks by the Catholic church and medical profession would also be revealing. The Puerto Rican case, then, provides another piece in the puzzle and increases our understanding of the historical development of Spiritism in Latin America, but it also demonstrates the need for more comparative analysis.

NOTES

Introduction

1. I refer here to sociological and anthropological formulations such as Bastide's ([1960] 1978) on interpenetration and Kirsch's (1977) on complexity. It is left up to the reader to determine whether or not recognizing an implicit order implies the label "modern" or "postmodern," a criterion that Jameson (1984) invokes in his distinction between pastiche and collage.

2. See, for example, the studies by the sociologists Roger Bastide ([1960] 1978, 1967) and Cândido Camargo (1961, 1973); the articles of the historian Donald Warren (1968a, 1968b, 1984) on nineteenth-century Spiritism; the sociologist J. Parke Renshaw's dissertation (1969), which focused on the Spiritist movement in Campinas; the anthropologist Sidney Greenfield's research (1986, 1987) on patronage relations and Spiritist healers; an article on the medium Francisco Cândido "Chico" Xavier by the anthropologist Luiz Eduardo Soares (1979); and the anthropologist Maria Cavalcanti's ethnography (1983) of a Spiritist center and institute in Rio. Cavalcanti noted the absence of work on the intellectual elite of the Spiritist movement, and she suggested that it "would be interesting to research the relationship between Spiritism and official science, whose theories and currents the Spiritists discuss" (1983: 76).

3. Umbanda is a spirit-mediumship religion that emerged in twentieth-century, urban Brazil. "Umbanda" and many related terms are defined in the Glossary.

4. Cavalcanti (1983: 26–29) has discussed a division, parallel to the second and third of Bastide's categories, between "evangelical" and "intellectual" Spiritists. Spiritists reject the inclusion of Umbanda under the umbrella term "Spiritism," and in this study I will follow the Spiritists' usage of the term. Thus, "Spiritist" will mean someone who follows the teachings of Allan Kardec and belongs to the Kardecist movement (again, see the Glossary).

5. Brandão's division of the mediumistic area into three stratified domains corresponds in a rough way to Bastide's distinctions among Spiritism, Umbanda, and Macumba magic (Bastide [1960] 1978; Bastide 1967: 11; cf. Hess 1991e). Umbanda, however, is very difficult to characterize, and social scientists disagree among themselves regarding the relative importance of middle-class participation and bourgeois ideology in Umbanda (e.g., Brown 1986; Ortiz 1978; Negrão 1979), but these differing positions share with Bastide and Brandão the assumption that Umbanda plays a mediating role in the religious system. On the whole, the evidence supports the argument that Umbanda mediates class and status conflicts and even articulates and dramatizes them. Because of this, many of the recent studies on Umbanda implicitly put this religion in an intermediary position at the "center" of the spirit-mediumship field: an "Umbanda centrism." While this framework is correct as far as it goes, in effect it diverts interest from Spiritism and blinds us to its own mediating position in a broader field of ideologies.

6. For example, recent studies on Umbanda by Birman (1985), Brown (1977, 1979, 1985, 1986), Concone and Negrão (1985), Negrão (1979), Ortiz (1978), and Pechman (1982) consider relations between Umbanda and the Catholic church, political parties, the state, and political ideologies. Another group of studies has examined Spiritist and Umbanda healing as a form of parallel or complementary medicine. For example, Milner's dissertation (1980) examines the healing practices of Umbanda and a Spiritist federation in Rio in the framework of complementary medical systems; Droogers has examined Spiritist healing from the perspectives of national ideology (1988) and symbolic efficacy (1989); and studies by Loyola (1984), Montero (1985), and Perelberg (1980) have examined the issue of parallel or complementary medical systems, even though they have not examined Spiritist medicine in detail. Also see the bachelor's thesis by Keefe (1976), who provides a case study of healing in an Umbanda center and in a mixed Spiritist-Umbanda center in Rio, and the chapter in Brody 1973 that includes descriptions of his visits to Spiritist centers in Rio. Perhaps closest to the perspective of the present book is the work of DaMatta (1981), B. Dantas (1982), and Maggie (1986, 1988), who consider the interrelations of elite ideologies, the state, and Afro-Brazilian religion and magic.

7. A similar point of reference is Jameson's (1984) discussion of the destruction of the "autonomy" of what he calls the "cultural sphere," or literary and artistic discourse; however, he seems to leave unquestioned the autonomy of scientific discourse.

8. I adopt the terminology of "orthodoxy" and "heterodoxy" in order to emphasize that such categories are coconstituted and reproduce themselves on multiple levels. One might distinguish between "heterodoxy," which refers to the status of ideas, and "marginal," which refers to the social position of the actors. (I resist the term "deviant science" because Spiritists do not see themselves as deviant.) Heterodox ideas and groups are generally marginal, but this is not always the case. On the sociology of "marginal" or "deviant" science, see Ben-Yehuda 1985, Dolby 1979, Tiryakin 1974, Truzzi [1971] 1974, Wallis 1979, and Wallis and Morley 1976. On the more specific topic of the social studies and parapsychology, see Collins and Pinch 1979, 1982, Allison 1979, and McClenon 1984. In the context of this literature, one might read *Spirits and Scientists* as an elaboration of the idea that Gieryn's concept of "boundary-work" can be viewed as cultural and social drama.

9. I will not argue that one of these systems of thought is "ideology" as opposed to some other "true knowledge" represented by another system. Rather, I will examine the

ideological dimension of each system, including that of the social scientist. The phrase "ideological dimension" does not refer only to the narrow, instrumentalist aspect of an ideology, the aspect that Geertz describes as "strain and interest" (1973: 201); the term also includes the social meaning or the cultural values that the thought articulates, including the way each group's ideas mark the group diacritically with respect to other groups. As a result, the method here involves moving back and forth between the structural question of how ideology marks social differences and articulates cultural values and the instrumental question of how it serves social interests. My goal, therefore, is to strike a balance between the symbolic approach (e.g., Durkheim and Mauss 1963; Lévi-Strauss [1962] 1966: ch. 2; Geertz 1973: ch. 8) and the instrumentalist approach (e.g., Bourdieu 1975; Bourdieu 1982; Giddens 1988). This goal provides a second reason for using the term "ideological arena" instead of ideology as a "cultural system" or a "field."

10. My occasional use of wordplay is also part of this strategy. With plays on the meaning of words such as "poltergeist" and "trance," I hope to signal how patterns at one level of discourse recur at other levels. For a more chronological view of the history of the Spiritist movement in Brazil, see Hess 1987b.

11. The term "reference text" intentionally invokes a loose comparison with the organization of Lévi-Strauss 1975 around a "reference myth," but the adoption of shifting perspectives on the ideological system might also be compared to Gregory Bateson's approach to the Naven ritual (1958). Boon's (1982: 9–21) discussion of Frazer, Lévi-Strauss, Bateson, and the functionalist monograph was influential, as was Michael Taussig's monumental, interdisciplinary synthesis of criticism, history, and ethnography (1987).

Chapter 1: The Elements of Spiritism in Brazil

1. The terms "mediate," "mediation," and "intermediary" may refer either to a structural position between two points or an active, intentional effort to adjudicate or synthesize two opposing positions. Throughout this book, the term will be used in the first sense.

2. A small group of Spiritists accepts the teachings of Kardec's contemporary, Jean-Baptiste Roustaing, who promulgated a Docetic Christian doctrine. Although this group controls the national federalizing body, Roustaingism has little influence at the local level outside the state of Rio de Janeiro. Ubaldists are the followers of Pietro Ubaldi, a twentieth-century, mystical Spiritist from Italy.

3. Spiritists view reincarnation as one of the crucial distinguishing features between Spiritism and Spiritualism, but as Macklin (1974: 390) points out, this should not be confused with the key historical factors that influenced the differences in reception of Spiritism and Spiritualism in Latin America.

4. Barnes (n.d.: 37). Spiritists believe that the reason Spiritualists do not accept reincarnation is that they are racist: they think white North Americans are unwilling to accept the possibility that they might have had African blood in one of their past existences. Although this theory is interesting because it reveals Brazilian perceptions of the United States, as an explanation it is rendered problematic by the fact that nineteenth-century Spiritualists were actively involved in antislavery campaigns (Moore 1977: 77ff.). Renshaw provides the alternative explanation that in Britain "Anglican orthodoxy and the traditional directions of English philosophy have militated against the acceptance of the idea of reincarnation" (1969: 61). It is doubtful, however, that North American Spiritualists, who in the nineteenth century often came from backgrounds in Unitarianism and Universalism, were concerned with this issue (Moore 1977: 49): the leading figure of nineteenth-century

Spiritualism, Andrew Jackson Davis, denied that he or Spiritualism were Christian (Ellwood 1979: 97). An alternative approach might examine how the strong emphasis on individualism in Anglo-Saxon cultures conflicts with the pluralistic (or relational) notion of identity implied in reincarnation; however, one would also have to take into account how North American New Age thought has refashioned reincarnation into an acceptable part of the quest for personal identity (Hess 1991d).

5. In addition, some categories of Spiritists—Roustaingists, Ubaldists, and others—accept Kardec's teachings only with qualifications. One Spiritist intellectual (Abreu 1950: 71) distinguishes between "Spiritists"—those who accept the fundamental principles of Kardec's doctrine in *The Book of the Spirits*—and "Kardecists," or "Christian Spiritists," who accept the evangelical aspect of Kardec's teachings (what I am calling evangelical Spiritism). On the question of Spiritism as a religion, see Dias 1985.

6. Some Spiritists even refer to Xavier as the "pope" of Brazilian Spiritism, and they speak of the younger medium Divaldo Franco as the heir apparent. Although Spiritist intellectuals reject this comparison with Catholicism, they still place a great value on the writings of Kardec and Xavier and, like the evangelists, refer to Kardec as "the codifier" and to his doctrine as "the basis" of Spiritism.

7. In contrast, Spiritualist publications occasionally mention Kardec as an important Spiritualist of the nineteenth century, but for Spiritualists his writings do not have the canonical status that they have in Brazil. Spiritists believe that this is because North Americans have their own Kardec: namely, the nineteenth-century medium Andrew Jackson Davis. However, Davis's writings do not receive nearly the same attention in Spiritualist services that Kardec's writings receive in Spiritist meetings. Although the National Spiritualist Association of Churches keeps a backlist of Davis's writings, his writings do not have the same authority that those of Kardec have for Brazilian Spiritists, and in general North American Spiritualism has no central figure similar to Kardec in Brazilian Spiritism. This difference in the role of a mediating doctrine corresponds to the Protestant value of a direct relationship between the believer and God, in contrast to the Catholic value of the intermediary institutions of the church and church doctrine. In short, although the Spiritist view of the discovery of spirit communication as the "third revelation" (after those of Moses and Christ) represents a Protestant-like revision of theology, Spiritists value the doctrine that resulted from this third revelation in a way that resonates with the values of the surrounding Catholic culture.

8. Some Spiritists divide their sessions into a "theoretical" and a "practical" part; that is, doctrinal study versus works of mediumship and charity. Cavalcanti (1983: 62–63) found a slightly different division: the Spiritists she studied in Rio divided their activities into sessions of study and practice versus works of charity. She adds that in the everyday language of the center, the Spiritists spoke of sessions of study, charity, and mediumship. In her center, then, there appear to have been three major categories.

9. Relying on his research in Rio de Janeiro, Milner (1980: 112–19) adds to these three basic types of *passes* four others: the "animic" or "animistic" shock; the Pasteur; *passes* for children; and self-placement or self-*passes*. Of these four types, I sometimes saw self-*passes* but witnessed the first type on only one occasion, during a disobsession.

10. "Our Home" (Nosso Lar) is both the name of the Spiritist "heaven" as well as the name of the medium Chico Xavier's famous center, which is located in Uberaba, Minas Gerais.

11. In his later work (1985, 1986), DaMatta tends to substitute the term "relational society" for the ethic of the "person," a term he used in *Carnavais* (1978). DaMatta uses the term "individual" both for actors not related by personal ties and for actors related by universalistic values. Since it is possible to confuse these two meanings, I use the term "outsider" for the first type of relationship.

12. See Parsons' comparison of North American and Latin American "value-orientation patterns" (1951: 182–200). Regarding Anglo-Saxon religious values, this study draws on Bellah 1974, Thomas 1971, and Weber [1904–5] 1958.

13. Interviews with the FEERJ leadership (November 12, 1984) and with representatives of the Union of Spiritist Societies of the State of Rio de Janeiro (USEERJ, November 7, 1985). The latter group is allied politically with the FEB but does not follow its Roustaingist ideology.

14. Interview with João Bovino, president of the Spiritist Federation of the State of São Paulo (June 12, 1985). When Antônio Schileiro of USE São Paulo visited the Spiritist Medical Association of São Paulo on April 13, 1985, he presented a very different description, which was accompanied by an organizational diagram that located USE São Paulo at the top and FEESP as just one of the federations under its auspices. I also spoke with Paulo Toledo Machado, the former general secretary of USE São Paulo (July 26, 1985), who explained that at one point USE and the FEESP had interlocking boards of directors.

15. Soares makes this point as an aside in his article. Although he promised to develop this interesting suggestion in another article, such a piece, as far as I have been able to ascertain, has never been written. Integralism was a Brazilian fascist movement similar to the contemporary Italian fascism of Benito Mussolini.

16. These ministries are organized spatially into two overlapping triangles. On the triangle and the Brazilian cultural preference for mediation, see DaMatta 1982. The government engulfs the entire formal structure of the colony; in Erving Goffman's terms (1961), Nosso Lar is a "total institution."

Chapter 2: Spiritist Intellectuals and Their Work

1. Although it is true that to some extent most Spiritists at times play the role of intellectual, the term "Spiritist intellectual" will be used here to refer to the actor who plays the role of intellectual consistently and who is affiliated with the specialized, Spiritist intellectual organizations. Although Spiritist intellectuals form an elite in terms of their class and educational background, they do not form a political elite in terms of control of the Spiritist movement's federations. These federations generally have a mixture of intellectual and evangelical Spiritists at the helm, and it is among the leaders of the federations that the two roles tend to merge.

2. Before he died, Deolindo Amorim was the leader of the ICEB, and when I visited the institute in 1985, its leadership rested with Krishnamurti de Carvalho Dias and the psychiatrist Jorge Andrea. I did not spend a great deal of time researching the ICEB, because Maria Cavalcanti has discussed it in her ethnographic study O Mundo Invisível (1983) and because Cary Milner (1980) has done research on the union affiliated with it. I did meet with Andrea and Dias several times, and I gave a guest lecture (comparing Brazilian Spiritism and North American Spiritualism) for the members of the União Espírita do Estado do Rio de Janeiro.

3. Again, any one actor may fit within several of these categories—and frequently does in this land of syncretisms—but as roles these categories are analytically distinguishable.

4. I attempted an interview with Quevedo on July 4, 1985, which he declined. On the silencing of Quevedo, see Veja magazine, October 22, 1986, p. 85. During my summer trip in 1988, I met with one of his colleagues, Padre Edvino Friderichs, who informed me that the prohibition had since been lifted.

5. Interview (February 4, 1986). Kloppenburg stated that Quevedo was under prohibition because "he did not stay within the boundaries of science."

6. Also see Brown 1986 and Greenfield 1986 on the relationship between personalism (or patron-client ties) and spirits.

7. There are striking parallels between the way Spiritist scientific thought reifies spirits and the way social science thought "relativizes" them. The Spiritists' strategy—to make the spirits scientifically real—is in a sense the opposite of the social scientists' strategy to make the spirits "symbolic," to treat them under the rubric of "social fact" or "cultural relativism." Yet relativism has much the same double result as reification. On the elite side, both reification and relativism make spirits into objects of scientific inquiry and therefore desacralize them. On the popular side, just as reification legitimizes spirits by making them scientifically real, so relativism legitimizes spirits by finding in them a source of social meaning and political expression. Thus, the social sciences operate on a two-way street of elite and popular ideology which is similar to that of Spiritism, and the Spiritists' move to encompass the popular discourse of the spirit world with a science of the spirit world is parallel to the social scientists' move to encompass Spiritist science with a social science of the science of the spirit world. The destabilizing implications of outflanking the "science of the spirits" with a "science of the science of the spirits" will be examined in more detail at the end of this book, where I discuss one Spiritist's solution to the problem of cultural relativism. For now, the purpose is to map out in detail the various types of elite/popular mediation in Spiritist scientific thought.

8. DaMatta (1986: 31) notes that the Portuguese word for "work," *trabalho*, is derived from the Latin word for "torture." (Less seriously, one might apply the same etymology to the English word "travel," or the torture of not working in a culture that embraces the work ethic.) See the comparison of work ethics in Moog 1964: 116–18, 134–37.

9. Of course, most recent social studies of science indicate that, in the arena of borderline science certainly, Mertonian norms—universalism, communality, organized skepticism, and disinterestedness (Merton 1973)—are not the norm (e.g., Ben-Yehuda 1985: 171–74; McClenon 1984: 26–37; Pinch 1979; Pinch and Collins 1984; see also Merton 1976 on counternorms). My point here is not to make any dubious claims about the nature of science as a normative activity; instead, I am merely making the comparative point that the parapsychology of the Parapsychological Association comes much closer to a pattern of universalism than does the parapsychology of Brazilian Spiritism or Catholicism.

10. What they perhaps do not realize is the extent to which this tradition of debate is based on the model of parliamentary democracy, in which actors may exchange heated opinions without causing violent ruptures, because they agree to follow the rules and speak as scientific citizens and not as self-motivated individuals. (On the "citizen" in the Brazilian context, see DaMatta 1985.) The research on European and North American parapsychology that is presented in this section is based on extensive journal reading, attendance at several conferences of the Parapsychological Association, and informal conversations with members of this organization. I am merely attempting to reflect their own views of themselves, and I use a description of their conventions of social action as a point of comparison in order to make it easier to understand Brazilian Spiritist parapsychology.

11. It is difficult to translate the ostensibly simple phrase "debates e perguntas" into English, because translation here also involves a transliteration of values, as Lima has noted in his comments on *discutir*, "to discuss," and *debater*, "to debate" (1985: 51). Translation of the phrase as "debates and questions" might offer a literal solution, but it would pass over the cultural nuances. The studied politeness of Brazilians who are *debatando* might be best translated into English as "discussing" rather than "debating." Likewise, *perguntar* is closer to the English word "to ask" or even "to request" than "to question," especially in the sense

of critically questioning ideas, texts, and so on, for which the Portuguese word *questionar* would come closer. Thus, the difference in Portuguese between *debater* or *perguntar* versus *discutir* and *questionar* would correspond, at least in some usages, to the difference between the insider and the outsider within a framework of particularistic values.

Chapter 3: Kardec's *Book of the Spirits*

1. "Banquét. Réponse de M. Allan Kardec," *Revue Spirite*, 1860, p. 301.

2. "Le Spiritisme à Lyon," *Revue Spirite*, 1861, p. 290. For his earlier statements, see "Propagation du spiritisme," *Revue Spirite*, 1858, p. 241, and "Réponse de M. Allan Kardec a Monsieur le rédacteur de la *Gazette de Lyon*," *Revue Spirite*, 1860, p. 294.

3. Regarding the size of the Spiritist movement, a survey conducted by the *Revue Spirite* shortly after Kardec's death in 1869 claimed 600,000 Spiritists in France and 1 million in Europe (Vartier 1971: 308). The total population of France at the time, according to the general census of 1875, was about 37 million. The Spiritist estimates are probably exaggerated; they should be compared to the French estimate of 3 million U.S. Spiritualists in 1854 (Vartier 1971: 68), contrasting with McCabe's (1920: 64ff.) early-twentieth-century history, which puts the membership peak of the U.S. Spiritualist movement in the mid-1850s at one-half to three-quarters of a million people in a total population of 25 million. In Britain, the "Two Worlds' First Annual Census of Spiritualist Societies," dated 1868, estimated the average attendance, a more restricted statistic, at below 30,000 in a total population of 22 million (Nelson 1969: app. table 3A; Lewis 1873: 34). All of this could lead to an essay on the cultural variations of statistical measurement.

4. "Réponses à l'invitation . . ." *Revue Spirite*, 1862, p. 278.

5. There was also a rival group of Spiritualists in Paris, but they do not appear to have been very important numerically. This group published a *Revue Spiritualiste* and, like the British Spiritualists, did not accept Kardec's endorsement of reincarnation (Salgues 1862).

6. "Variétés. L'Index de la cour de Rome," *Revue Spirite*, 1864, p. 191; Kardec [1868] 1944c: ch. 15, #65–#67.

7. See Kardec [1859] 1944e: chs. 8, 14. The historian Donald Warren (1984: 59–60) argues that after the Lourdes phenomena Kardec developed a "miraclephobia" and that the second edition of *The Book of the Spirits* omits a significant paragraph on healing that appeared as question #245 in the first edition of 1857. That paragraph, however, appears in chapter 10 of the first edition; and many other paragraphs of chapter 10 appeared again, not in the second edition of *The Book of the Spirits* but in *The Book of the Mediums*. Among the paragraphs that reappear in *The Book of the Mediums*, one finds the question on healing ([1859] 1944e: ch. 26, §293, #24) with a similar answer. Although the tone of the answer is slightly less enthusiastic than that in *The Book of the Spirits*, there is no significant difference in meaning. Thus, Kardec's lack of support for the curing mediumship is still dubious; one is on firmer ground regarding Kardec's rejection of miracles (which, however, appears to be more generalized and not limited to the issue of healing). Kardec's negative attitude toward miracles may also have been a response to the more favorable use of the term in the rival *Revue Spiritualiste* (e.g., 1858: 200–205; 1859: 143–53, 450; 1861, 4.1: 12).

8. On the Morzines studies, see "Étude sur les possédés de Morzine," *Revue Spirite*, 1862, pp. 353–63; and 1863, pp. 1–9, 33–41, 101–3, 133–42.

9. Among the studies of the early history of psychical research and its relationships to Spiritualism, see Cerullo 1982, Gauld 1968, Moore 1977, and F. Turner 1974.

10. Charles Richet (1923: 33) notes that the short-lived Société de Psychologie Physiologique preceded the *Annales*.

11. This idea recalls the seventeenth-century pansophists, philosophers who attempted to forge a unity among Christian sects through their new science (Manuel and Manuel 1979: 206ff.).

12. The historical Fénelon openly criticized Jansenism, perhaps because he hoped to return to the good graces of the Catholic church, from which he had fallen after his defense of quietism, another Catholic reform movement. Fénelon also defended Augustinian ideas on grace and free will, ideas that are comparable to Kardec's doctrine on karma, reincarnation, and free will (see Chapter 1 above).

13. "Cours publics de Spiritisme à Lyon et à Bordeaux," *Revue Spirite*, 1864, pp. 152–55. For an early Catholic-Spiritist interchange, see "Réponse à la réplique de M. l'abbé Chesnel, dans *l'Univers* [May 28, 1859]," *Revue Spirite*, 1859, pp. 191–92. Also see the discussion in Wantuil and Thiesen 1980: 267ff., 282.

14. Kloppenburg 1960: 113 and "Variétés. L'Index de la cour de Rome," *Revue Spirite*, 1864, p. 191. The position did not change with the successors of Pius IX; for example, in 1898 Pope Leo XIII added automatic writing to the list of injunctions (Thurston 1933: 17).

15. See Wantuil and Thiesen 1980: 221. Kardec's report of his travels in 1862, which was published separately from the *Revue Spirite*, does not discuss the auto-da-fé, although it mentions attacks against the Spiritist movement. (Also see "Voyage Spirite en 1862," *Revue Spirite*, 1862, pp. 321–22.) There is no mention of the auto-da-fé in the travel reports of 1861 published in the *Revue Spirite*, despite the fact that Kardec's meetings with Spiritists in Bordeaux took place only a few days after the auto-da-fé. See "Réunion générale des Spirites bordelais. Le 14 octobre 1861," *Revue Spirite*, 1861, p. 330, and "Discours et toast de M. Allan Kardec" *Revue Spirite*, 1861, p. 356.

16. The historical account that follows is based on Downs 1975: 71–77 and Silber 1960: 235–49.

17. There is some disagreement among biographers regarding Kardec's activities between 1818 and 1824; the most probable accounts have him staying in the Pestalozzi school (Blackwell 1875: 9) or studying drafting at a school led by one of Pestalozzi's students (Vartier 1971: 27).

18. The biographical materials of this paragraph are collated (codified?) from Blackwell 1875, Moreil 1961, Sausse 1952, and Vartier 1971.

19. It is likely that his experience with stage magic enhanced his sense of sophistication and allowed Kardec to believe that he would easily have caught the mediums if they had been cheating.

20. Following Kardec, Mesmerism and magnetism are treated here as synonyms. Mesmerism/magnetism is the precursor of hypnotism, but it differs from hypnotism in both technique and theory. Whereas hypnotism tends to use verbal suggestion and envisions the resulting trancelike state as a natural process, Mesmerism used magnetic *passes* and envisioned the resulting trancelike state as caused by the flow of vital fluids. Several sources document the links between Mesmer and hermeticism. See Pattie 1956 for the influence of John Mead on Mesmer; Darnton 1968: 14 and Wyckoff 1975: 26 for that of Fludd, Van Helmont, and Maxwell; and Roberts 1972: 102 for the influence of Rosicrucian freemasonry.

21. A "somnambule" is someone who is in a sleeplike or trancelike condition due to magnetism. Darnton adds that Willermoz was also a good friend of Louis-Claude de Sainte-Martin, France's leading proponent of Martinism, a doctrine that mixed cabalism and mystic Catholicism (1968: 68–69). Colinon (1959: 41) speculates that Kardec met

Willermoz, but Vartier (1971: 116) argues from a study by Antoine Faivre of Willermoz's correspondence that such a meeting did not take place.

22. Respectively "Le magnétisme et le spiritisme," *Revue Spirite*, 1858, p. 92, and "Variétés: Les banquets magnétiques," *Revue Spirite*, 1858, p. 176. Also see "Le magnétisme devant l'Académie," *Revue Spirite*, 1860, pp. 6–11.

23. Samuel Hahnemann, founder of homeopathy, used the similar term "vital force," and he and Kardec both lived in Paris during the 1830s. Although there is no evidence that Kardec knew Hahnemann personally, the former wrote favorably of homeopathy in the *Revue Spirite* and stated that the majority of doctors who accepted Spiritism were homeopaths. See "Jean Reynaud et les précurseurs du Spiritisme," *Revue Spirite*, 1863, p. 234. In addition, the discarnate Hahnemann was one of the first spirits with whom Kardec spoke (Kardec [1890] 1944f: 280).

24. This move is similar to that of Kardec's German precursor, Johann Heinrich Jung-Stilling (1834: 372). See also Podmore 1902: 95.

25. "Charles Fourier, Louis Jordan et la réincarnation," *Revue Spirite*, 1862, p. 374. Kardec responded (pp. 375–76) that reincarnation was a law, not someone's opinion. For his later response, see "Jean Reynaud et les précurseurs du Spiritisme," *Revue Spirite*, 1863, p. 232.

26. See Yates's discussion (1964: 36) of the *Asclepius* of Ficino.

27. The Brazilian Spiritist medium Hercílio Maes later wrote a book called *Life on the Planet Mars* (1965), which describes a world strikingly similar to life on the planet Brazil (Hess 1989b). Unlike Kardec's spirit, Maes's spirit describes Martians as a more highly evolved people.

28. Darnton 1968: 67, 139; Podmore 1902: 82; Roberts 1972: 104, 294–99. On Swedenborg as a hermetic philosopher, see the comparisons with Fludd, Ripley, Norton, Van Helmont, and others in Hitchcock 1865: 204. Furthermore, one finds in Swedenborg's descriptions of "the sun in heaven" and "the four quarters of heaven" echoes of the City of Adocentyn of the *Picatrix;* that is, the Egyptian City of the Sun with the animated statues (Yates 1964: 54ff.). Yates (1972) further traces the image of the animated statues in the Palatinate of Frederick the Elector; and it does not seem too far-fetched to see in the somnambules and mediums of Willermoz and, in the later Kardec, a transformation of this hermetic image.

29. This edition and the FEB edition ([1860] 1944d) make a mistake in numbers after #1010; in the IDS edition ([1860] 1983) this question is #1016.

30. Renshaw (1969: 177–80) compares and contrasts the two groups, but he does not suggest any connection.

31. Although in Brazil Spiritists as well as positivists were republicans, I found no overlap when I compared the leadership of the two movements (using Costa 1964; Nachman 1977; Wantuil 1969) at the end of the nineteenth century. Furthermore, the journalist Ubiratan Machado suggests (1983: 175) that the relationship between the positivists, who were "materialists," and the Spiritists was antagonistic. Machado uncovers two interesting cases: one intellectual who was first a Spiritist then became a positivist (p. 114) and another (a character taken from the literature of the period) who was a positivist before becoming a Spiritist (p. 185). This pattern of complementary distribution provides further evidence in favor of the interpretation that the relationship between positivism and Spiritism was oppositional, if not antagonistic. Likewise, Adolfo Bezerra de Menezes, the "Brazilian Kardec," effected a sustained critique of the materialist tendency of positivists (1939: 30ff.), and the positivist influence of the first years of the Old Republic (the 1890s) contributed to the atmosphere of state repression of the Spiritist movement.

32. Respectively: Dr. Déchambre, "La Doctrine spirite," *Gazette Médicale, Hebdomaire de*

Médicine et Chirurgie, cited in Machado 1983: 99; and *Presse,* January 8, 1863, cited in "Sur la folie spirite," *Revue Spirite,* 1863, pp. 51–59.

33. See "Les muscle craquers," *Revue Spirite,* 1859, pp. 141–49, and Moore 1977: 27.

34. Michael Kenny (1986; cf. Hess 1987d) makes the similar but narrower point that the idiom of spirits is very similar to the idiom of multiple personalities.

Chapter 4: Menezes' *Insanity Through a New Prism*

1. Some Spiritists today add that the clients must also study Kardec, since their thoughts may continue to attract obsessing spirits, but Menezes does not discuss this point.

2. The Biblioteca Nacional houses some Spiritist periodicals from this period, but most were not available for consultation due to their poor condition. Likewise, the Brazilian Spiritist Federation houses a Rare Books Collection, but the FEB leaders would not make these documents available for my research because they were "too delicate to be touched." I was unable to locate any Spiritist documents from the nineteenth century in São Paulo and Curitiba; therefore, I had to work from secondary sources that are written either from a pro-FEB and Roustaingist perspective (e.g., Wantuil 1969) or from a Paulista or Kardecist perspective (e.g., Abreu 1950). Thus, one does not find a biography of Angeli Torteroli in Wantuil's collection of biographies, even though Torteroli appears to have been a major figure and a leader of the scientific Spiritists, but Torteroli does figure in the articles of the Paulista Spiritist Mauro Quintella in the *Jornal Espírita* (January 1988, and September 1985). An additional problem is that some secondary sources (e.g., Aquarone 1982; S. B. Soares 1962) integrate fictionalized conversations into their narratives. Given these circumstances, I was unable to confirm the original date of publication of Menezes (1897) 1939, which appears to have been first published as a series of articles in *O Reformador.*

Several of the secondary sources are written in the form of biographies of Bezerra de Menezes and other early Spiritist leaders, and this brings up another interesting question (in addition to those discussed in Appendix 1) regarding genres and cultural values: Spiritists tend to write their history in a personalistic way, seeing it through the prism of people rather than institutions, a perspective which also allows them to smooth over the numerous factional divisions that punctuate Spiritist history. These divisions come out in some of the earlier documents still in circulation (e.g., Cirne 1935; Richard 1914; Richard in G. Ribeiro 1941) and in histories not published by the FEB (e.g., Abreu 1950; Aquarone 1982; Dos Anjos 1978, 1979, 1980). For a more complete overview of the history of the Spiritist movement, see Hess 1987b; and for a comparative history of Spiritism in Brazil and Puerto Rico, see Appendix 3.

3. Canuto Abreu (1950: 58), himself a "scientific" Paulista Spiritist of the twentieth century, describes the division in terms of "scientists" (psychical researchers, occultists, and Kardecists) versus "mystics" (Roustaingists, Swedenborgians, and Theosophists). The term "Kardecists" is not clearly defined, but it seems to include intellectual as well as evangelical Spiritists.

4. The inevitable question emerges: Was Menezes a Roustaingist? Boaventura Kloppenburg (1960: 45) and Canuto Abreu (1981: 67) claim that he was, and Luciano Dos Anjos (April 1979: 3) states that in 1895 Menezes supported the change in the FEB statutes in favor of studying Roustaing. However, Francisco Aquarone (1982: 95) calls him a Kardecist, and the issue is still being debated between Paulista and FEB Spiritists (Innocencio 1986).

5. *Revista Espírita do Brasil,* May 1930, p. 117; July 1930, p. 181; August 1930, pp. 217–18.

6. Dos Anjos (June/July 1979: 15). Further evidence in favor of the *receitista*-Roustaingist linkage is Ubiratan Machado's point (1983: 148) that Bittencourt Sampaio, who was a *receitista* medium, was one of the first Brazilians to embrace Roustaingism. Dos Anjos (April 1979: 14) notes that in 1902 FEB President Cirne supported the deletion of the federation statutes favoring the study of Roustaing. That same year, Cirne also began the project for a school for mediums, but it lasted only a few years and was abandoned until 1911, when Cirne attempted to revive the project. Cirne claims that this second attempt led to a "block of resistances" within the FEB board of directors and that the *receitistas* (homeopathic mediums) threatened to leave if Cirne were reelected (Cirne 1935: 268–70). The *receitistas* proved to have enough power to wrest the presidency from Cirne, and he lost his reelection bid in 1914. His failure to win reelection meant that the *receitistas* remained loyal to the FEB, but Cirne claims (1935: 273) that more than two-fifths of the FEB membership left during 1913 and 1914 (perhaps later forming the Spiritist League of Brazil). Dos Anjos (June/July 1979: 3) states that the school for mediums was closed immediately after Cirne left office; he also states that Cirne's successor, Aristides Spínola, was an arch-Roustaingist who supported new statutory reforms that reestablished the study of Roustaing in 1917 (June/July 1979: 3, 14; August/September 1979: 2)

7. Menezes was himself cured by a homeopathic medium, and this may have been a key factor in his conversion to Spiritism (Warren 1984: 61).

8. *O Reformador,* September 1965, pp. 19–20. A similar example of the hostile relations between the Spiritist movement and the Catholic church is the heated exchange between *O Reformador* and the Catholic organ *O Apóstolo* (U. Machado 1983: 153).

9. Because of the absence of official statistics for the period, indices of this rapid growth are problematic. One convenient index is the explosion of new Spiritist journals at the turn of the century, documented in C. Ramos 1978. Another is the growth of state Spiritist federations: by the mid-1930s, all of the major Spiritist state federations or leagues had been founded (Kloppenburg 1960: 20).

10. Donald Warren (1984: 77) makes the interesting point that one source of Menezes' doctrine might have been the popular healers of the Northeast, where Menezes grew up.

11. One exception was Henrique Roxo, professor and department chair of the College of Medicine of Rio de Janeiro (and known for having instituted the first courses in psychiatry there). Roxo argued that while the *espiritismo* of the Candomblés "should be banned as [it is] a source of insanity," the scientific *espiritismo* of Charles Richet "should be studied" (Roxo [1918] 1946). In neither case did Roxo use the word *espiritismo* in Kardec's sense, and he shows some confusion regarding the difference between Spiritism and psychical research; however, this lack of differentiation between Spiritism, psychical research, and dynamic psychiatry at the beginning of the twentieth century, together with the dominance of neurology, is what allowed Spiritists like Menezes to believe that they might revolutionize official medicine. See also R. Machado 1978.

12. See the Spiritist accounts by Inácio Ferreira (1962), Freitas Nobre (1981), and Jorge Rizzini (1979).

13. Although Menezes only poses his disobsession therapy as an alternative to neurological treatment, the Catholic rite of exorcism is also an implicit point of comparison (e.g., Menezes [1897] 1939: 170).

14. This student apparently did not attend the disobsession, and for Spiritists the absence of the client provides an argument in favor of the spiritic interpretation of the

treatment, in contrast to a skeptical interpretation that might attribute success to suggestion or to catharsis via dramatization.

Chapter 5: Poltergeists and Bricoleurs

1. Although the poltergeist-philosopher Jacques Derrida (1978: 285–87) "deconstructs" Claude Lévi-Strauss's (1966) division between the mythic thought of the bricoleur and the scientific thought of the engineer, it is quite possible that Lévi-Strauss had already recognized implicitly the bricolage-like nature of science when he referred to his work on myths as myths about myths, in which case Derrida's critique would represent a bricolage of elements already "present" in Lévi-Strauss's work. For our purposes, one need only assume that, at least in the case of heterodox science, scientific thought is also subject to a process of bricolage or reworking as it passes across cultures.

2. The poltergeist's work is therefore opposite to that of the bricoleur, the jack-of-all-trades who takes miscellaneous objects that are gathered together without any special order and finds for them some kind of useful role. The poltergeist takes things that are in place and creates mischief by disorganizing them, whereas the bricoleur takes things out of place and creates utility by organizing them.

3. The quotation marks in the title are original. Suzano is a city on the outskirts of São Paulo. Andrade has subsequently republished this study as part of a book on Brazilian poltergeists (1988a).

4. Andrade focuses his discussion on practitioners of Quimbanda or black magic, but many Spiritists are less specific. Frequently they lump together Umbanda, Quimbanda, Candomblé, Macumba, and other more or less Afro-Brazilian magico-religious systems under the rubric of "black magic."

5. I reveal the identity of "Lawrence Blacksmith" with Andrade's permission.

6. Ironically, this comment associates Spiritist parapsychology with the leftist (and perhaps implicitly "materialist") third party; certainly the commonality that Andrade saw was that both were underdogs. However, Andrade also distances himself from Spiritist orthodoxy, and probably this is why he says he is "not even Eduardo Supplicy."

7. See Andrade 1984a for a detailed discussion of the differences among the astral body, the vital body, the BOM, and the "cúpula."

8. Quevedo 1969 (Portuguese edition, 1974).

9. For historical accounts of these movements, see Cerullo 1982, Gauld 1968, and R. L. Moore 1977.

10. See McVaugh and Mauskopf 1976 and Mauskop and McVaugh 1980.

11. Alvarado 1984: 392–95. For another English-language account of the Suzano poltergeist, see Playfair 1975. Playfair worked with Andrade and provides a report very similar in perspective to that of his mentor.

12. During my field trip in June and July of 1988, I met with Edvino Friderichs, S.J., who said that Quevedo has since been released from the prohibition.

13. Faria has since pointed out to me that the word *anômalo* in Portuguese means "pathological" or "abnormal." Here I am using the term more in Thomas Kuhn's (1970) sense—that which does not fit the existing paradigms. In this case, the framework is parapsychology in Brazil, which generally is either Catholic or Spiritist.

14. Anthropologists use the Polynesian term "mana" to refer to a magical or supernatural power, and the Greek term "doxa" to refer to the realm of accepted opinion and assumptions that underlies disputes over orthodoxies and heterodoxies.

Chapter 6: Spirit Surgeons and Wounded Laws

1. "Campanha de Esclarecimento Sobre Trabalhos de Cura, Segunda Fase—VII," in *Folha Espírita* 12: 136 (July 1985): 6.

2. Lecture given at the First Brazilian Symposium on Parapsychology, Medicine, and Spiritism, São Paulo, October 26, 1985.

3. On the comparison of Arigó and Aleijadinho, see the Spiritist J. Herculano Pires (1963, c. 1973).

4. Some versions of the Arigó biography discuss a multinational "phalanx" of spirit doctors, but Dr. Fritz is by far the most important of Arigó's spirit controls.

5. See Jorge c. 1964; Pires 1963, c. 1973; Rizzini 1963; and Tourinho and Imbassahy c. 1967. The version presented here is based on the fuller account in Fuller (1974) and on a conversation with the widow and children of Arigó in Congonhas do Campo (January 1985).

6. Lex notes (1985: 6) that Pires was at the same time writing a series of articles on Arigó for the rival *Diário de São Paulo* (July 27 and 29, August 2, 3, and 9, 1962).

7. For the most detailed popular survey of the post-Arigó spirit surgeons, see *Revista Planeta* no. 134-B, a (n.d.) special issue on "As Curas Paranormais," pp. 39–55. Also see Sidney Greenfield's more thorough, anthropological description (1987) of the medium Edson Queiroz and the Spiritist account by Lima and Neiva (1972).

8. *Jornal Espírita*, July 1988, p. 11; *Jornal do Brasil*, June 2, 1988, p. 8.

9. Spiritists, especially the homeopathic *receitista* mediums of Rio discussed in Chapter 4, have long incorporated homeopathy into their mediumistic activities, although the AMESP doctors are not homeopaths and did not seem very interested in the topic. See Lauro Thiago's (1972) account of the affinities between Spiritism and homeopathy.

10. Visit to Mendes's clinic (June 1985). Also see Mendes 1976, 1980a, 1980b, 1980c, 1985.

11. Although the procedure is reminiscent of acupuncture, Queiroz denies that it has anything to do with the Chinese traditional medicine. Instead, he uses the needles to operate on the perispirit (Greenfield 1987). The North Americans with whom I spoke felt pain during these treatments, perhaps because they had a lower level of belief and suggestibility than the Brazilians who volunteered for treatment.

12. On the articles concerning the illegal practice of medicine and stellionate, see Delmanto 1981: 291–92. On the history of this and related legal measures, see Maggie 1988: 24–31.

13. Article 22.3, "Normas Gerais sobre Defesa e Proteção de Saúde" (Lei 2.312, September 3, 1954), *Lex. Legislação Federal* 18 (1954): 491. Also see the similar regulation for the state of São Paulo: Article 497, Decreto-Lei 52.497, *Lex Legislação do Estado de São Paulo* 34 (1970): 895.

14. In my visits to Spiritist psychiatric hospitals and in my discussions with hospital administrators, I did not encounter any case in which the health regulations had been applied. Nevertheless, Spiritist administrators were aware of these regulations, and this motivated them to maintain a low profile with respect to the official medical profession.

15. On the *passe* or blessing as *curandeirismo*, see *Revista dos Tribunais* 221/344, 241/419, 287/434, 292/398, 292/444, 325/383, 384/251, 395/88, and 395/298. On the *passe* or blessing as religious practice, see 298/449, 307/565, 318/320, 319/318, 330/508, 340/274, 370/269, 404/282, and 464/391. See Maggie 1988 for a more detailed discussion of the history and development of the conflicting "schools" of legal thought on the related issue of "low Spiritism."

16. I am also indebted to Marlene Nobre, who answered my questions on this topic.

More recently, an article in the *Jornal do Brasil* (July 31, 1987, p. 3) reported that Spiritists have proposed an article for the Constitution that states: "The following shall be guaranteed: the right of exercising and practicing mediumship with ends of spiritual assistance and auxiliary aid in the treatment of psychological, spiritual, and physical infirmities, including the use of *passes*, so long as that right is exercised without charge and without causing any harm to the patient." The medical profession was against this proposal. My most recent information (late 1989) is that Spiritists were still working to have these reforms accepted.

17. The first, introduced in 1965 by Deputy Campos Vergal, was inspired by the Sociedade de Medicina e Espiritismo do Rio de Janeiro; see Projeto No. 2.915, *Anais da Câmara dos Deputados* 14 (June 18–24, 1965): 681–89. The second, introduced in 1975 by then Deputy Amaral Furlan, was less detailed but contained a long quotation from the Spiritist intellectual J. Herculano Pires; see *Diário do Congresso Nacional*, sec. 1, August 27, 1975, p. 635. The third bill was introduced in 1982 by Deputy Freitas Nobre; see Projeto-lei No. 6.162, April 29, 1982. The first and third of the bills contained long outlines defining parapsychology in a way that was consistent with Spiritist doctrine.

Chapter 7: Obsessions and Disobsessions

1. This comparison of theories of the religious system draws on Carlos Rodrigues Brandão's analysis of different maps of the religious system in Itapira, São Paulo (1980: 228–34).

2. See, for example, Boaventura Kloppenburg's comparison of the 1940 and 1950 census figures (1960: 26). These figures showed an increase of 78 percent for Spiritists, 62 percent for Protestants, and only 24 percent for Catholics.

3. See Kloppenburg 1961a for his reply.

4. Cosmetic changes are likely to bring cosmetic responses: on October 20, 1984, while I visited one Umbanda *terreiro* (which was evolving toward Candomblé), I watched the members hide images of the African *orixás* and create a Christian-style altar for a mass to be held by a visiting Catholic priest. After the priest left, the members reconverted the *terreiro* and held a *caboclo* session, that is, a session dedicated to the spirits of Indians.

5. A. Guimarães Filho, cited in Ribeiro and Campos 1931: 61–62; Cesar 1931; A. X. Oliveira 1931: 193.

6. For the Spiritist response, see Amorim (1955) 1978 and Imbassahy 1935, 1943, and 1949; see also Fróes 1928.

7. Videotaped interview of Deolindo Amorim by Krishnamurti de Carvalho Dias, Archives of the Institute of Brazilian Spiritist Culture (ICEB). Amorim had died shortly before I began doing research in Rio in 1984, so I never had the opportunity to meet him.

8. The Hospital Espírita de Porto Alegre was founded in 1926 (*Relatório da Diretoria do Hospital Espírita de Porto Alegre*, 1984). Inácio Ferreira founded his clinic in Uberaba, Minas Gerais, around 1940, and the Sanatório Américo Bairral of São Paulo was founded in 1936. On the latter, see Bianchi 1984.

9. This strategy affected at least two members of the medical profession in São Paulo who had an interest in psychical research (Cesar 1941, 1942; Whitaker 1942).

10. The title of the Spanish-language edition was also different: *Aspectos sociológicos del espiritismo en São Paulo* (1961). Several months after I finished writing this section, I was saddened to learn that Professor Camargo had died.

11. Several scholars have recently recognized in other contexts the Afro-Brazilian bias

in Bastide's writings (Cavalcanti 1986, Dantas 1982, Fry 1984, Lapassade and Luz 1972, Maggie 1986, and Monteiro 1978; see also Hess 1989a, 1991e); the present chapter adds to these studies by showing how Bastide's Afro-Brazilian bias created distortions in his interpretations of Spiritism.

12. This same supplementary status of a relativizing, critical anthropology occurs to a large extent within the discipline of medical anthropology (at least its noncritical variants), which, instead of inverting the hierarchy of psychiatric/anthropological knowledge, often preserves it.

13. His argument is similar to that of two other Spiritist psychiatrists, Denizard Souza and Teresinha Fátima Deitos, who suggest that Spiritist therapies in psychiatric hospitals might be considered as just one more type of "group support therapy" (1980: 194). Souza and Deitos compare Spiritist therapies with other group therapies—such as the transactional and psychoanalytic approaches—and find that Spiritist "group therapy"—which includes *passes*, doctrinal study, and disobsession—may even perhaps be superior according to some criteria, such as duration of treatment.

14. Also see Pires 1980, which traces the evolution of mediumship from tribal practices through Christianity to Spiritism. I have chosen not to discuss this text, which is based on a nineteenth-century model of cultural evolution, because the more sophisticated anthropology of Amorim and Mundim raises more interesting issues regarding the relationships between anthropology and Spiritism in the ideological arena. In Pires's study, the modern/primitive hierarchy is obvious.

15. I also summarized Patric Giesler's ideas (1984, 1985) on parapsychology and anthropology, as well as his experimental studies of Umbanda and Afro-Brazilian religions.

16. If I never went into trance while in Brazil, I still achieve a trancelike state when I reflect on the possible meanings of this rite of cultural trancelation. When teaching Mauss and informing the students, to their evident surprise and chagrin, that Carlos Castaneda had made up most of his materials, was I serving as a medium between Spiritism and orthodox anthropology? In this case, I thought I was just doing good anthropology, which is, after all, an act of cultural mediumship. Or was it all less innocent: could one see it through the more paranoid prism of discursive obsessions and disobsessions, perhaps a good root metaphor for the entire ideological arena? Was my presentation of orthodox anthropology and parapsychology a ritual of discursive disobsession of Spiritist parapsychology and para-anthropology, just as these discourses attempt to disobsess orthodox parapsychology and anthropology from positivism and materialism? And was the very use of any kind of anthropology in this context—be it "para" or "ortho"—merely a means for marking Spiritists as scientific with respect to Umbanda, the Afro-Brazilian religions, and popular Catholicism, which, by becoming objects of anthropological study, are marked as primitive? Or did it provide an idiom that might make possible a more equal dialogue with these other groups? Was Spiritism obsessing my own discourse of anthropology, or was such an obsession a fine act of par(a)ticipant-observation and discursive mediumship—and therefore not an obsession at all? Such are the paradoxes of having anthropology as a paramour in the land of trances and *transas*.

GLOSSARY

ANIMISM, ANIMISTIC PHENOMENA. In Spiritism, the term for paranormal phenomena caused by the psychic abilities of the living rather than of spirits. "Animistic" is contrasted with "spiritic."

CANDOMBLÉ. An Afro-Brazilian spirit-mediumship religion. The best known and most influential, the Candomblé Nagô, derives from Yoruba religion. A Candomblé "priest" is called *mãe-de-santo* (mother of the saints) or *pai-de-santo* (father of the saints); the temples of Candomblé are called *terreiros;* and Candomblé priests receive Yoruba spirits called *orixás.*

CURANDEIRISMO. Folk or popular healing, the efficacy of which is often attributed to spiritual forces and/or beings. In medical circles and among some Spiritists, the term *curandeiro* has the meaning of "quack" or "charlatan."

DESENCÔSTO. A type of disobsession, associated more with Umbanda than with Spiritism.

DESOBSESSÃO (DISOBSESSION, DEOBSESSION). In Spiritism, the practice whereby mediums receive lost or perturbing spirits and whereby another member of the center talks to the spirit and educates, evangelizes, or "indoctrinates" it. These lost or perturbing spirits are not necessarily linked to specific victims, and the afflicted do not need to be present during the disobsession meeting. Frequently, though, victims are present and, as a result, non-Spiritists may refer to disobsession as "exorcism" (a word that Spiritists reject because it implies demons or other, nonhuman spirits).

DISSOCIATION. Among certain psychologists (e.g., Pierre Janet, Ernest Hilgard), the belief that the mind may split into two or more separate and relatively independent units or streams of consciousness.

ESPIRITISMO. This word has two meanings in Brazil, depending on who uses it: (1) the followers of Kardec's doctrine, who are sometimes called *kardecistas*, although they generally prefer to be called *espíritas;* and (2) any group that practices spirit mediumship and believes in communication with spirits through mediums. In the former context, I have translated *espiritismo* as "Spiritism"; in the latter, as "spirit-mediumship religions" ("spiritic" for the adjective).

ESPIRITUALISMO. Spiritists use this term to refer to any doctrine or group that endorses the idea of the soul. Thus, *espiritualismo* is the opposite of "materialism." I have translated this term as "spiritualism" (with a lower-case "s"). See *mediunismo*, Spiritualism, and spiritualism.

EXTRASENSORY PERCEPTION (ESP). Acquisition of information paranormally; that is, without explanation in terms of "normal" sensory perception or memory. Extrasensory perception is generally subdivided into telepathy, clairvoyance, and precognition.

FREQUENTERS (*FREQÜENTADORES*). Laypeople who are not members of a Spiritist center but who attend sessions irregularly.

INCORPORATION. What happens when a medium receives a spirit and the spirit takes control of the medium's body. Spiritists generally think of incorporation as a more profound form of communication with the spirits, because the statements of incorporated spirits involve less animism, that is, are less influenced by the medium's own unconscious.

JEITINHO, DAR UM JEITINHO ("Deal," "To figure out a way"). This important Brazilian expression refers to the way Brazilians try to figure out ways around institutionalized regulations by means of personal networks (see DaMatta 1986: 95–105).

KIRLIAN PHOTOGRAPHY. Sometimes known as the phantom-leaf effect or photography of the aura, Kirlian photography involves passing an electric charge between two photographic plates with a finger or leaf and a piece of film in between. Although Hernani Guimarães Andrade first introduced this Soviet invention to the West, he now accepts the conclusions of North American and West European parapsychologists and scientists, who attribute its effect to pressure and moisture artifacts. Most Spiritists, however, still believe that Kirlian photography provides a picture of the spiritual body, or "perispirit," and even those who understand the electrical mechanism believe that it somehow reveals the status and health of the perispirit.

MACUMBA. The word has two usages. In popular parlance, one "does a *Macumba*," which is understood to be a kind of "black magic" spell or offering; and "Macumba" may refer to any kind of black magic practice or Afro-Brazilian religion. In academic parlance, such as in the work of Roger Bastide ([1960] 1978), the term refers to Afro-Brazilian religious practices, generally in Rio and São Paulo, associated with the descendants of Bantu slaves. There are few historical documents on Macumba, and today most practitioners appear to have abandoned the term in favor of Umbanda or Quimbanda (q.v.).

MÃE-DE-SANTO (MOTHER OF THE SAINTS). A medium in Umbanda and a priestess in the Afro-Brazilian religions.

MATERIALIST. Literally, anyone who does not believe in God or in a spiritual aspect to human existence; but Spiritists use this term loosely to refer to anyone whom they view as anti-Spiritist.

MEDIUMISTIC SURGERY (*CIRURGIA MEDIÚNICA*). In Brazil, generally associated with Spiritist mediums but not limited to them. It involves biomedical-like operations with the intent to heal, and it can be classified into two major types: (1) the physical-intervention type, in which the medium uses a scalpel or knife and cuts the patient's body; (2) the nonphysical type, in which the medium operates only on the patient's perispirit in pantomime-like operations that do not involve breaking the skin.

MEDIUNISMO. LITERALLY "MEDIUMISM," BUT TRANSLATED AS "SPIRIT MEDIUMSHIP." The Spiritist term for the belief and practice of spirit mediumship regardless of acceptance of Allan Kardec's doctrine. Sometimes Spiritists use this term almost pejoratively to refer to spirit-mediumship religions such as Umbanda, which "lack" the Kardecian doctrine; at other times, they use it as a general term for spirit mediumship that includes Spiritism. Some Spiritists confuse this term with *espiritualismo* (q.v.).

METAPSÍQUICA. From the French word *métapsychique*, associated with the psychic research of Charles Richet. See psychical research.

OBSESSION. See spirit obsession.

ORIXÁS. Yoruba deities. Though recognized by Umbandists, the *orixás* generally descend only among the Candomblés.

PAI-DE-SANTO (FATHER OF THE SAINTS). A medium in Umbanda and sometimes in other Afro-Brazilian religions.

PARANORMAL PHENOMENA (PSI PHENOMENA, PSYCHIC PHENOMENA). Any phenomena alleged to involve the direct interaction between the mind (spirit, consciousness, soul) and the world, for which no known physical explanation is available. Parapsychologists generally divide paranormal phenomena into extrasensory perception and psychokinesis. Some parapsychologists accept a third category of paranormal phenomena known as survival, or psi-theta, phenomena; others believe that these phenomena can be subsumed under the first two categories.

PARAPSYCHOLOGY. The study of paranormal phenomena. The term "parapsychology" is used in two ways: (1) it is associated with the Rhinean school (q.v.), which limited itself to the study of ESP and psychokinesis, was skeptical of the ability to prove spirit communication, and emphasized the value of laboratory over field research; (2) it is used as a general name for all the schools that study paranormal phenomena, including *métapsychique*/psychical research, psychobiophysics, psychotronics, and post-Rhinean parapsychology.

PASSE ("pass," laying-on of hands). The donation of spiritual energies or vital fluids from a medium and/or spiritic source to a patient. Spiritists divide *passes* into three types: (1) magnetic, in which the energy source is the medium; (2) spiritual, in which the energy source is a spirit; and (3) mixed, in which the source is both. Spiritists believe that, in practice, most *passes* are of the third type.

PERISPIRIT. The Spiritist term for the semimaterial body made of vital fluids or energies. Upon death, the perispirit and the spirit leave the body, and the perispirit becomes the spiritual body of the "discarnate" spirit. In English, the rough equivalents of the term "perispirit" are "astral body," "beta body," or "subtle body."

PESQUISA PSÍQUICA. See psychical research.

PK. See psychokinesis.

POLTERGEIST. According to psychical researchers and Spiritists, an unexplained outbreak of uncontrolled object movements, falling stones, water leaks, fires, and so on that usually takes place inside a home or workplace. Poltergeists usually center around a person or persons who are called the agent. In Brazil, the afflicted generally associate poltergeist outbreaks with spirit attacks, the devil, or "black magic." Psychologists and parapsychologists have offered many alternative explanations, including rats, seismographic activity, electrical failure, pranks, dissociated action, and agent-driven unconscious psychokinesis (recurrent spontaneous psychokinesis).

PSYCHICAL RESEARCH. The older name for the discipline presently known as parapsychology, although some people consider psychical research to be a separate discipline rather than just an older name for parapsychology. In contrast to parapsychology, psychical research is characterized by more observational and field-oriented methods; its research is oriented toward proof of survival of the soul after death and spirit communication. Rhinean parapsychologists consider it to represent an earlier, less scientific phase or "paradigm" for the field of parapsychology.

PSYCHIC SURGERY. See mediumistic surgery.

PSYCHOBIOPHYSICS (PSICOBIOFÍSICA). Hernani Guimarães Andrade's term for a Spiritist-oriented parapsychology.

PSYCHOGRAPHY (PSICOGRAFIA). The practice of receiving spirit communications via automatic writing.

PSYCHOKINESIS (PK). Alleged direct action by the mind or consciousness on the physical world with no known physical channel, such as the body or electromagnetic, gravitational, or other physical forces.

PSYCHOTRONICS. Frequently, the name used for parapsychology in Soviet-bloc countries, implying somewhat different assumptions from those of most European and North American parapsychologists.

QUIMBANDA. A type of Afro-Brazilian religious practice associated with "black magic"; often this term is used by Umbandists, who wish to distinguish their own religious and magical practices as "white magic," or "on the side of the good."

RECEITISTA MEDIUMS. Spiritist mediums who give homeopathic prescriptions.

RHINEAN, POST-RHINEAN. A school of parapsychology, associated with the North American Joseph Banks Rhine, emphasizing laboratory research and maintaining that questions of soul survival or spirit communication cannot be answered until more is known about the paranormal processes among the living.

SPIRITIC. Of or related to spirits; sometimes used in opposition to "animistic phenomena," or paranormal phenomena of human origin.

SPIRITISM. Sometimes called "Kardecism," the movement that follows the teachings of Allan Kardec. Some English-language texts use the term "spiritist" to mean anyone who accepts the idea of spirit communication, in contrast to "Spiritualist," which implies being part of the religious movement. To avoid confusion, this study uses only "Spiritist" (with an upper-case "S").

SPIRIT MEDIUM. A person, not necessarily Spiritist, who relays spirit communications or physical effects generally by appearing to go into a trance and incorporating the spirit. Anthropologists sometimes use Erika Bourguignon's category of "possession trance"; however, her terminology is not adopted here because for Spiritists possession implies something unwanted and uncontrolled, and spirit mediums do not always relay spirit communications by incorporating a spirit (mediums may simply hear a voice, for example, and relay it to the sitters).

SPIRIT-MEDIUMSHIP RELIGIONS. Used here as an equivalent of the Portuguese *religiões mediúnicas, mediunismo,* or, when used to refer to all spirit-mediumship religions and not just the Spiritist (or Kardecist) variant, *espiritismo.*

SPIRIT OBSESSION. The influence of a perturbing or earthbound spirit on a living human's thoughts and actions. Spiritists divide spirit obsession into three categories—simple obsession, fascination, and subjugation—the first of which is the least serious and the last the most serious.

SPIRIT SURGERY. See mediumistic surgery.

SPIRITUALISM. The sibling of Spiritism in English-speaking countries. Spiritualists do not follow Allan Kardec but share many other beliefs and practices with Spiritists. The main doctrinal difference is that reincarnation is an optional belief for Spiritualists. Note that "Spiritualism" is not the equivalent of the Portuguese term *espiritualismo* (q.v.). When used with a lower-case "s," the term "spiritualism" will mean some belief in God or supernatural beings; that, in fact, is how Kardec used the term in the introduction to *The Book of the Spirits.*

SPONTANEOUS CASE RESEARCH. Case or field studies of apparently paranormal phenomena that are generally uncontrolled and/or nonrepeatable, hence "spontaneous." Contrasted with laboratory research.

SURVIVAL PHENOMENA (PSI-THETA PHENOMENA). A class of paranormal phenomena believed to be suggestive of the survival of the personality after death. Survival phenomena include reincarnation, mediumistic communication, hauntings, apparitions, and (sometimes) poltergeists. Many North American and European parapsychologists (as well as Catholic parapsychologists in Brazil) believe that survival phenomena do not constitute a separate class and can instead be subsumed under the categories of extrasensory perception and psychokinesis. For example, a successful mediumistic communication might be explained as the result of a secondary personality dramatizing a spirit and employing unconscious extrasensory perception; this is known as the "super-psi theory."

TELERGY. An unknown physical energy that drives poltergeists; discussed by Pedro Oscar González Quevedo (following other parapsychologists).

TERREIRO. Literally "open ground"; in practice, the building or temple in which Candomblé and some Umbanda sessions are held.

UMBANDA. A spirit-mediumship religion that originated in Brazil during the early twentieth century, Umbanda has a pantheon of Brazilian spirits that includes *pretos velhos* (old black slaves) and *caboclos* (Amerindians). Umbanda is sometimes considered part of Spiritism (see Chapter 7), but some scholars think of Umbanda as an Afro-Brazilian religion while others think of it as just "Brazilian," without the prefix. The anthropologist Diana DeGroat Brown (1986) distinguishes two lines of Umbanda, one more African and the other closer to Spiritism, and the sociologist Cândido Procópio Ferreira de Camargo has argued that a "continuum" exists between Spiritism and Umbanda (see Chapter 7). The name of the place where Umbanda rituals take place varies; it may be called a *terreiro*, a center, or a temple. See Quimbanda.

UMBRAL. In Spiritist doctrine, the threshold zone between the terrestrial plane and Nosso Lar, the colony for Brazilians in the otherworld.

BIBLIOGRAPHY

Abreu, Canuto
   1950   *Adolpho* [sic] *Bezerra de Menezes.* São Paulo: Livraria Allan Kardec. (Republished as *Bezerra de Menezes,* São Paulo: FEESP, 1981.)
Abreu, Canuto, and J. Herculano Pires
   1973   *O Verbo e a Carne. Duas Análises do Roustaingismo.* São Paulo: Caibrar.
AEPR (Asociación Espiritista de Puerto Rico)
   1934   *Manifiesto a los espiritistas de Puerto Rico.* Santurce: Asociación Espiritista de Puerto Rico.
Allison, Paul
   1979   "Experimental Parapsychology as Rejected Knowledge." In *On the Margins of Science: The Social Construction of Rejected Knowledge.* Sociological Review Monograph no. 27, ed. Roy Wallis. Keele, Staffordshire: University of Keele.
Alvarado, Carlos
   1979   "Psychical Research in Puerto Rico." *Parapsychology Review* 10(6): 23–24.
   1980   "Apuntes sobre la *Historia del espiritismo en Puerto Rico,* del. Lic. Nestor A. Rodríguez Escudero." *Puerto Rico Espírita* 2(7): 21–25.
   1984   Review of *O "Poltergeist" de Suzano. Journal of the Society for Psychical Research* 52(798): 392–95.

Amorim, Deolindo
1949   *Africanismo e Espiritismo.* Rio de Janeiro: Gráfico Mundo Espírita (orig. 1946).
1955   *O Espiritismo à Luz da Crítica.* Curitiba: Federação Espírita do Paraná.
1957   *O Espiritismo e as Doutrinas Espiritualistas.* Curitiba: Federação Espírita do Paraná.
1958   *Africanismo y espiritismo.* Buenos Aires: Editorial Constancia (orig. 1946).
1978   *O Espiritismo e Criminologia.* Curitiba: Federação Espírita do Paraná (orig. 1955).
c. 1980   *Idéias e Reminiscências Espíritas.* Juiz de Fora, M.G.: Instituto Maria.
Andino, Telesforo
1937   *El espiritismo en Puerto Rico y la reforma.* San Juan: Tip. San Juan.
Andrade, Hernani Guimarães
1980   *O Caso Ruytemborg Rocha.* São Paulo: IBPP.
1982   *O "Poltergeist" de Suzano.* São Paulo: IBPP.
1983   *Morte, Renascimento, Evolução.* São Paulo: Pensamento.
1984a   *Espírito, Perispírito, e Alma.* São Paulo: Pensamento.
1984b   *Parapsicologia Experimental.* São Paulo: Pensamento (orig. 1967).
1986   *Psi Quântico.* São Paulo: Pensamento.
1988a   *Poltergeist. Algumas de Suas Ocorrências no Brasil.* São Paulo: Pensamento.
1988b   *Reencarnação no Brasil. Oito Casos Que Sugerem Renascimento.* São Paulo: Pensamento.
Andrade, Hernani Guimarães (Lawrence Blacksmith)
1979a   "As Três Faces de Parapsicologia (I). A Face Soviética." *Folha Espírita* 6(63): 5.
1979b   "As Três Faces de Parapsicologia (II). A Face Ocidental." *Folha Espírita* 6(64): 4–5.
1979c   "As Três Faces de Parapsicologia (III). A Face Brasileira." *Folha Espírita* 6(65): 4–5.
Andrade, Mário de
1975   *Macunaíma, o Herói sem Nenhum Caráter.* São Paulo: Livraria Martins (orig. 1928).
Andrea, Jorge
1980   *Nos Alicerces do Inconsciente.* Rio de Janeiro: Caminho de Liberdade.
1982   *Palingênese, a Grande Lei (Reencarnação).* Rio de Janeiro: Caminho de Liberdade.
1984   *Correlações Espírito-Matéria.* Rio de Janeiro: Samos.
Aquarone, Francisco
1982   *Bezerra de Menezes, o Médico dos Pobres.* São Paulo: Aliança.
Aresi de Garibaldi, Albino
1975   *Homen Total: Dinamismo, Educação, Desajuste, e Parapsicologia.* São Paulo: Loyola.
1976   *I Congresso de Parapsicologia e Medicina.* São Paulo: Mens Sana.
1978   *Fundamentos Científicos de Parapsicologia.* São Paulo: Mens Sana.
1979   *II Congresso de Parapsicologia e Medicina.* São Paulo: Mens Sana.
1984   *Método de Terapia Noossofrológica das Clínicas Frei Albino.* São Paulo: Mens Sana.

Armond, Edgard
1978   *Cromoterapia.* São Paulo: Aliança.
Azevedo, Fernando de
n.d.   *As Ciências no Brasil.* Vol. 2. São Paulo: Melhoramentos.
Azzi, Rolando
1977   "Catolicismo Popular e Autoridade Eclesiástica na Evolução Histórica do Brasil." *Religião e Sociedade* 1: 125–49.
Bacón, Hemeterio
1910   *Memorias de un maniático, o Apuntes históricos del espiritismo en Puerto Rico de los años 1872 al 1876.* Mayagüez: Imp. "La Bandera Americana."
Barnes, Peggy
n.d.   *The Fundamentals of Spiritualism.* Indianapolis: NSAC Publishing Center.
Barreto, Djalma
1972   *Parapsicologia, Curandeirismo, e Lei.* Petrópolis: Vozes.
1978   *O Alienista, o Louco, e a Lei.* Petrópolis: Vozes.
Barreto, Paulo (João do Rio)
1951   *As Religiões no Rio.* Rio de Janeiro: Organização Simões (orig. 1904).
Bastide, Roger
1967   "Le Spiritisme au Brésil." *Archives de Sociologie des Religions* 24: 3–16.
1974   "The Present Status of Afro-American Research in Latin America." *Daedalus* 103(2): 111–23.
1978   *The African Religions of Brazil.* Baltimore: Johns Hopkins University Press (orig. 1960).
Bateson, Gregory
1958   *Naven.* Stanford, Calif.: Stanford University Press (orig. 1936).
Bellah, Robert
1974   *The Broken Covenant: American Civil Religion in Time of Trial.* New York: Seabury Press.
Ben-Yehuda, Nachman
1985   *Deviance and Moral Boundaries.* Chicago: University of Chicago Press.
Bianchi, Cesar
1984   *A História do Sanatório "Américo Bairral."* São Paulo: Livraria Espírita "Katie King"/Lar da Família Universal.
Birman, Patrícia
1985   "Registrado em Cartório, com Firma Reconhecida. A Mediação Política das Federações de Umbanda." In *Umbanda e Política.* Cadernos do ISER no. 18. Rio de Janeiro: Marco Zero.
Blackwell, Anna
1875   "Translator's Introduction." In *Spiritualist Philosophy: The Spirits' Book,* by Allan Kardec. London: Trubner & Co.
Boon, James A.
1982   *Other Tribes, Other Scribes.* Cambridge: Cambridge University Press.
1985   "Mead's Mediations: Some Semiotics from the Sepik, by Way of Bateson, on to Bali." In *Semiotic Mediations,* eds. E. Mertz and R. Parmentier. New York: Academic Press.
1987   "Between-the-Wars Bali: Rereading the Relics." In *Malinowski, Rivers, Benedict, and Others,* ed. George Stocking, Jr. Madison: University of Wisconsin Press.

Bourdieu, Pierre
1975   "The Specificity of the Scientific Field and the Social Conditions of the Progress of Reason." *Social Science Information* 14(6): 19–47.
1982   *A Economia das Trocas Simbólicas.* São Paulo: Edicel.
Brandão, Carlos Rodrigues
1980   *Os Deuses do Povo. Um Estudo sobre a Religião Popular.* São Paulo: Brasiliense.
Brody, Eugene B.
1973   *The Lost Ones: Social Forces and Mental Illness in Rio de Janeiro.* New York: International Universities Press.
Brown, Diana DeGroat
1977   "O Papel Histórico da Classe Média na Umbanda." *Religião e Sociedade* 1: 31–59.
1979   "Umbanda and Class Relations in Brazil." In *Brazil: Anthropological Perspectives,* eds. M. Margolis and W. Carter. New York: Columbia University Press.
1985   "Uma História da Umbanda no Rio." In *Umbanda e Política.* Cadernos do ISER no. 18. Rio de Janeiro: Marco Zero.
1986   *Umbanda: Religion and Politics in Urban Brazil.* Ann Arbor, Mich.: UMI Press.
Bruneau, Thomas
1974   *The Political Transformations of the Brazilian Catholic Church.* Cambridge: Cambridge University Press.
Camargo, Cândido Procópio Ferreira de
1961   *Kardecismo e Umbanda.* São Paulo: Pioneira. (Spanish-language edition: *Aspectos sociológicos del espiritismo en São Paulo.* Fribourg and Bogotá: Oficina Internacional de Investigaciones Sociales de FERES, Federación Internacional de los Institutos Católicos de Investigaciones Sociales y Socio-religiosos, 1961.)
1973   *Católicos, Protestantes, e Espíritas.* Petrópolis: Vozes.
Casella, V. O.
1961   "Espiritismo, Hipnose, e Letargia." *Revista Internacional do Espiritismo* (March–May).
1961/62   "Revides aos Rebates do Dr. Osmard." *Revista Internacional do Espiritismo* (August 1961–July 1962).
1962   "Esclarecimentos sobre os Nossos Debates com o Dr. Osmard." *Revista Internacional do Espiritismo* (July).
Cavalcanti, Maria Laura
1983   *O Mundo Invisível. Cosmologia, Sistema Ritual, e Noção de Pessoa no Espiritismo.* Rio de Janeiro: Zahar.
1986   "Origens, para Que as Quero?" *Religião e Sociedade* 13(2): 84–101.
Ceccarini, Natalio
1952   "Umbanda y Espiritismo." *Cosmos* 12(139): 18–19.
Cerullo, John
1982   *The Secularization of the Soul.* Philadelphia: ISHI.
Cesar, Osório
1931   "Contribuição para o Estudo do Espiritismo como Fator Predisponente de Perturbações Mentais." *Revista Nova* (São Paulo) 1(4): 563–81.
1941   "Fenomenologia Supernormal." *Revista Paulista de Medicina* 19(5): 273–95.

1942   "Experiências Metapsíquicas, com Provas Fotográficas, sobre Algumas Curiosas Formações Teleplásticas." *Revista Paulista de Medicina* 20(3): 119–36.
Cirne, Leopoldo
1913/14   *Mensagem aos Meus Consócios na FEB*. Rio de Janeiro: n.p.
1935   *Antichristo, Senhor do Mundo*. Rio de Janeiro: Bedeschi.
Clifford, James
1983   "On Ethnographic Authority." *Representations* 1: 118–46. (Also in Clifford, *The Predicament of Culture*. Cambridge: Harvard University Press, 1988.)
Clifford, James, and George Marcus (eds.)
1986   *Writing Culture*. Berkeley and Los Angeles: University of California Press.
Cobêro, Marcia Regina
1983   "Diálogo com os Amigos. Formação de Parapsicólogos." *Boletim do Centro Latino-Americano de Parapsicologia* 28: 3–5.
Colinon, M.
1959   "Comment M. Rivail devint Allan Kardec." *Miroir de l'Histoire* 112: 544–52.
Collins, H. M., and T. J. Pinch
1979   "The Construction of the Paranormal: Nothing Unscientific Is Happening." In *On the Margins of Science: The Social Construction of Rejected Knowledge*. Sociological Review Monograph no. 27, ed. Roy Wallis. Keele, Staffordshire: University of Keele.
1982   *Frames of Meaning: The Social Construction of Extra-ordinary Science*. London: Routledge & Kegan Paul.
Colón, William, and Isaac Irizarry Sasport
1939   *La nueva educación*. New York: self-published.
Comte, Auguste
1858   *The Catechism of Positive Religion*. London: Chapman (orig. 1852).
Concone, Maria Helena, and Lísias Negrão
1985   "Umbanda. Da Representação à Cooptação." In *Umbanda e Política*. Cadernos do ISER no. 18. Rio de Janeiro: Marco Zero.
Costa, João Cruz
1964   *A History of Ideas in Brazil*. Berkeley and Los Angeles: University of California Press (orig. 1956).
Costa, Jurandir Freire
1976   *História da Psiquiatria no Brasil*. Rio de Janeiro: Documentário.
Cruz Monclova, Lidio
1952   *Historia de Puerto Rico. Siglo XIX*. Vol. 1 (1808–68). San Juan: Editorial Universitaria, Universidad de Puerto Rico.
DaMatta, Roberto
1978   *Carnavais, Malandros, e Heróis. Para uma Sociologia do Dilema Brasileiro*. Rio de Janeiro: Zahar.
1981   "The Ethic of Umbanda and the Spirit of Messianism." In *Authoritarian Capitalism: Brazil's Contemporary Economic and Political Development*, eds. T. Bruneau and P. Faucher. Boulder, Colo.: Westview.
1982   "*Dona Flor e Seus Dois Maridos:* A Relational Novel." *Social Science Information* 21(1): 19–46.
1984   *Relativizando*. Petrópolis: Vozes.

1985   *A Casa e a Rua*. São Paulo: Brasiliense.
1986   *O Que Faz brasil, Brasil?* Rio de Janeiro: Rocco.
Dantas, Beatriz
1982   "Repensando a Pureza Nago." *Religião e Sociedade* 8: 15–20.
Darnton, Robert
1968   *Mesmerism and the End of the Enlightenment in France.* Cambridge: Harvard University Press.
Dean, Douglas
1985   "Infra-red Measurements of Healer-Treated and Magnetically-Treated Water." In *Proceedings and Abstracts, the First International Congress on Alternative Therapies.* São Paulo: International Association for Alternative Therapies.
Della Cava, Ralph
1970   *Miracle at Joaseiro.* New York: Columbia University Press.
Delmanto, Celso
1981   *Código Penal Anotado. 1981.* São Paulo: Saraiva.
Derrida, Jacques
1978   *Structure, Sign, and Play in the Discourse of the Human Sciences: Writing and Difference.* Chicago: University of Chicago Press.
Dias, Krishnamurti Carvalho de
1985   *O Laço e o Culto. É o Espiritismo uma Religião?* Santos, São Paulo: Divulgação Cultura Espírita.
Dolby, R. G. A.
1979   "Reflections on Deviant Science." In *On the Margins of Science: The Social Construction of Rejected Knowledge.* Sociological Review Monograph no. 27, ed. Roy Wallis. Keele, Staffordshire: University of Keele.
Dos Anjos, Luciano
1978   "A Posição Zero." *Obreiros do Bem* (June, August, and October).
1979   "A Posição Zero." *Obreiros do Bem* (April, June/July, and August/September).
1980   "A Posição Zero." *Obreiros do Bem* (January/April).
Downey, Gary L.
1988   "Structure and Practice in the Cultural Identities of Scientists: Negotiating Nuclear Wastes in New Mexico." *Anthropological Quarterly* 61(1): 26–38.
Downs, Robert
1975   *Heinrich Pestalozzi: Father of Modern Pedagogy.* Boston: Twayne.
Droogers, André F.
1989   "The Enigma of the Metaphor That Heals: Signification in an Urban Spiritist Healing Group." Paper presented at the 88th Annual Meeting of the American Anthropological Association, November 15–19, Washington, D.C.
1988   "Brazil as Patient: Political Healing in a Spiritist Group." Paper prepared for the symposium on "Religion, Power, and Ideology in Latin America and the Caribbean," 46th International Congress of Americanists, July 4–9, Amsterdam, the Netherlands.
Dumont, Jean-Paul
1978   *The Headman and I: Ambiguity and Ambivalence in the Fieldworking Experience.* Austin: University of Texas Press.

Dumont, Louis
1980   *Homo Hierarchicus.* Chicago: University of Chicago Press (orig. 1966).
Durkheim, Émile
1965   *The Elementary Forms of the Religious Life.* New York: Free Press (orig. 1915).
Durkheim, Émile, and Marcel Mauss
1963   *Primitive Classification.* Chicago: University of Chicago Press.
Ellenberger, Henri
1970   *The Discovery of the Unconscious.* New York: Basic Books.
Ellwood, R. S., Jr.
1979   *Alternative Altars: Unconventional and Eastern Spirituality in America.* Chicago: University of Chicago Press.
Escholier, Marc
1968   *Port-Royal: The Drama of the Jansenists.* New York: Hawthorne Books.
Faria, Osmard Andrade
1959   *Hipnose e Letargia.* Rio de Janeiro: Atheneu.
1961/62   "Hipnose e Espiritismo." *Revista International do Espiritismo* (July 1961–July 1962).
1979   *Manual de Hipnose Médica e Odontológica.* Rio de Janeiro: Atheneu.
1981   *Parapsicologia.* Rio de Janeiro: Atheneu.
1984   *O Que É Parapsicologia.* São Paulo: Brasiliense.
FEB (Federação Espírita Brasileira)
1904   *Memória Histórica do Espiritismo. Publicação Comemorativa do Centenário de Allan Kardec.* Rio de Janeiro: Federação Espírita Brasileira.
1907   *As Curas Espíritas perante a Lei.* Rio de Janeiro: Federação Espírita Brasileira.
1912   *Esboço Histórico da Federação Espírita Brasileira.* Rio de Janeiro: Federação Espírita Brasileira.
Ferreira, Inácio
c. 1940   *Espiritismo e Medicina.* Uberaba, M.G.: Flama.
1946   *Novos Rumos à Medicina.* Uberaba, M.G.: Flama.
1962   *Subsídio para a História de Eurípedes Barsanulfo.* Uberaba, M.G.: self-published.
1963   *A Psiquiatria em Face da Reencarnação.* São Paulo: Difusora Cultural.
Figueira, Sérvulo A.
1978   "Notas Introdutórias ao Estudo das Terapêuticas I: Lévi-Strauss e Peter Berger." In *Sociedade e Doença Mental,* ed. S. A. Figueira. Rio de Janeiro: Campus.
Finkler, Kaja
1983   *Spiritualist Healers in Mexico.* South Hadley, Mass.: Bergin & Garvey.
Fitzpatrick, John
1983   *O Poder de Fé.* São Paulo: Pensamento (Earlier edition: São Paulo: Milesi Editora, 1970.)
Fodor, Nandor
1948   "The Poltergeist Psychoanalyzed." *Psychiatric Quarterly* 22: 195–203.
Foucault, Michel
1973   *Madness and Civilization.* New York: Vintage Books (orig. 1961).
Franco, Divaldo P.
1982   *Nas Fronteiras da Loucura. Pelo Espírito Manoel P. de Miranda.* Salvador: Livraria Espírita Alvorada.

Freixedo, Salvador
    1973   *El diablo inconsciente. Parapsicología y religión.* Mexico, Puerto Rico, Vene-
            zuela: Editorial Isla.
Friderichs, Edvino A.
    1979   *Panorama da Parapsicologia ao Alcance de Todos.* São Paulo: Loyola.
Fróes, A. de Lima
    1928   *O Espiritismo e a Sociedade de Medicina do Rio de Janeiro.* Pelotas, R.S.:
            Barcellos, Bertaso & Cia.
Fry, Peter
    1984   "Gallus Africanus Est, ou, Como Roger Bastide se Tornou Africano no
            Brasil." *Folhetim* (São Paulo, July 15): 7–10.
Fuller, John
    1974   *Arigó: Surgeon of the Rusty Knife.* New York: Thomas Crowell.
Galvão, Luiz de Almeida Prado
    1967   "Notas para a História da Psicanálise em São Paulo." *Revista Brasileira
            de Psicanálise* 1(1): 46–64.
Garcia, Wilson
    1983   *Médicos Médiuns.* São Bernardo do Campo, S.P.: Editora Espírita
            Correio Fraterno do ABC.
Garrison, Vivian
    1977   "The 'Puerto Rican Syndrome' in Psychiatry and Espiritismo." In *Case
            Studies in Spirit Possession,* eds. Vincent Crapanzano and Vivian Garri-
            son. New York: John Wiley & Sons.
Gasparetto, Zibia
    n.d.   *O Mundo em Que Eu Vivo.* São Paulo: Associação Cristã de Cultura
            Espírita "Os Caminheiros" (c. 1983).
Gauld, Alan
    1968   *The Founders of Psychical Research.* New York: Schocken.
Geertz, Clifford
    1973   *The Interpretation of Cultures.* New York: Basic Books.
    1983   *Local Knowledge.* New York: Basic Books.
Giddens, Anthony
    1988   "Ideology and Consciousness." In *Central Problems in Social Theory.*
            Berkeley and Los Angeles: University of California Press.
Gieryn, Thomas
    1983   "Boundary-Work and the Demarcation of Science from Non-Science."
            American Sociological Review 48: 781–95.
Giesler, Patric
    1984   "Parapsychological Anthropology: I." *Journal of the American Society for
            Psychical Research* 78(4): 289–330.
    1985   "Parapsychological Anthropology: II." *Journal of the American Society for
            Psychical Research* 79(2): 113–66.
Goffman, Erving
    1961   *Asylums: Essays on the Social Situation of Mental Patients and Other Inmates.*
            Chicago: Aldine.
Gratton, Henri, O.M.I.
    1955   *Psychanalyses d'hier et d'aujourd'hui, comme thérapeutiques, sciences, et phi-
            losophies.* Paris: Editions du Cerf.
Greenfield, Sidney
    1986   "Psychodrama, Past Life Regression, and Other Therapies Used by

Spiritist Healers in Rio Grande do Sul, Brazil." *Association for the Anthropological Study of Consciousness Newsletter* 2(2): 1ff.
1987   "The Return of Dr. Fritz: Spiritist Healing and Patronage Networks in Urban, Industrial Brazil." *Social Science and Medicine* 24(12): 1095–1108.

Harwood, Alan
1987   *Rx: Spiritist as Needed.* New York: John Wiley & Sons.

Hess, David
1987a   "O Espiritismo e as Ciências." *Religião e Sociedade* 14(3): 41–54.
1987b   "The Many Rooms of Spiritism in Brazil." *Luso-Brazilian Review* 24(2): 15–34.
1987c   "Religion, Heterodox Science, and Brazilian Culture." *Social Studies of Science* 17: 465–77.
1987d   Review of Michael Kenny, *The Passion of Ansel Bourne: Multiple Personality in American Culture. Transcultural Psychiatric Research Review* 24: 210–13.
1989a   "Disobsessing Disobsession: Religion, Ritual, and the Social Sciences in Brazil." *Cultural Anthropology* 4(2): 182–93.
1989b   "On Earth as It Is in Heaven." Manuscript.
1989c   "Psychical Research and Cultural Values: A Comparison of Two Theories of the Poltergeist." *Newsletter for the History and Sociology of Marginal Science* 1(2): 1–4.
1991a   "The Anthropology of Science and the New Ethnography." Manuscript.
1991b   "Ghosts and Domestic Politics in Brazil." *Ethos* (in press).
1991c   "Religious Pluralism and the Rhetoric of Encompassment: Four Perspectives from Brazil." Manuscript.
1991d   "Science in the New Age: A Cultural Critique of Skepticism and the Paranormal in the United States." Manuscript.
1991e   "Umbanda and Quimbanda Magic in Brazil: Rethinking Aspects of Roger Bastide's Work." *Archives de Sciences Sociales des Religions* (in press).

Hitchcock, Ethan Allen
1865   *Swedenborg, a Hermetic Philosopher.* New York: James Miller.

Holston, James
1989   *The Modernist City: An Anthropological Critique of Brasília.* Chicago: University of Chicago Press.

Hutchinson, Bertram
1966   "The Patron-Dependent Relationship in Brazil: A Preliminary Examination." *Sociologia Ruralis* 6(1): 3–29.

Imbassahy, Carlos
1935   *O Espiritismo à Luz dos Fatos.* Rio de Janeiro: Federação Espírita Brasileira.
1943   *A Mediunidade e a Lei.* Rio de Janeiro: Federação Espírita Brasileira.
1949   *Espiritismo e Loucura.* São Paulo: LAKE.
1950   *À Margem do Espiritismo.* Rio de Janeiro: Federação Espírita Brasileira.
1955   *A Evolução, com uma Reposta a Crítica sobre o Livro "A Reencarnação e Suas Provas."* Curitiba: Federação Espírita do Paraná.
1961   "Sessões, Médiuns, e Débeis." *Revista Internacional do Espiritismo* (February–May).
1962a   "De Flammarion a Richet." *Revista Internacional do Espiritismo* (July).

242   Bibliography

1962b   "É Inacreditável." *Revista Internacional do Espiritismo* (July).
1962c   "O Espiritismo, o Hipnotismo, e os Estados d'Alma." *Revista Internacional do Espiritismo* (August).
1962d   "O Fenômeno Espírita e a Hipnose." *Revista Internacional do Espiritismo* (October).
c. 1965   *A Farsa Escura da Mente.* São Paulo: LAKE.
1967   *Enigmas da Parapsicologia.* São Paulo: Calvário.
1969   *Freud e as Manifestações da Alma.* Rio de Janeiro: Eco.
Imbassahy, Carlos, and Pedro Granja
1950   *Fantasmas, Fantasias, e Fantoches.* São Paulo: Edipo.
Imbassahy, Carlos, and Mário Cavalcanti de Mello
c. 1945   *A Reencarnação e Suas Provas.* Foreword by Pedro Granja. Curitiba: Federação Espírita do Paraná.
Innocencio, José Dias
1986   "Bezerra de Menezes ante Roustaing." *O Reformador* (September): 268–70.
James, William
1950   *The Principles of Psychology.* Vol. 1. New York: Dover (orig. 1890).
1961   *The Varieties of Religious Experience.* New York: Macmillan (orig. 1902).
Jameson, Frederic
1984   "Postmodernism, or the Cultural Logic of Late Capitalism." *New Left Review* 146: 53–93.
Janet, Pierre
1899   *L'Automatisme psychologique.* Paris: Alcan (orig. 1889).
Jesús López, Antonio de
1936   *Ante el espiritismo kardeciano. Réplica.* Utuado, P.R.: n.p.
Joralemon, Don
1990   "The Selling of the Shaman and the Problem of Informant Legitimacy." *Journal of Anthropological Research* (in press).
Jorge, Moacyr
c. 1964   *Arigó: A Verdade Que Abala o Brasil.* Second edition. São Paulo: Edicel.
Jung-Stilling, Johann Heinrich
1834   *Theory of Pneumatology.* London: Longman, Rees.
Kardec, Allan
1875   *Spiritualist Philosophy: The Spirits' Book.* Trans. Anna Blackwell. London: Trubner & Co. (orig. 1860; first ed. 1857).
1944a   *Ceu e Inferno.* Rio de Janeiro: Federação Espírita Brasileira (orig. 1865).
1944b   *O Evangelho Segundo Espiritismo.* Rio de Janeiro: Federação Espírita Brasileira (orig. 1864).
1944c   *A Genêse.* Rio de Janeiro: Federação Espírita Brasileira (orig. 1868).
1944d   *O Livro dos Espíritos.* Rio de Janeiro: Federação Espírita Brasileira (orig. 1860; first ed. 1857).
1944e   *O Livro dos Médiuns.* Rio de Janeiro: Federação Espírita Brasileira (orig. 1859).
1944f   *Obras Posthumas.* Rio de Janeiro: Federação Espírita Brasileira (orig. 1890).
1983   *O Livro dos Espíritos.* São Paulo: Instituto de Difusão Espírita (orig. 1860; first ed. 1857).

Keefe, David
1976   "Interaction of Spiritualism and Western Medicine in Rio de Janeiro, Brazil." B.A. thesis, Committee on History and Science, Harvard University.
Kenny, Michael
1986   *The Passion of Ansel Bourne.* Washington, D.C.: Smithsonian Institution Press.
Kirsch, A. Thomas
1977   "Complexity in the Thai Religious System: An Interpretation." *Journal of Asian Studies* 26(21): 241–66.
Kloppenburg, Boaventura
1957   *A Reencarnação. Exposição e Crítica.* Petrópolis: Vozes.
1960   *O Espiritismo no Brasil. Orientação para os Católicos.* Petrópolis: Vozes.
1961a   *O Reencarnacionismo no Brasil.* Petrópolis: Vozes.
1961b   *A Umbanda no Brasil. Orientação para os Católicos.* Petrópolis: Vozes.
1967   "Brazil: Spiritism." *The New Catholic Encyclopedia.* Vol. 2. New York: McGraw-Hill.
1972   "Ensaio de uma Nova Posição Pastoral perante a Umbanda." In *Cultos Afro-Brasileiros.* Rio de Janeiro: Sóno-Víso do Brasil.
Koss, Joan
1976   "Religion and Science Divinely Related: A Case History of Spiritism in Puerto Rico." *Caribbean Studies* 16(1): 22–43.
Kuhn, Thomas
1970   *The Structure of Scientific Revolutions.* Chicago: University of Chicago Press (orig. 1962).
Lapassade, Georges, and Marco Aurélio Luz
1972   *O Segredo da Macumba.* Rio de Janeiro: Paz e Terra.
La Porta, Ernesto
1979   *Estudo Psicanalítico dos Rituais Afro-Brasileiros.* Rio de Janeiro: Atheneu.
Latour, Bruno
1988   "The Politics of Explanation: An Alternative." In *Knowledge and Reflexivity,* ed. Steve Woolgar. Beverly Hills: Sage.
Leach, Edmund
1968   "Ritual." In *The International Encyclopedia of the Social Sciences.* Vols. 13 and 14. New York: Macmillan.
Le Goff, Jacques
1984   *The Birth of Purgatory.* Chicago: University of Chicago Press.
Leme-Lopes, José
1979   "Psiquiatria e Antropologia." *Neurobiologia* (Recife) 42(1): 3–12.
Lessa, Adelaide Petters
1975   *Precognição.* São Paulo: Duas Cidades.
Lévi-Strauss, Claude
1961   *Tristes Tropiques.* New York: Atheneum (orig. 1955).
1963   "The Effectiveness of Symbols." In *Structural Anthropology.* New York: Basic Books (orig. 1949).
1966   *The Savage Mind.* Chicago: University of Chicago Press (orig. 1962).
1975   *The Raw and the Cooked.* New York: Harper (orig. 1964).
Levy Júnior, Maurício
1970   "Contribuição para o Estudo Psicanalítico dos Sonhos Telepáticos." *Revista Brasileira de Psicanálise* 4(2): 191–239 and 4(3): 317–52.

244   Bibliography

Lewis, James
    1873   Digest of the English Census of 1871. London: Edward Stanford.
Lex, Ary
    1985   "As Operações Espirituais." Folha Espírita 12 (July/136): 6.
Lima, Luiz da Rocha, and Lauro Neiva
    1972   Forças dos Espíritos. Rio de Janeiro: Artenova. (Later edition: Rio de
           Janeiro: Lar de Frei Luiz/Livraria Atheneu, 1981.)
Lima, Roberto Kant de
    1985   A Antropologia da Academia. Petrópolis: Vozes; Niterói: Universidade
           Federal Fluminense.
Loewe, Ronald
    1990   "Continuity and Change in the Folk Medicine of Yucatan." Manuscript.
Loyola, Maria Andréa
    1984   Médicos e Curandeiros: Conflito Social e Saúde. São Paulo: Difel.
Lyra, Alberto
    1976a "Parapsicologia: Teoria Geral e Fenomenologia." In Psicologia Médica,
           ed. Darcy de Mendonça Uchôa. São Paulo: Sarvier.
    1976b "Precognição. Um Enfoque Psicológico e Filosófico." In Psicologia
           Médica, ed. Darcy de Mendonça Uchôa. São Paulo: Sarvier.
    1983   "Parapsicologia no Brasil." Manuscript (São Paulo).
    1984   "Psiquiatria, Parapsicologia, e os Fenômenos de Obsessão Espírita e
           Possessão Demoníaca." Boletim Médico-Espírita 1(2): 35–91.
McCabe, Joseph
    1920   Spiritualism: A Popular History from 1847. New York: Dodd, Mead.
McClenon, James
    1984   Deviant Science: The Case of Parapsychology. Philadelphia: University of
           Pennsylvania Press.
Machado, Roberto
    1978   Danação da Norma. Rio de Janeiro: Graal.
Machado, Ubiratan
    1983   Os Intelectuais e o Espiritismo. Rio de Janeiro: Antares; Brasília: Instituto
           Nacional do Livro.
Machado de Assis, Joaquim Maria
    1956   Diálogos e Refelexões de um Relojoeiro. Rio de Janeiro: Civilização
           Brasileira.
Macklin, June
    1974   "Belief, Ritual, and Healing: New England Spiritualism and Mexican-
           American Spiritism Compared." In Religious Movements in Contemporary
           America, ed. Irving Zaretsky and Mark Leone. Princeton: Princeton
           University Press.
McVaugh, Michael, and Seymour Mauskopf
    1976   "J. B. Rhine's Extrasensory Perception and Its Background in Psychi-
           cal Research." Isis 67: 161–89.
Maes, Hercílio
    1965   A Vida no Planeta Marte. Rio de Janeiro: Bastos.
Maggie, Yvonne
    1986   "O Medo do Feitiço." Religião e Sociedade 13(1): 72–86.
    1988   "Medo do Feitiço. Relações entre Magia e Poder no Brasil." Ph.D.
           dissertation, Anthropology Department, Museu Nacional, Universi-
           dade Federal do Rio de Janeiro.

Manuel, Frank, and Fritzie Manuel
    1966   *French Utopias: An Anthropology of Ideal Societies.* New York: Free
            Press.
    1979   *Utopian Thought in the Western World.* Cambridge: Harvard University
            Press.
Marcus, George, and Michael Fischer
    1986   *Anthropology as Cultural Critique.* Chicago: University of Chicago
            Press.
Mariante, João Gomes
    1975   "Aspectos Mágico-Terapêuticos nos Rituais Afro-Brasileiros." *Revista
            Brasileira de Psicanálise* 9(1): 51–61.
Marinho, Jarbas George
    1974   "Brazilian Research on Paraphenomenal Events." *Impact of Science on
            Society* 24(4): 365–69.
Martínez Barrena, Jesús, C.M.
    1948   *La democracia, el espiritismo, la masonería. Tres conferencias científico-
            religiosas.* San Juan: La Milagrosa.
Martins, Clóvis
    1969   "Psiquiatria Transcultural e Países em Desenvolvimento." *Revista Bra-
            sileira de Psiquiatria* 3(1): 31–62.
Martins, Clóvis, and Fernando Oliveira Bastos
    1963   "Estado Atual da Psicoterapia no Brasil." *Boletim da Clínica Psiquiátrica
            da Faculdade de Medicina da Universidade de São Paulo* 2(2): 49–53.
Mauskopf, Seymour H., and Michael R. McVaugh
    1980   *The Elusive Science: Origins of Experimental Psychical Research.* Baltimore:
            Johns Hopkins University Press.
Mello, Antônio da Silva
    1949   *Mistérios e Realidades Dêste e do Outro Mundo.* Rio de Janeiro: J. Olympio.
            (English-language edition: *Mysteries and Realities of This World and the
            Next.* London: Weidenfeld & Nicholson, 1960.)
Mello, Mário Cavalcanti de
    c. 1958   *Como os Teólogos Refutam. . . .* Curitiba: Federação Espírita do Paraná.
Melo, Rui, and Cesário Morey Hossri
    1962   "Milagre ou Farsa?" In *Folha Ilustrada* of *Folha de São Paulo* (July 4–7
            and 9–11): 1 and (July 8): 8.
Melo, Wilson Ferriera de
    1984   "Das Obsessões." *Boletim Médica-Espírita* 1(2): 16–29.
Mendes, Eliezer
    1976   *Personalidade Subconsciente.* Bahia: self-published.
    1980a   *Personalidade Hiperconsciente.* São Paulo: Pensamento.
    1980b   *Personalidade Instrusa.* São Paulo: Pensamento (orig. 1974).
    1980c   *Psicontranse.* São Paulo: Pensamento.
    1985   *Sexo em Transe.* São Paulo: Edições para Agora.
Menezes, Adolfo Bezerra de
    1939   *A Loucura sob Novo Prisma.* Rio de Janeiro: Federação Espírita Bra-
            sileira (orig. c. 1897).
    1977   *Estudos Filosóficos.* São Paulo: Edicel.
Merton, Robert
    1973   *The Sociology of Science: Theoretical and Empirical Investigations.* Chicago:
            University of Chicago Press.

1976   *Sociological Ambivalence and Other Essays.* New York: Free Press.
Milner, Cary
1980   "God, Saints, and Spirits: A Comparative Analysis of Brazilian Urban
        Medical Systems." Ph.D. dissertation, Sociology Department, Univer-
        sity of Toronto.
Monteiro, Duglas
1978   "Roger Bastide. Religião e Ideologia." *Religião e Sociedade* 3: 11–24.
Montero, Paula
1985   *Da Doença a Desordem. A Magia na Umbanda.* Rio de Janeiro: Graal.
Moog, Viana
1964   *Bandeirantes and Pioneers.* New York: Braziller.
Moore, R. Laurence
1977   *In Search of White Crows.* New York: Oxford University Press.
Moore, Sally F., and Barbara Myerhoff
1977   *Secular Ritual.* Assen and Amsterdam: Van Gorcum.
Morales, Agapito
1904   *Breve tratado de hipnotismo, magnetismo, espiritismo, y sugestoterapia.* San
        Juan: El Alba-Marina.
Moreil, André
1961   *La Vie et l'œuvre d'Allan Kardec.* Paris: Sperar.
Moura, D. Odilão
1978   *As Idéias Católicas no Brasil.* São Paulo: Convívio.
Mundim, Pedro de Oliveira
1985   "Terapêuticas Espiritualistas ('Nooterapias') e Psicopatologia." Paper
        presented at the First International Conference on Mind-Matter Inter-
        action, July 22–24, São Paulo.
Myers, F. W. H.
1903   *Human Personality and Its Survival of Bodily Death.* London: Longmans,
        Green.
Nachman, Robert
1977   "Positivism, Modernization, and the Middle Class in Brazil." *Hispanic
        American History Review* 57(1): 1–23.
Negrão, Lísias Nogueira
1979   "A Umbanda como Expressão da Religiosidade Popular." *Religião e
        Sociedade* 4: 171–91.
Negromonte, Álvaro
1954   *O Que É Espiritismo.* Second edition. Rio de Janeiro: Santa Maria (orig.
        1949).
Nelson, Geoffrey K.
1969   *Spiritualism and Society.* London: Routledge & Kegan Paul.
Nobre, Freitas
1981   *A Perseguição Policial contra Eurípedes Barsanulfo.* São Paulo: Edicel.
Nunes, René
1981   *Cromoterapia. A Cura através da Cor.* Brasília: Papelaria ASA-SUL.
Oliveira, Antônio Xavier de
1931   *Espiritismo e Loucura.* Rio de Janeiro: A. Coelho Branco.
Oliveira, Pedro A. Ribeiro de
1985   *Religião e Dominação de Classe.* Petrópolis: Vozes.
Ortiz, Renato
1978   *A Morte Branca do Feiticeiro Negro.* Petrópolis: Vozes.

Paixão, Paulo
1981   Letargia e Hipnose sem Magia. São Paulo: Organização André Editora.
Paixão, Paulo, and César Santos Silva
1974   Parapsicologia. Ciência ou Magia? Rio de Janeiro: Interinvest Editora.
Parsons, Talcott
1951   The Social System. New York: Free Press.
Passos, A. C. de Moraes
1964   "Percepção Extra-sensorial e Hipnose." Revista de Psicologia Normal e Patológica 10(3–4): 555–62.
Pattie, Frank
1956   "Mesmer's Medical Dissertation and Its Debt to Mead's De Imperio Solis ac Lunae." Journal of the History of Medicine and Allied Sciences 11: 275–87.
Pechman, Tema
1982   "Umbanda e Política no Rio de Janeiro." Religião e Sociedade 8: 37–44.
Peixoto, Isadora Durval
1980   Superstição e Crime no Brasil. São Paulo: Revista dos Tribunais.
Pereira, Sérgio Gischkow
1981   "Curandeirismo." Revista dos Tribunais 547: 216–82.
Perelberg, Rosine Jozef
1980   "Umbanda and Psychoanalysis as Different Ways of Interpreting Mental Illness." British Journal of Medical Psychology 53: 323–32.
Peres, Maria Júlia
1985   "Terapia Espírita." In Proceedings and Abstracts, the First International Congress on Alternative Therapies. São Paulo: International Association for Alternative Therapies.
Peres, Ney Prieto
1984   "Ações Magnéticas no Perispírito—Nas Obsessões e nas Curas. Boletim Médico-Espírita 1(2): 212–43.
Pinch, Trevor
1979   "Normal Explanations of the Paranormal: The Demarcation Problem and Fraud in Parapsychology." Social Studies of Science 9: 329–48.
Pinch, T. J., and H. M. Collins
1984   "Private Science and Public Knowledge: The Committee for the Scientific Investigation of the Paranormal and Its Use of the Literature." Social Studies of Science 14:521–46.
Pinho, Álvaro Rubem de, et al.
1975   "Tratamentos Religiosos das Doenças Mentais." Revista da Psiquiatria Clínica 4(4): 183–92.
Pires, J. Herculano
n.d.   Parapsicologia e Suas Perspectivas. São Paulo: Edicel.
1963   Arigó. Um Caso de Fenemologia Paranormal. São Paulo: Paulo de Azevedo.
1964   O Espírito e o Tempo. São Paulo: Pensamento.
c. 1973   Arigó. Vida, Mediunidade, e Martírio. São Paulo: Edicel.
1980   O Espírito e o Tempo. Fourth edition. São Paulo: Edicel.
Playfair, Guy
1975   The Flying Cow. London: Souvenir Press.
Podmore, Frank
1902   Modern Spiritualism. Vol. 1. London: Methuen & Co.

Ponte Jiménez, Francisco
  1914   *Conferencia dada en la Biblioteca Insular de San Juan.* San Juan: The Times.
Queiroz, Maria Isaura Pereira de
  1977   "Messiahs, Miracle Workers, and 'Catholic Duality' in Brazil." *International Social Science Journal* 29(2): 298–312.
Quevedo, Pedro Oscar González
  1962   "Telepatia ou Clarividência?" *Revista de Psicologia Normal e Patológica* 8(1–4): 132–42.
  1964   *A Face Oculta da Mente.* São Paulo: Loyola.
  1968   *As Forças Físicas da Mente.* São Paulo: Loyola.
  1969   *¿Que es la parapsicología?* Buenos Aires: Editorial Columbia.
  1974   *O Que É a Parapsicologia?* São Paulo: Loyola.
  1978   *Curandeirismo: Um Mal ou um Bem?* São Paulo: Loyola.
Rabinow, Paul
  1986   "Representations Are Social Facts: Modernity and Post-Modernity in Social Anthropology." In *Writing Culture,* ed. J. Clifford and G. Marcus. Berkeley and Los Angeles: University of California Press.
Ramos, Arthur
  1940   *O Negro Brasileiro.* São Paulo: Nacional.
  1946   *As Culturas Negras no Novo Mundo.* São Paulo: Nacional.
Ramos, Clóvis
  1978   *A Imprensa Espírita no Brasil. 1869–1978.* Juiz de Fora, M.G.: Instituto Maria.
Ranieri, R. A.
  n.d.   *Materializações Luminosas.* São Paulo: LAKE.
Rauscher, Elizabeth
  1985   "Human Volitional Effects on a Model Bacterial System." In *Proceedings and Abstracts, the First International Congress on Alternative Therapies.* São Paulo: International Association for Alternative Therapies.
Renshaw, J. Parke
  1969   "A Sociological Analysis of Spiritism in Brazil." Ph.D. dissertation, Sociology Department, University of Florida at Gainesville.
Riasanovsky, Nicholas
  1967   "Charles Fourier." *The Encyclopedia of Philosophy.* Vol. 3. New York: Macmillan.
  1969   *The Teaching of Charles Fourier.* Berkeley and Los Angeles: University of California Press.
Ribas, João Carvalhal
  1966   "Parapsicologia. Estado Atual." *Revista de Psicologia Normal e Patológica* 12(3–4): 427–29.
Ribeiro, Guillon
  1941   *Trabalhos do Grupo "Ismael" da Federação Espírita Brasileira.* Vol. 1. Rio de Janeiro: Federação Espírita Brasileira. (Includes materials drawn from *Reformador,* September 15, 1901.)
Ribeiro, Leonídio
  1975   "Curandeirismo." In *Memórias de um Médico Legista.* Rio de Janeiro: Sul Americano.
Ribeiro, Leonídio, and Murillo de Campos
  1931   *O Espiritismo no Brasil. Contribuição ao Seu Estudo Clínico e Médico-Legal.* São Paulo: Editora Nacional.

Richard, Pedro
1914   Carta Aberta ao Presidente da Federação Espírita Brasileira. Rio de Janeiro: self-published.
Richet, Charles
1923   Traité de métapsychique. Paris: Félix Alcan. (English-language edition: Thirty Years of Psychical Research. New York: Macmillan, 1923.)
Rizzini, Jorge
1963   Caso Arigó. São Paulo: Gráfica.
1979   Eurípedes Barsanulfo, o Apóstolo da Caridade. São Paulo: Correio Fraterno.
Roberts, J. M.
1972   The Mythology of Secret Societies. New York: Scribner's.
Rodrigues, Raimundo Nina
1901   "La folie des Foules." Annales Médico-Psychologiques 49 (January–February): 19–32; (March–April): 189–99; (May–June): 370–81; (July–August): 5–18; (September–October): 202–9.
1932   Os Africanos no Brasil. São Paulo: Nacional.
1935   O Animismo Fetishista dos Negros Bahianos. Rio de Janeiro: Civilização Brasileira (orig. 1896).
Rodríguez Escudero, Nestor A.
1979   Historia del espiritismo en Puerto Rico. Aguadilla, P.R.: self-published.
Roll, William
1977   "Poltergeists." In Handbook of Parapsychology, ed. Benjamin Wolman. New York: Van Nostrand Reinhold.
Roustaing, Jean-Baptiste
c. 1900   Os Quatro Evangelhos. Revelação da Revelação. Rio de Janeiro: Federação Espírita Brasileira (orig. 1866).
Roxo, Henrique de Brito Belford
1946   "Delírio Espírita Episódica." In Manual de Psiquiatra. Rio de Janeiro: Guanabara (orig. 1918).
Ruby, Jay
1982   A Crack in the Mirror: Reflexive Perspectives in Anthropology. Philadelphia: University of Pennsylvania Press.
Salgues, M.
1862   "Les Spirites et leurs reincarnations." Revue Spiritualiste 4(10): 321–25.
Sausse, Henri
1952   Biografía de Allan Kardec. Buenos Aires: Editorial Víctor Hugo (orig. 1927).
Silber, Kate
1960   Pestalozzi: The Man and His Work. London: Routledge & Kegan Paul.
Soares, Luiz Eduardo
1979   "O Autor e Seu Duplo. A Psicografia e as Proezas do Simulacro." Religião e Sociedade 4: 121–40.
Soares, Sylvio Brito
1962   Vida e Obra de Bezerra de Menezes. Rio de Janeiro: Federação Espírita Brasileira.
Sobral, Raul
1984   "Sensitivo. Recurso Terapêutico?" Boletim Médico-Espírita 1(2): 163–86.
1985   "PK Biológico. Evidências Sugestivas de Ação Terapêutica." In Proceed-

ings and Abstracts, the First International Congress on Alternative Therapies. São Paulo: International Association for Alternative Therapies.

Soler, Luis M. Díaz
1960 *Rosendo Matienzo Cintrón.* Vol. 1. San Juan: Universidad de Puerto Rico.

Sousa do Prado
1932 *Padres, Médicos, e Espíritas (Refutação aos "Leonídios").* Rio de Janeiro: self-published.

Souza, Denizard
1983 "Metapsiquiatria e a Vida após a Morte." *Revista da Psiquiatra* 37(39): 22–33.
1985 *Alucinações.* Santa Maria, R.S.: self-published.

Souza, Denizard, and Teresinha Fátima Deitos
1980 "Terapia Espírita em Hospitais Psiquiátricos." *Revista da Associação Brasileira de Psiquiatria* 2(3): 190–94.

Souza, Márcio
1983 *The Order of the Day: An Unidentified Flying Opus.* New York: Avon.

Spínola, Aristides, and Luiz de Mesquita Barros
1915 *Caridade Perseguida.* Recurso Criminal no. 247. Rio de Janeiro: Cadaval.

Stepan, Nancy
1976 *Beginnings of Brazilian Science: Oswaldo Cruz, Medical Research, and Policy, 1890–1920.* New York: Science History Publications.

Stevenson, Ian
1972 "Are Poltergeists Living or Are They Dead?" *Journal of the American Society for Psychical Research* 66(3): 233–52.

Stocking, George (ed.)
1983 *Observers Observed: Essays on Ethnographic Fieldwork.* Madison: University of Wisconsin Press.

Suárez, Francisca
1892 *Nuestra réplica articulada del Dr. Don Manuel Guzmán Rodríguez.* Mayagüez, P.R.: Tip. Comercial.

Swedenborg, Emanuel
1867 *Heaven and Its Wonders, the World of Spirits, and Hell (From Things Heard and Seen).* New York: American Swedenborg Printing and Publishing Society.

Taussig, Michael
1987 *Shamanism, Colonialism, and the Wild Man.* Chicago: University of Chicago Press.

Thiago, Lauro
1972 *Homeopatia e Espiritismo.* Rio de Janeiro: Federação Espírita Brasileira.

Thomas, Keith
1971 *Religion and the Decline of Magic.* New York: Scribner's.

Thurston, Herbert
1933 *The Church and Spiritualism.* Milwaukee: Bruce Publishing Co.

Tinôco, Carlos Alberto
1982 *O Modelo Organizador Biológico.* Curitiba: Veja.

Tiryakin, Edward (ed.)
1974 *On the Margin of the Visible: Sociology, the Esoteric, and the Occult.* New York: John Wiley & Sons.

Tourinho, Nazareno
1983   *Edson Queiroz, o Novo Arigó dos Espíritos.* São Bernardo do Campo, S.P.: Editora Espírita Correio Fraterno do ABC.
Tourinho, Nazareno, and Carlos Imbassahy
c. 1967   *O Poder Fantástico da Mente.* Rio de Janeiro: Eco.
Truzzi, Marcello
1974   "Definition and Dimensions of the Occult: Towards a Sociological Perspective." In *On the Margins of the Visible,* ed. Edward Tiryakian. New York: John Wiley & Sons (orig. 1971).
Turner, Frank Miller
1974   *Between Science and Religion.* New Haven: Yale University Press.
Turner, Victor
1974   *Dramas, Fields, and Metaphors.* Ithaca: Cornell University Press.
Uchôa, Darcy de Mendonça
1976   *Psicologia Médica.* São Paulo: Sarvier.
1981   *Organização da Psiquiatria no Brasil.* São Paulo: Sarvier.
Valle, Sérgio
c. 1954   *Silva Mello e os Seus Mistérios.* São Paulo: LAKE.
Vartier, Jean
1971   *Allan Kardec. La Naissance du spiritisme.* Paris: Hachette.
Vieira, Waldo
1986   *Projeciologia. Panorama das Experiências da Consciência Fora do Corpo Humano.* Rio de Janeiro: self-published.
Vincenty, Francisco
1907   *Controversia religiosa.* Ponce, P.R.: El Sol.
Wallis, Roy (ed.)
1979   *On the Margins of Science: The Social Construction of Rejected Knowledge.* Sociological Review Monograph no. 27. Keele, Staffordshire: University of Keele.
Wallis, Roy, and Peter Morley
1976   *Marginal Medicine.* London: Peter Owen.
Wantuil, Zêus
1969   *Os Grandes Espíritas do Brasil.* Rio de Janeiro: Federação Espírita Brasileira.
Wantuil, Zêus, and Francisco Thieson
1980   *Allan Kardec.* Vol. 2. Rio de Janeiro: Federação Espírita Brasileira.
Warren, Donald
1968a   "The Portuguese Roots of Brazilian Spiritism." *Luso-Brazilian Review* 5(2): 3–33.
1968b   "Spiritism in Brazil." *Journal of Inter-American Studies* 10: 393–405.
1984   "A Terapia Espírita no Rio de Janeiro por volta de 1900." *Religião e Sociedade* 11(3): 56–83.
1986   "A Medicina Espiritualizada. A Homeopatia no Brasil do Século XIX." *Religião e Sociedade* 13(1): 88–107.
Watson, Graham
1987   "Make Me Reflexive—But Not Yet." *Journal of Anthropological Research* 43: 29–41.
Weber, Max
1958   *The Protestant Ethic and the Spirit of Capitalism.* New York: Scribner's (orig. 1904–1905).

1978   *Economy and Society.* Berkeley and Los Angeles: University of California Press.

Whitaker, E. de Aguiar
1942   "Manifestações Psíquicas Inconscientes ou Raras e Espiritismo." *Revista de Neurologia e Psiquiatria de São Paulo* 8: 1–10.

Wittkower, Eric
1968   "Perspectives of Transcultural Psychiatry." *Revista Brasileira de Psiquiatria* 2(3): 61–78.

Woolgar, Steve
1982   "Laboratory Studies: A Comment on the State of the Art." *Social Studies of Science* 12: 481–98.

Woolgar, Steve (ed.)
1988   *Knowledge and Reflexivity: New Frontiers in the Sociology of Knowledge.* Beverly Hills: Sage.

Wyckoff, James
1975   *Franz Anton Mesmer: Between God and Devil.* Englewood Cliffs, N.J.: Prentice-Hall.

Xavier, Francisco Cândido
1944   *Nosso Lar. Pelo Espírito de André Luiz.* Rio de Janeiro: Federação Espírita Brasileira.

1947   *No Mundo Maior. Pelo Espírito de André Luiz.* Rio de Janeiro: Federação Espírita Brasileira.

1964   *Desobsessão. Pelo Espírito de André Luiz.* Rio de Janeiro: Federação Espírita Brasileira.

1984   *Cidade no Além.* Araras, S.P.: Instituto de Difusão Espírita.

Xavier, Francisco Cândido, and Waldo Vieira
1958   *Evolução em Dois Mundos.* Rio de Janeiro: Federação Espírita Brasileira.

1959   *Mecanismos da Mediunidade.* Rio de Janeiro: Federação Espírita Brasileira.

Yáñez, Vda. de Otero, Teresa
1963   *El espiritismo en Puerto Rico.* San Juan: n.p.

Yates, Frances
1964   *Giordano Bruno and the Hermetic Tradition.* Chicago: University of Chicago Press.

1972   *The Rosicrucian Enlightenment.* London: Routledge & Kegan Paul (U.S. edition: Boulder, Colo.: Shambhala).

Zaluar, Alba
1983   *Os Homens de Deus.* Rio de Janeiro: Zahar.

NAME INDEX

SUBJECT INDEX

Printed in the United States
204408BV00001B/356/A

9 780271 033679

Made in the USA
Lexington, KY
27 April 2011